Wake Up Church: The End is Nigh!

By

Dennis Crump

This book is a work of non-fiction. Names and places have been changed to protect the privacy of all individuals. The events and situations are true.

© 2002 by Dennis Crump. All rights reserved.

No part of this book may be reproduced, restored in a retrieval system, or transmitted by means, electronic, mechanical, photocopying, recording, or otherwise, without written consent from the author.

ISBN: 0-7596-9790-6

This book is printed on acid free paper.

1st Books - rev. 4/12/02

Dedications:

to a very dear friend of mine who demonstrated to me what it means to courageously press forward against all odds, though not in concern for yourself. Sandi Willis, my dear sister in Christ, died of cancer on Easter Sunday of 2001. She was one of my former helpers in the ministry and even while battling this enemy of cancer, she continuously demonstrated a concern for others far more greater than most others that I know. She deserves to be honored.

Acknowledgments

People who have greatly influenced me in the study of the end-times: Colin Deal and Marvin Byers.

People who have helped to inspire the outcome of this book: In great measure, my dear wife Rhonda and my mother Betty Crump. Others: Carrie Vergin, Karen Galske, Michelle Wilke, Jeff Murphy, John Cogswell, Richard Price, John Kearns, Jr., Jody Mull, Ricky Tucker, Chris Powers, Jody Noe, Cathy Adair, Joann Hancock, Donna and Amanda Partin, Jeremy Walker, the Youth Group I pastored at First Baptist Church, the Youth Group I pastored at Open Door Baptist Church, and the Believers I pastor at Believers Assembly.

TABLE OF CONTENTS

Preface ("Why this Book?") xi

- Part 1 – "The End-Time Introduction" 1

- Part 2 - "The End-Time Period" 11

Chapter 1 "The Tribulation" 13

- Part 3 - "The End-Time Players" 29

Chapter 2 "Israel" 31
Chapter 3 "Mystery Babylon" 34
Chapter 4 "The Beast: The Arab Empire!" 40
Chapter 5 "The 10 Horns" 45
Chapter 6 "The 7 Heads" 51
Chapter 7 "The 7 Kings" 57
Chapter 8 "Nebuchadnezzar's Image" 61
Chapter 9 "The King of the North vs The King of the South" 69
Chapter 10 "The Little Horn" (Yasser Arafat?) 76
Chapter 11 "The PLO & Hamas" 94
Chapter 12 "The Origin of the Beast: The Bottomless Pit (or Abyss)!"
.... 106
Chapter 13 "The Family Feud: A Landmark Issue!" 111
Chapter 14 "The Mark of the Beast" 118
Chapter 15 "The Apostasy" 128
Chapter 16 "666" 133
Chapter 17 "The Antichrist?" 140
Chapter 18 "The Locusts" 147

- Part 4 - "The End-Time Pieces" 152

Chapter 19 "A Thief in the Night!" 154
Chapter 20 "Peace & Safety" 160
Chapter 21 "The Abomination of Desolation" 163
Chapter 22 "The Rapture" 167
Chapter 23 "The Wrath of God" 171
Chapter 24 "The Marriage Supper" 186

Chapter 25 "The New Jerusalem" 192
Chapter 26 "But What About My Mansion?" 200
Chapter 27 "The 144,000" 205
Chapter 28 "The Fullness of Times" 211
Chapter 29 "Which Generation?" 217
Chapter 30 "Heaven and Earth Pass Away" 222
Chapter 31 "The Third Heaven (or Paradise!)" 230
Chapter 32 "Holy Days: The Seven Feasts of Israel" 238
Chapter 33 "The 7 Day Principle" 245
Chapter 34 "No Man Knoweth the Day and the Hour!" 256

- Part 5 - "The End-Time Conclusion" **268**

Chapter 35 "The Two Witnesses" 270
Chapter 36 "What to Expect for Believers" 286
Chapter 37 "What about the United States?" 297

Appendix 306

A: A Possibility Worth Considering ("1260, 1290, and 1335 Days") 308

Preface

"Why this Book?"

The end-times. Certainly it is popular because of its controversial and yet sensational subject matter. Essentially, it refers to the great conflict that approaches as the world seemingly nears its end, climaxed by the Second Coming of Jesus Christ. But why another book on prophecy or the end-times? Aren't there enough out there in the market already. Interestingly enough, the answer is, "Yes..., and then again, no!" Yes because there are plenty of prophecy books out there, but no because <u>this particular book addresses these end-time issues in a way that few, if any, of the others do</u>. Of course, to be very honest with you, I must admit that I did not want to write this book. In a sense, you could call this, "The book that <u>refused</u> to NOT be written!" That's right, it is as if, <u>against my very own wishes</u>, the writing of this book would eventually prevail. What do I mean by this? Let me explain.

I suppose it all began when I was just 15 or 16 years old. I believe it was back in 1978, while I was just a sophomore in high school, that I was on a return trip home from another town in which my dad was interviewing for a job. Riding in our car with both my parents, I clearly remember a conversation that we had about the return of Jesus Christ — this conversation most likely the result of a Bible conference that had just taken place at our church in which the speaker had addressed this very same topic. But what I remember most about this trip was a statement that I had made and my feelings which followed. The statement that I made was that I truly believed that we would not see the year 2000 because I felt that Christ would return by then. Of course I was a youth then and had no real knowledge whatsoever regarding prophecy, and therefore my statement was more or less given as a youthful "hunch," if you will. Nevertheless, the emotion I experienced was that of feeling honored on the one hand, yet disappointed on the other — a very real contrast of feelings. Honored to think that Christ might possibly choose my lifetime to make His return in. Disappointed however because I was still young and would then only reach, at most, a short 37 years in age before it all ended. Of course, this belief did not make me a prophet, for in no way did I consider myself as having some form of "inside information" regarding the end-times. After all, I was just a youth, discussing the Lord's return, probably experiencing similar emotions as just about any other youth would have. Still, there was one other vivid reality that came out of this experience and that was that I had this growing fascination for this unusual subject. I was intrigued. I was even captivated. In fact, I was hooked.

However, it wasn't until almost 10 years later, having by this time genuinely committed my life to Christ, that I first began to seriously study prophecy. Of course, as with most anybody else, my method of studying was very simple – you know, get a copy of a book in which the author's viewpoint is one that fits together with what I know should already be my viewpoint, that is, a viewpoint which is of the same position as that of my church, my parents, etc.. For myself, this viewpoint would be the same as what is considered to be the traditional viewpoint of most conservative protestant churches regarding the end-times. And with that, I studied (or actually, I read!). Of course, once again I was captivated. In fact, I soon thereafter got to the point where I not only read about it, but actually "studied" prophecy, even up to the point where I had a handle well enough on it that I myself could teach it. And soon I did just that – I was teaching it. And then came the year 1988.

In 1988, a very stirring book hit the Christian community by storm, bringing both revival and controversy with it. The book was called, "88 Reasons Why The Rapture Will Be In 1988," authored by a man named Edgar Whisenant. The central point of this book was that the rapture of the Church would take place in September of 1988. Being "enraptured" myself by prophecy, I read this book with both great interest and yet a bit of skepticism. So complex was the detail within it that I found myself on the one hand, unable to refute it and yet on the other hand, unsure of its validity. Thus, I only found myself more deeply driven to study the end-times while at the same time, more enthusiastic in the anticipation of (for I no longer feared Christ's return) the rapture, just in case...

Of course, the rapture never came and, although the teaching was supposedly refined for the same possibility to take place one year later in 1989, I found myself only more impassioned with this subject. And then something so incredible, and yet so simple, happened for me. While continuing in the diligent study of Bible prophecy, through another author I was introduced to a principle of study that would forever change my method of studying the Bible. The principle was basic and yet it also was profound — "Use Scripture to interpret Scripture." So basic it was, in fact, that I discovered that it was included as one of the normal rules for studying the Bible that was taught in my seminary course on Hermeneutics (meaning how to study the Bible). Yet it was profound in that when it came to the study of end-time prophecy, it seemed that away from this principle so often scholars would deviate. In many cases, as a matter of fact, without them ever even realizing it.

Of course, I am sure that you probably know how it goes. For example, you are told that you really should not study the book of Revelation until you get a good handle on the rest of God's Word. Otherwise, they say that you will not be able to understand it. Of course, when that time finally comes, you then go out and get a copy of some generally accepted author's teaching on this subject in order to familiarize yourself with it and better prepare you for this study. Then when it comes to you doing your own study, you pull out your favorite Bible commentaries and away you go. As you study, you then make sure you do not get lost or confused by frequently referencing these other resources as needed and in many cases, whenever possible. And then, just as I also did, you become one of those so-called well versed and intelligible students (or teachers!) of prophecy. And this cycle continues as more and more join the fold.

But let's consider for a moment some of the problems with this approach. Essentially, the way it really works is that after one becomes well versed in another person's teachings (via books, commentaries, or your church's teachings), you then begin the pursuit of your own study. But what really happens is that instead of actually becoming well versed in the Scriptures prior to, during, and after a study of the book of Revelation, you instead become well versed in what another person's teachings are, which quite often have become traditional. And yet, we are warned in God's Word to be careful of and not fall captive to the traditional teachings of man (Col. 2:8). Another problem that occurs is in this overall approach — that is, in the approach of requiring that one gets a grasp on the rest of God's Word prior to their tackling the book of Revelation. In a sense, I have found that this is somewhat backwards. After all, in just the 3rd verse of Revelation we are told regarding the attempted study of this book that "<u>Blessed</u> is he that readeth, and they that hear the words of this prophecy" (Rev. 1:3). In other words, God is telling us that there is a blessing that comes to those who study Revelation – at <u>any</u> particular time — and I myself only found this out the hard way, due to my waiting until I felt I was "prepared" to study it. I mean really, if you think about it, why would God encourage us to study this book if He knew it would "hurt" or "damage" us? Of course, the reality is that it doesn't "hurt" us, but rather helps us. And yet, from the Body of Christ in general, we often and unfortunately are discouraged from studying the book of Revelation and it is often due to fear — fear more or less on the part of the teacher, believing that the student might become frightened, confused, or even lost in their effort.

For me however, as I said earlier, my life would never be the same again as a result of this study. For as soon as I seemed to clearly understand this principle of using other Scripture to interpret Scripture, I found myself in an unusual set of circumstances in which I had no excuse but to try this principle out in a very in-depth manner. Ironically, I had just departed from seminary and was back in my hometown, serving in my childhood church as an Intern Pastor for just a brief period of time, anticipated to be about 6 months or so. While in this position, my responsibilities were limited and as a result, I soon found my situation to be very flexible with alot of time to freely fill as I chose. Thus, it was in this situation that I soon found myself beginning an in-depth study of the book of Revelation, utilizing this "profound" principle.

Beginning with the very first word in the first verse of the first chapter, I began my study. Using only the Bible, a concordance, and a Bible dictionary, I began to research how each word in Revelation was used in the Bible, referencing and cross-referencing, until after over a thousand hours and many months later, it seemed I began to better understand how the Bible actually interpreted itself. During this process, I began to uncover and discover many seemingly new things in Scripture which would alter my formerly embraced preconceived positions. Amazingly, I even discovered another principle along the way which was unlike any that we are generally told. In other words, <u>rather than the key to understanding the book of Revelation being an understanding of the rest of the Bible, I found</u>

<u>that the key to understanding the rest of the Bible was actually an understanding of the book of Revelation</u>. Ironically, it seemed that in obtaining a Scriptural understanding of what Revelation was really about, invaluable keys and insights within the rest of the Bible would thereby result as well. And this too became a very exciting discovery.

Still, as a result of these discoveries, I found myself also coming to many a crises concerning the various other teachings and positions on the end-times. These crises really were within myself, for I soon found myself often having to struggle in many cases with what I "wanted" to believe versus what I was now actually "seeing" in Scripture. This was because as I more and more studied, so also the more I found my former understanding to be unravelling in and of itself.

At the same time however, I also found myself now growing more concerned, zealous, and yet uneasy all at once. I was concerned because of the potential ramifications of what I was discovering in Scripture. Essentially, if what I was seeing was right, or even close to being right, then I couldn't help but wonder what this would mean for me with respect to the rest of the Body of Christ in general who basically saw things differently. Fortunately, I was aware that there were some others at least who were "seeing" these same and/or similar things. At the same time, as with anybody when for themselves they encounter new Biblical insights, I was zealous to share with others what I had discovered. Yet this too caused a great uneasiness within me because of what I felt others might think, especially in light of my conclusions. Being already one who was in the ministry, too well I knew what some of these reactions might be.

Nevertheless, I still considered myself as a student who was neither unteachable nor stubborn. Certainly I was fully aware, just as I am now, that there was room for error in my conclusions. Just as certain, however, was that I had a thirst for the truth. Personally, I can best describe this quest as being of the same desire as was described of the Berean people in the book of Acts who "searched the scriptures daily, (to see) whether those things were so" (Acts 17:11). Thus, I even yearned for responses regarding these insights. Again, one thing that I knew was that I was not the only one who was "seeing" many of these same insights. For example, the person from whom I learned that profound principle of interpretating the Scriptures from was also one who was seeing the same or somewhat similar findings. Incidentally, as this verse in Acts seems to imply, this same rule of interpretation seems to be descriptive of the method used by these Berean Believers as well. As a matter of fact, it is for this same reason that they were highly commended by God, actually being characterized in Scripture as being "noble" (Acts 17:11).

At any rate, I soon began to seek out various fellow Believers who were both respected and knowledgeable, most often being pastors, missionaries, lay leaders or teachers. My approach, of course, was for me to initiate going to them, asking them to consider looking at some things that I was seeing in Scripture. During these meetings I would carefully and gradually build my case, only to eventually encounter what would become a predictable reaction or response of resistance. Of course this resistance would come in many forms. For example, I often would be given a couple of books that the person owned that better explained their end-time positions so that they would not have to deal with me any longer. Or in other cases, they would do this because they disagreed and therefore just wanted to avoid potentially offending me. However, as more and more I experienced this pattern, it also became clear that this was a way for them to avoid having to examine these insights by researching them themselves. Still other times, as I would gradually be building up towards my conclusion, I would get cut off as an issue of lesser importance became the topic of discussion. Then, as the balance of time for our meeting would run out, I would be left there without ever having been able to fully share my point.

There were other times, however, in which I would be able to make my point. Yet even then it would often lead to an unfortunate result, for I would find myself being questioned as to whom I was because it seemed that they thought that I was thinking that I was one supposedly receiving insight that nobody else was. In other words, instead of them addressing (or attacking) the Scriptural arguments, I would find that it was myself (or my character) that was being attacked. This was all too unfortunate and thus, in a very precarious situation I soon found myself in — that is, wondering what it was that I was going to do?

Well, some five years soon followed and I found myself in the position of being able to really only do one thing – wait on God! If the insights that I was finding were of God, then He would have to order my steps and create the interest for them, knowing of my availability to share them as opposed to the other way around, as was earlier tried. And so, over the course of this time, I found myself sharing and teaching this material in very limited contexts, but generally based upon the other person's expressed desire or interest. In many cases, these people were either youth-aged or else young in the faith. Seldom did I find myself able to share in any depth this material with a more studied individual. Yet in the process of these various times of sharing, one thing that became invaluable was the resultant development of how I could better package this material. At one point, having had another individual express an interest in hearing this material, I found myself at one more crossroads. Although I was wanting to share this material via conversation, which in the least would require our getting together for no less than four hours, this individual preferred and therefore requested that I write my arguments down so that he could more closely study and evaluate them. Of course to me, knowing the volume of material that I had and the process involved in evaluating it, I felt that he had no real idea of what he was truly asking for from me. Yet after my initial resistance to his request and upon further reflection regarding it, for the first time I began to realize the meaning of the circumstances that I now found myself in – I sensed that it was really God who was leading me to write this material down, which would then be developed into a book. This had become obvious to me and with that, my assignment from Him had been realized. And thus, because at first I really did not want to ever write this material down, I refer to this as "the book that refused to NOT be written!"

But that was back in 1995. I finally completed the book and had it first printed (though not published) in 1996. With no real circulation, I was left to more or less sit on this material for the years that followed. Plus, during this same period of time, the current events of the world didn't seem to be as captivating with respect to the book. However, God began to work on my heart again in December of 2000. I could sense Him beginning to stir up the need to revise and update this book, although I could not seem to find the time to do so. However, on the eve of September 10th, 2001, I happened to mention to my wife, Rhonda, that I could sense God's stirring within my spirit and that His desire for me was to begin writing again. By the end of the next day, I knew exactly why. The terrorist attacks on the World Trade Centers would begin to set the stage for a renewed interest in, and possibly even fresher look at, the subject of the end-times. Thus, I set to writing again and have now completed this assignment, realizing even more so just how timely God's direction seems to always be.

Incidentally, before you begin reading this book, let me at least share with you a helpful hint to consider while reading it. Probably the best thing you can do is to just read it fully through before really researching in greater depth the many references. In a sense, you will then have a better overview from which to consider these details and Scriptural proofs. After all, end-time prophecy is similar to a very difficult puzzle, such as one of those 1,000 or more piece puzzles that you might try to put together. If you were to only buy from a store the puzzle without the box top's picture to work from, then you would have for yourself an even greater or more complicated challenge. Yet even with the box top, you quickly notice that its picture essentially communicates one major idea — or that it is one large picture consisting of a compilation of many smaller or mini-pictures, each made up of intricate little details from which ultimately is done the cutting to give you the many little puzzle pieces. As a result, you quickly discover that while putting the overall puzzle together, each piece, though unique individually in and of itself, quite often is found to be very similar to many of the other various pieces. Thus, it is often either overlooked or else the attempt is incorrectly made to fit it together with the other pieces that make up these various smaller pictures, which again collectively make up this overall large picture. This is a very challenging process indeed and yet, this too is the case in the attempt to piece together our end-time picture's many puzzle pieces. By reading through "WAKE UP CHURCH: THE END IS NIGH!" first, you will have begun to grasp the bigger picture with its various parts. Then, upon a further evaluation of the many Scriptural references cited within, you can more thoroughly investigate the various details of each particular piece. At this, you will begin to see the beauty of the whole picture as well as the amazing complexity, depth, and wisdom of the artist's mind, of whom is God Himself. As in the case of any genuine work of art, this picture of the end-times likewise needs time for its pieces to be fully understood and therefore truly appreciated. And so with the understanding of this helpful hint, I ask you to now begin reading "WAKE UP CHURCH," hoping that you will enjoy and appreciate, as I too have, this incredibly mysterious art piece, fashioned by the Master Artist, of which I believe I have only somewhat begun to understand from a Scriptural standpoint — indeed a masterful "end-time puzzle!"

- Part 1 -

"The End-Time Introduction"

Dennis Crump

The End-Time Introduction

"9-1-1"

Terrible Tuesday! The day was Tuesday, September 11, 2001 or 9-11 (9-1-1). Like any other day, people got up and went about their day as with any other. Life was normal. Unfortunately, this was no "normal" day. By day's end, people all over the world were mesmerized, grieved, shocked, and horrified. With the hijacking of four American airliners, the collapse of New York City's 100-plus story twin tower World Trade Centers, the additional damage to the military's central command center known as the Pentagon in Washington D.C., and the resultant loss of countless lives, the United States, even the world, had become engulfed in the shock and fear of being a victim of a sinister and monstrous enemy. Terrorism! The evil force of terrorism had risen to the forefront of everyone's concerns. And Osama bin Laden, the wealthy financier being holed up within the borders of the Middle East's Taliban-ruled country of Afghanistan, had become the prime suspect. And this was not the first time…

Osama bin Laden

Is this the beginning of the end?

The year is 2001. Palestinian leader Yasser Arafat continues to forge ahead, aiming to make Palestine a legitimate nation. The peace process that had been fueling this goal since 1993 had changed its shape. An escalating force had become the new operandus modi for achieving this destiny. The victim? Not the United States. Rather, in this case Israel. The monstrous force? Again, terrorism. Suicide bombings had plagued the nation of Israel and the streets of Jerusalem with constant fear. And the source of this fear was once again coming from within the territory known as the Middle East.

Does this have anything to do with the end?

Imagine this response, if you will. The United States declares a war against terrorism. It seeks to unravel the mysterious web spun by its prime target, Osama bin Laden. It directs itself into the borders of Afghanistan. It definitely wreaks some havoc, but struggles in unearthing the evasive and hidden bin Laden. Although generally experiencing global support in its response, the United States is not without dissidents. Most notably, Afghanistan and some of its neighbors. The common denominator – they are of Arab descent, fundamentally Islamic, and from the Middle East. As the U.S. acts, they react. The outcome? A sudden counter-reaction. Although the U.S. may have support (possibly United Nations support, or even some southern Arab countries such as Egypt and/or Saudi Arabia), its enemy nevertheless responds back. First directly against the U.S.. Yet as they respond against the U.S., they coincidentally turn on their Arab neighbors to the south. Aggressively and surprisingly, they successfully continue on only to make a sudden and what appears to be an irrational turn to their west. Their aim – Israel. Specifically, Jerusalem! By this time it is the spring, around the time of the Jewish Passover season. Iraq, led by its terrifying dictator and leader, Saddam Hussein, unleashes its 300,000 plus volunteer army, called the Al-Quds – or Jerusalem – Army, with one aim - to free Jerusalem from Israeli control.

Saddam Hussein

Amazingly, it works!

Somehow, behind it all and yet ironically, at the forefront, is one man. Yasser Arafat. This time, it is not the nation of Israel that relents, but rather the Palestinians. Or for that matter, the Arabs united. Israel falls to knees. Rapidly, the Jewish state begins to fear for their lives and they choose their safest recourse - to flee! Jerusalem becomes a hotbed of contention. And the Jews flee to the wilderness and/or mountains that surround it. And so this goes on for some time. A pre-determined period of time for that matter. Three and one-half years!

Fortunately, this does not last forever. Near the end of that three and one-half years, a breakthrough takes place. Israel, depleted and defeated, cries out for help. But this cry is unlike any other. Specifically because of whom they cry out to. For the very first time, as a nation, Israel pleads to Yeshua for help. That's right! Yeshua – or Jesus. In desperation, they acknowledge that it was Yeshua who was their long awaited Messiah. And they now realize this and therefore plead for His help.

And help He does!

Yeshua, with His very own army, comes to the rescue, to battle on their behalf. Where? To the Valley of Meggido. Why? To avenge His people – the Jews. The result – Arab chastisement, meaning that they too experience God's wrath, now resulting in their destruction.

Ultimately, Yeshua comes to establish His Kingdom – a Kingdom of peace and righteousness here on earth!

Could this scenario really take place? Yes it could. Will it happen? Possibly! Is it Scriptural? Well, there is a Scriptural basis for this possible outcome and it is found in the book of Daniel (see Daniel 11:40-45). Although the details may end up being different, the basic idea for an outcome such as this could be the intent of what Daniel suggests.

Incidentally, it is my aim that your attention not only be gained, but that the Church Body of the Lord Jesus Christ <u>WAKE UP</u> and not remain in darkness regarding His Word on the subject of the end-times and His return. And it is for this matter that I humbly write and cry out to God to open our eyes on this subject. Too long we as a Church have reproduced an end-time theology that has been based upon traditional and yet sensational teaching, only to unfortunately become blinded to the very truths of Scripture that therein lie.

And it is now time to wake up!

For as the Apostle Paul wrote in First Thessalonians 5:5-6,

> "But you, brethren, are not in darkness, so that this Day should overtake you as a thief. You are sons of the light and sons of the (D)ay. We are not of the night nor of darkness. Therefore let us not sleep, as others do, but let us watch and be sober."

<u>Author's Note</u>: Each chapter in this book is written in the form of an overview first followed by a Scriptural explanation. I have chosen to do this for a couple of reasons. First, the end-time subjects in and of themselves can be very detailed, complex, confusing, and difficult

to follow. Thus, so as not to lose readers in the process, I have chosen to provide the overview in the first part of each chapter which should be easier to read, simpler to understand, and easier to follow. Then, in the second part, I will provide the Scriptural basis and explanation, which of course, will be more complex and detailed. Quite possibly, and this is my prayer, it will provide a much easier way to follow along in this difficult subject of the end-times!

"9-1-1"
Scripturally Explained

As mentioned already, Daniel 11:40-45 is the basis for this chapter. Although a more detailed explanation will be provided later in this book, I will provide at least a general explanation right now. Daniel writes, "And <u>at the time of the end shall the king of the south push at him</u>: and <u>the king of the north shall come against him</u> like a whirlwind, with chariots, and with horsemen, and with many ships; and <u>he shall enter into the countries</u>, and shall overflow and pass over" (vs. 40). The "him" in this verse is the "little horn" of Daniel 8. Although I will share more later in this book regarding this "little horn," this very well could be the Palestinian leader Chairman Yasser Arafat. The "king of the south" is a character originating from the southern kingdom, historically known as the Ptolemaic empire which, incidentally, on a map would include what is present day Egypt and Saudi Arabia. Any alliance the United States would have with any countries from this southern kingdom would potentially allow them to indirectly be considered as a part of this reference to the "king of the south." This, by the way, took place during the Gulf War in 1991 when the U.S. defended Kuwait against Iraq. This is because Kuwait lies within the geographic boundaries of the southern kingdom while Iraq lies within the boundaries of the northern kingdom. Incidentally, the "king of the north" obviously originates from the "northern kingdom" which historically included what today would be Iraq, Afghanistan, Pakistan, Iran, and Syria, to name a few. Again, I will provide greater detail and explanation regarding these subjects in later chapters of this book. Nevertheless, a counter-reaction on their part would therefore constitute a move on the part of this "king of the north."

Daniel continues in verse 41, "He shall enter also into the <u>glorious land</u>, and <u>many countries shall be overthrown</u>: but these shall escape out of his hand, even Edom, and Moab, and the chief of the children of Ammon." In this case, the "glorious land" happens to be the nation of Israel of which encounters a sudden turning by them against itself. Edom, Moab, and Ammon happen to represent present day Jordan which for some reason seems to be immune from this conflict.

It is at this point that what Jesus described in Luke 21:20 will have come to pass, "And when ye shall see <u>Jerusalem compassed with armies</u>, then know that <u>the desolation thereof is nigh</u>." This sudden surrounding of it will take place by armies of Arab descent with one aim in mind – the destruction of and taking over of Jerusalem. When this happens, the result will be that the Jewish people will run for their lives, as Jesus described in Luke 21:21-22, "Then <u>let them which are in Judea flee to the mountains</u>; and let them which are in the midst of it depart out; and let not them that are in the countries enter thereinto. <u>For these be the days of vengeance, that all things which are written may be fulfilled.</u>"

How long will this take place? The Apostle John provides this answer in Revelation 11:2, "But the court which is without the temple leave out, and measure it not (which speaks of Jerusalem); for it is given unto the Gentiles: and <u>the holy city shall they tread under foot forty and two months</u>." Incidentally, forty-two months represents three and one-half years - the length of the tribulation period of which Israel suffers from.

Daniel continues with verse 42, "He shall stretch forth his hand also upon the countries: and the land of Egypt shall not escape. But he shall have power over the treasures of gold and of silver, and over all the precious things of Egypt: and the Libyans and the Ethiopians shall be at his steps. But <u>tidings out of the east and out of the north shall trouble him</u>: therefore he shall go forth with great fury to destroy, and utterly to make away many. And <u>he shall plant the tabernacles of his palace between the seas in the glorious holy mountain; yet he shall come to his end</u>, and none shall help him." It is at this point that Israel will turn to Jesus as their Messiah. As the Prophet Zechariah recorded in Zechariah 13:9, "And <u>they shall call on my name</u>, I will hear them: I will say, It is my people: and they shall say, The Lord is my God." The result — Jesus will exact revenge against the Arabs in the valley of Meggido, a day known as the battle of Armageddon, "And it shall come to pass in that day, that <u>I will seek to destroy all the nations that come against Jerusalem</u>. In that day shall there be a great mourning in Jerusalem, as the mourning of Hadad-rimmon <u>in the valley of Megiddon</u>" (Zechariah 12:9,11). Or as John put it in Revelation 16:16, "And he gathered them together into a place called in the Hebrew tongue <u>Armageddon</u>."

This would complete the period known as the tribulation. But what really is the tribulation and how long is it? As I mentioned earlier, I will provide further detail regarding some of these above mentioned end-time subjects in later chapters of this book. Nevertheless, it is in the next chapter that I would like to say more on this topic of the tribulation, otherwise known in Scripture as "the time of Jacob's (<u>Israel's</u>) trouble" (Jeremiah 30:7).

- Part 2 -

"The End-Time Period"

Dennis Crump

Chapter 1

"The Tribulation"

It has been generally accepted that the length of the tribulation is to be seven years long. It is said that this seven year tribulation is further broken down into two periods each of three and one-half years. Although, the first period is often referred to as just the "tribulation," the second period has been coined the "<u>great</u> tribulation." This view is so prominent and so accepted that seldom, if ever, will one even dare to challenge it. But what if one were to question the length? Is it really seven years? What if one were, perhaps, to at least ask for the scriptural references to support a tribulation period that totals seven years? What would they find?

Unfortunately, it is this very question that leads to a conclusion that should raise further questions for one quickly finds that there really is only one, that's right, <u>ONE</u> passage of Scripture that has been used to teach a tribulation period that totals seven years. Oh yes, there are numerous other passages that speak of three and one-half year periods and of course, adding any two of these together will equal seven years. Nevertheless there still is only one passage that actually addresses a full seven-year period in the reference. So let me challenge this teaching with the question, "What if that one passage has been misinterpreted?" Is it possible? Sure. Is it probable?

The passage is Daniel 9:24-27 – a difficult passage to read, let alone understand. However when explained properly, it is fairly obvious what it is saying. Let me share with you what I mean.

In the book of Daniel, chapter 9, the Prophet Daniel cries out to God to have mercy on His people, the nation of Israel. At the time, Israel was not a free people and it was getting to the point where one began to wonder if freedom would ever come. Even more frustrating was the fact that the people of Israel had been told by God that they would be given a land flowing with milk and honey, or a haven, if you will – the Promised Land! Since God was not a liar, if definitely raised questions for them and most likely stirred up a great deal of frustration. Some of them even began to lose hope that they would ever be free again. It is in this state of affairs that Daniel appeals to

God based upon His promise - (my paraphrase) **"Don't You want Your people to be free? You promised...?"**, to which God actually responded. His response (again paraphrased by myself) went something along the lines of this:

> "My servant Daniel: There will be 490 years that will be used to define the period from the point that the command was given to rebuild Jerusalem unto the time that the Messiah will be set up as your King in order to bring in righteousness for the rest of eternity. At this point, there will no longer be a need for any more sacrifices and thus all sins will finally be forgiven. This period of 490 years will be further subdivided into a period of 483 years (made up of two successive periods of 49 years and 434 years) and a period of 7 years. In fact, sometime after this 483 year period the Messiah will go to the cross, but not for Himself. He will actually be doing it for others. Unfortunately, Jerusalem will then be destroyed, as well as its Temple. In fact, I will hold the Jewish people responsible for this outcome. Their consequence will be that they will suffer a period of both desolation and continuous conflict. Nevertheless, the Messiah will usher in a NEW covenant, that is, a better and stronger covenant for My people. This covenant will be bookended by two periods of three and one-half years each with the final sacrifice of His own life taking place in between. It is at this point, with His death on the cross, that there will no longer be any additional need, EVER, for anymore sacrifices for sins! That need will cease. However since My people, the Israelites, failed in their responsibility of letting Me show Myself through her to her neighboring nations, but instead participated in an

> abundance of abominable practices, even encouraging these abominations, they will therefore suffer the consequence of becoming a desolate people right on up until the completion of this 490 year period!"

This was quite a mouthful, wouldn't you say? Incidentally, the two 3½ year periods are not, nor do they have to be, continuous or back to back in their occurrence. That is, there is a gap between these two periods of 3½ years. Actually, the first 3½ years have already been fulfilled in history. When? During Jesus's ministry term at His First Coming. From the time Jesus began His public ministry after being baptized in the Jordan River by John the Baptist up until His sacrificial death on the cross, there was a total of 3½ years. This is the first 3½ year period. The last 3½ year period has yet to be fulfilled and is what is referenced in Scripture as the great tribulation period. In between these two periods, of course, was the Messiah's being "cut off," or His death on the cross. And this is why the tribulation period is only 3½ years long — a considerable difference from the traditional teaching of seven years! So, how does tradition really explain Daniel 9:24-27? Basically, it goes something like this:

> "After the first 483 years following Daniel's prayer, the Messiah (Jesus) is cut off (crucified) by the Romans who then destroy the city of Jerusalem. The prince that shall come is the Antichrist and his people (the revived Roman empire) shall with war bring in the end of the age (the tribulation). This tribulation period will commence when the Antichrist signs a 7-year *peace* treaty (one week covenant) with Israel. However, in the middle of this seven year period (in the midst of the week), the Antichrist will go into the rebuilt temple, make himself out to be God, cause the reestablished Jewish system of sacrifices to stop, and pour out his wrath upon the whole world. This will be quite a horrific period of time and is

> known as both the "abomination of desolation" and "great tribulation," that is, the last 3½ year period prior to Christ's return."

Of course, you can see the considerable difference between the two interpretations. Were it not for the fact that this one passage in Daniel is the only place in Scripture used to teach a seven year period of tribulation, the length might not be in question. However, it is the only reference and in fact, it actually does not even say seven years, but rather just refers to a "week" of years, which though it totals seven, still demands further examination. This one subject, if in fact it has been traditionally misinterpreted, would actually impact many of the other teachings regarding the end-times as well. And its impact can be far reaching, of which much of the rest of this book will address. Nevertheless, for a more thorough and detailed explanation of Daniel 9:24-27, please continue on in reading the second half of this chapter before we get to the next topic addressing the question of who the major players will be during this end-time period?

"The Tribulation"
Scripturally Explained

Again, the reference in question is found in the Old Testament book of Daniel, specifically, chapter nine. In Daniel 9:24-27, Daniel receives an answer from God to a prayer of intercession that he had been offering up on the behalf of God's people, the nation of Israel. At the time of this prayer, Israel had been held captive by a Gentile people led by King Darius of the Medo-Persian empire. In response to Daniel's prayer, God finally gave him His answer through the angel Gabriel, recorded in these four verses (vs. 24-27). The answer, prophetic in nature, was that there would be a period of "seventy weeks" of years, or 490 years, of time to elapse prior to the fulfillment of what Daniel's prayer was really requesting. In verse 25, one quickly sees that the 490 years would not be one continuous period, but rather a period of seven weeks of years (49 years) first, followed by a period of 62 weeks of years (434 years). Then in verse 27, there follows an additional period of one week of years (7 years). We know that they are multiple periods because verse 26 explains that until the end comes, "desolations" (plural), meaning more than one period of desolation as opposed to just a single period of desolation (singular), are determined for Israel.

The first two periods (the 7 weeks and 62 weeks of years, or 483 years) historically have already been fulfilled. It is this last week of years that most people believe has yet to be fulfilled. But is this really the case?

A closer look at this passage should reveal some interesting things, to include just how long this tribulation period really is. The passage goes as follows:

> vs. 24 - "*Seventy weeks are determined upon thy people and upon thy holy city, to finish the transgression, and to make an end of sins, and to make reconciliation for iniquity, and to bring in everlasting righteousness, and to seal up the vision and prophecy, and to anoint the most Holy.*"
>
> vs. 25 - "*Know therefore and understand, that from the going forth of the commandment to restore and to build Jerusalem unto the Messiah the Prince shall be seven weeks,*

and threescore and two weeks: the street shall be built again, and the wall, even in troublous times."

vs. 26 - "And after threescore and two weeks shall Messiah be cut off, but not for himself: and the people of the prince that shall come shall destroy the city and the sanctuary; and the end thereof shall be with a flood, and unto the end of the war desolations are determined.

vs. 27 - "And he shall confirm the covenant with many for one week: and in the midst of the week he shall cause the sacrifice and the oblation to cease, and for the overspreading of abominations he shall make it desolate, even until the consummation, and that determined shall be poured upon the desolate."

The first thing to notice is that the "Messiah the Prince" of verse 25, the "Messiah" of verse 26, the "prince" of verse 26, and the "he" of verse 27 are all the same individual — that is, Jesus Christ. Most people will quickly point out that the "prince" in verse 26 and the "he" in verse 27 are not capitalized, and therefore cannot be Christ. Unfortunately, this is an argument that does not, rather cannot, exist. Why? Many fail to realize or else forget that the Bible you and I read is actually written in English, complete with capital letters, numbered verses, punctuation, etc.. Our English version however is a translation from the original version, that being in the Hebrew language. Unfortunately, in the Hebrew there is no such thing as upper and lower case letters. In other words, there are no capital letters. Thus, the words "Prince" and "prince" appear identical in the Hebrew. You would not know this without a prior understanding of the Hebrew language. This, unfortunately, is lost in the translation process. As a matter of fact, it is at this point that the biased interpretation of those doing the translating takes over, because it is they who have determined to make one ("Prince") capitalized while the other is not ("prince").

Another major factor that is lost in interpreting this passage is the very use of the English language's basic literary and grammatical rules. For example, just follow the rules and watch what you end up with:

Wake Up Church: The End is Nigh!

1. In verse 25, one character is introduced into the passage. He is identified with a specific and complete identity — the "Messiah the Prince."
2. Daniel, having now identified his only character specifically and completely in verse 25, is more general in verse 26, referring to this same character again, but only as "Messiah." This is found in the very first part of the first sentence. However, he refers to him again in the second part of this sentence only instead using the other part of his title - the "prince" — in the phrase "the people of the prince." Again, it would actually appear the same as the capitalized "Prince" had the translators left out their bias. Nevertheless, the most important point is that this is NOT to be understood as a new or different character. It would be grammatically incorrect to introduce a new character here within this same phrase in which the emphasis is on the "people" and not on the "prince." However, it is correct and is therefore assumed that the "people" emphasized belong to the already existing "prince" that was previously identified.
3. Now, having familiarized you both specifically (as in "Messiah the Prince") and in general (as in "Messiah" first and then "Prince") in verses 25 and 26, Daniel takes an even more general approach in verse 27. He refers to this character (which is still the first character — in fact, he is actually the only character referred to in this entire passage!) using only the general pronoun of "he" — three times. One should note that the rules of grammar prohibit you from the use of a pronoun without the original introduction of the character at first with a more specific identity. Therefore the "he" can only refer to the "Messiah the Prince."
4. To say that the "prince" in verse 26 was a reference to the Antichrist might be acceptable were it not for the prior introduction of the "Messiah the Prince" in verse 25. But having already been introduced, and being the only character thus far in this passage, this "prince" can be none other than the "Messiah."

5. To put it another way, an example of this would be for you to be talking to someone about myself, first identifying me in a specific manner, such as in "Pastor Dennis Crump." In the next sentence, you refer to me more casually — first as "Pastor" and then as "Dennis". Finally you then, having already identified me, refer to me in the remaining few times just as "he" or "him."

Of course, all this above explanation would not really matter if these new "changes" in explaining this passage did not even fit the interpretation. The following thus serves as an appropriate and more detailed interpretation of Daniel 9:24-27 beginning with verse 24:

> *vs. 24 - "Seventy weeks are determined upon thy people and upon thy holy city, to finish the transgression, and to make an end of sins, and to make reconciliation for iniquity, and to bring in everlasting righteousness, and to seal up the vision and prophecy, and to anoint the most Holy."*

In answering the prayer request of Daniel, God first indicates in this verse that there is a time period involved — "seventy weeks." Next, God reveals the recipient of this answer to prayer — "thy people and thy holy city." This, of course, refers to none other than the nation of Israel and the city of Jerusalem. At this, God then lists six things that will have taken place upon the completion of this stated time period, which reveals why this period is necessary:

1. To finish the transgression,
2. To make an end of sins,
3. To make reconciliation for iniquity,
4. To bring in everlasting righteousness,
5. To seal up the vision and prophecy, and
6. To anoint the most Holy.

Ironically, the ministry in the life of one man fulfilled the completion of all six of these objectives. That man, of course, was the "Messiah the Prince," or Jesus Christ, and His ministry lasted all of three and one-half years. Some cross references indicating the fulfillment of each of these six things listed above are as follows:

1. Is. 53:8; Gal. 3:19; Heb. 9:15 ("finish" = John 4:34; 5:36; 17:4)
2. 1 Jn. 3:5; Heb. 9:26; Mt. 1:21; Jn. 1:29; Acts 3:19; 1 Cor. 15:3; 1 Pt. 2:24; Heb. 10:4-12; Lk. 7:48
3. Is. 53:6; 2 Cor. 5:18-19; Tit. 2:14; Col. 1:20-21; Eph. 2:16; Heb. 2:17
4. Mt. 3:15; Rm. 3:21-26; 2 Cor. 5:21; Heb. 1:9; 9:12; 1 Cor. 1:30; 1 Pt. 2:24; 1 Jn. 2:29; Rm. 10:4
5. Acts 3:18; Mt. 11:13
6. Lk. 8:28; Acts 4:27; 10:38; Mk. 1:24; Heb. 1:9 (Note: "Messiah" actually means "Anointed one")

Some additional points to note are that the purpose God had for these "seventy weeks" is alluded to in the same chapter, only in an earlier verse. Note verse 2, "the word of the Lord came to Jeremiah the prophet, that he would accomplish seventy years in the desolations of Jerusalem." Thus, the seventy years is the timetable God uses to at last bring to an end the desolations of Jerusalem, only he discovers that it is actually to be seventy "weeks" of years (or 70 "7-year" periods).

It would serve to note also at this point that, conceivably, it could have only taken sixty-nine and one-half weeks of years had the Jewish people received Jesus Christ as the Messiah during His first coming. During that time, it was the nation of Israel that was considered God's people — they were the recipients of the Old Covenant. Quite often in their presence, Jesus (and John the Baptist) declared that "the kingdom was at hand" (Mt. 3:2; 4:17,23; etc.). Why and how could this be true? Jesus was the King of Kings and thus their King (Mt. 27:11,29,37). He was already prepared to go to Jerusalem and usher in the new era of His theocratic and Divine rule (Mt. 21). Unfortunately, the Scriptures say that they did not receive or even acknowledge Him as their King (Jn. 1:11). As a matter of fact, they would actually end up being the ones God would hold ultimately responsible for crucifying Jesus (Acts 2:22-23,36). As a result, God pronounced judgment upon them (Mt. 23; Lk. 21:24) and in turn offered the Kingdom, under a new and better covenant, unto the Gentiles (Rm. 11:11). This "new age" would begin, however, with Israel being instead made spiritually blind by God and it would last on up "until the fulness of the Gentiles be come in" (Rm. 11:25; Lk. 21:24), at which point Israel would finally humble themselves and acknowledge Jesus as their Messiah and Lord (Mt. 23:39). This last prophetic period of 3½ years serves as the judgment upon Israel by God which brings them to their knees and in turn, is thereby also known as the "time of Jacob's (or Israel's) trouble" (Jer. 30:7). Thus, this explains the need for the last half week (or 3½ years) of the seventy weeks of years prophesied about.

> *vs. 25 - "Know therefore and understand, that from the going forth of the commandment to restore and to build Jerusalem unto the Messiah the Prince shall be seven weeks, and threescore and two weeks: the street shall be built again, and the wall, even in troublous times."*

Incidentally, this verse has already been historically fulfilled and therefore, for our purposes today, has no further prophetic fulfillment. The "commandment" went forth during the reign of Cyrus (2 Chron. 36:20-23; Ezra 1:1-4; 4:4-5; 6:1-5) and the sixty-nine weeks of years were culminated upon the anointment of Jesus as "Messiah the Prince" at His baptism by John the Baptist in the Jordan River.

> *vs. 26 - "And after threescore and two weeks shall Messiah be cut off, but not for himself: and the people of the prince that shall come shall destroy the city and the sanctuary; and the end thereof shall be with a flood, and unto the end of the war desolations are determined."*

In examining verse 26, first notice the word "after" at the beginning of this verse. It does not say, "at the end of." The point here is that the Messiah was to be cut off at some point subsequent to or "after" the completion of the sixty-nine weeks, but not necessarily immediately at the end of it. As it turned out, this was the case because He was cut off during the seventieth week. The Messiah of course is Jesus Christ (the Greek word "Christ" and Hebrew word "Messiah" actually mean the same thing), His being "cut off" was the crucifixion (Is. 53:8; Mt. 27:35), and as it turned out, it was "not for himself" but rather for the "many" (Mt. 26:28), which actually included "the whole world" (Jn. 3:16).

Next, notice that in the phrase "the people of the (P)rince <u>that shall come</u>," that at the time of Daniel writing this, the Prince (Jesus) had yet to come. Most people today read this phrase thinking that the only prince yet to come is the Antichrist, the problem though being that they fail to read this verse from the perspective of the time that it was written – that is, at a time when Messiah had yet to come. Again, this too points to this prince's identity as being the Messiah, not the Antichrist.

In this same phrase we also see that it is God's people who "destroy the city and the sanctuary." But was it the Jews who destroyed Jerusalem? Not directly, anyway. However, they were held accountable for their role of being used by God to be the agent through whom God would choose to reveal Himself to the rest of the world. Thus, it was necessary for them to cooperate with Him. However, they did not and therefore ended up being a stumbling block for others. Thus, God held them responsible for this. As a result, this would be one of the primary reasons for their demise – a consequence for their own stubbornness. The result was that they would experience many "desolations" as well as ultimately be left "desolate," just as Jesus pronounced in Matthew 23:37-38, "O Jerusalem, Jerusalem, thou that killest the prophets, and stonest them which are sent unto thee, how often would I have gathered thy children together, even as a hen gathereth her chickens under her wings, and ye would not! Behold, <u>your house is left unto you desolate</u>." This Scripturally helps to explain why it is the Israelites who are accused of being the ones who "destroy the city and the sanctuary!"

Next, in the latter part of verse 26, we see that "the end thereof shall be with a flood." Did (or will) the destruction of Jerusalem take place with a flood? Yes... if you understand how the word "flood" is often used in Scripture. Many times the word "flood" is symbolic and denotes the taking place of "war" (see Dan.11:22; Is 59:19; Ps. 18:4; Jer. 46:7-9; 47:2) which was certainly the case with the destruction of Jerusalem then and will certainly also be the case just prior to Christ's return (Lk. 21:20).

Finally, the verse ends with, "and unto the end of the war (= flood = war!) desolations are determined." Is this to be true of Jerusalem? Again, notice the words of Jesus in Matthew 23:37-39, "O Jerusalem, Jerusalem, thou that killest the prophets, and stonest them which are sent unto thee, how often would I have gathered thy children together, even as a hen gathereth her chickens under her wings, and ye would not! <u>Behold, your house is left unto you desolate</u>. For I say unto you, Ye shall not see me henceforth, till ye shall say, Blessed is he that cometh in the name of the Lord."

> *vs. 27 - "And he shall confirm the covenant with many for one week: and in the midst of the week he shall cause the sacrifice and the oblation to cease, and for the overspreading of abominations he shall make it desolate, even until the consummation, and that determined shall be poured upon the desolate."*

Finally, in evaluating verse 27, first notice that the "he" throughout this verse again is the Messiah. Also, the word "shall" is a future tense verb that certainly was future in Daniel's day, but has since, from the perspective of our day, already been fulfilled.

In addition, a study of the word "confirm" ultimately makes an even stronger case for the "he" being the Messiah rather than the Antichrist. First of all, the word is associated with the word "covenant." Rather than speculating that this must be some form of a peace treaty, as is traditionally taught, one only has to go back a few verses within the same ninth chapter to determine exactly what Daniel means by "covenant." Notice that in verse 4, Daniel's petition to God for his people is in reference to a covenant already in existence – the one God had already made with Israel — a "covenant of mercy" (the Hebrew word translated here as "and" is interchangeable with "of," therefore rendering the phrase "covenant and mercy" to mean "covenant of mercy"). This same covenant is referred to as a "covenant of peace" in Numbers 25:12 (Wouldn't it be reasonable to reckon the "covenant of peace" as being made stronger by this "Messiah the Prince" – or the "Prince of Peace?"). In other words, this covenant actually is the first covenant that God made with His people – or the Abrahamic covenant (Gen. 17). It served its purpose, but God in His wisdom chose to improve upon it, thus making it the "old covenant" and instead bringing in the "new covenant," a covenant with "many," if you will (Matt. 26:28; Mk. 14:24; Lk. 2:34). And this is where the study of the word "confirm" comes in. The Hebrew word and its Greek counterpart "gabar" mean "to put to more strength" or "to make stronger," which is exactly what the Messiah did with His death on the cross (Gal. 3:15-17; 4:24; Heb. 8:6-7,13; Lk. 1:69-73; Acts 3:25-26)! That is, He made the new covenant a stronger one, which is also why His death was the final and complete sacrifice, ultimately satisfying the demands of God's justice.

Then in the next portion of verse 27 it says, "and <u>in the midst of the week</u> he shall cause the sacrifice and the oblation to cease." Rather than referring to the Antichrist, again the "he" is a reference to the Messiah. Actually, a study of Christ's ministry on earth will reveal that He again fits these parameters like a glove. Specifically, during the first coming of Christ, from the moment His ministry began with His baptism by John the Baptist to its end with His crucifixion, Jesus' ministry lasted all of three and one-half years. This 3½ year period is the first half of the last week, or seventieth week, referred to here by Daniel. Thus, in the midst of this week, or after 3½ years, Jesus was cut off, or crucified. Once again, His crucifixion was considered in God's eyes as the final sacrifice, thereby causing "the sacrifice and the oblation" required by the Jewish system "to cease" (Heb. 7:22,27; 9:26; 10:8-12).

Continuing on in verse 27, the next portion states, "and for the overspreading of abominations he shall make it desolate, even until the consummation." The intent of what Daniel is saying here in the Hebrew is, "because someone has caused an overspreading of abominations, he (the Messiah) shall make it (the land) desolate." This happens to be a reference to the works of and the corresponding judgment upon the nation of Israel. The religious leaders of this Hebrew nation were the pharisees and God hated their works. The word "abomination" means "something that God hates or detests" and this was definitely true of the works of the pharisees and scribes. The entire 23rd chapter of Matthew, by the way, consists of Jesus rebuking them for their works and it ends with Jesus pronouncing judgment upon the city of Jerusalem (vs. 37) and the house (or nation) of Israel (vs. 38 — "Behold, your house is left unto you desolate"). This, of course, is what is meant by the "abomination of desolation" that Jesus referred to as recorded in Matthew 24:15-16. However, a more proper rendering of this phrase would be the "abomination that maketh desolation." In other words, the ultimate desolation of Israel/Jerusalem takes place during the last 3½ year period of this seventieth week of Daniel (or during the great tribulation period). Compare Matthew 24:15-21 with Luke 21:20-24 and you will see that "abomination of desolation" in Matthew 24:15 is the same thing as, and therefore occurs, "when ye shall see Jerusalem compassed with armies" (Luke 21:20). Of course, this desolation will continue to take place, as it states, "even until the consummation," which is a reference to the end of the seventieth week or end of the tribulation period.

Finally, the judgment that falls upon Israel/Jerusalem during the great tribulation period (or last 3½ years) is reflected by the last part of verse 27 of Daniel chapter 9, "and <u>that determined</u> (judgment) shall be poured upon the desolate (Israel/Jerusalem)." The following timeline thus illustrates the prophetic record of these 70 weeks of years:

Daniel's 70 Weeks of Years

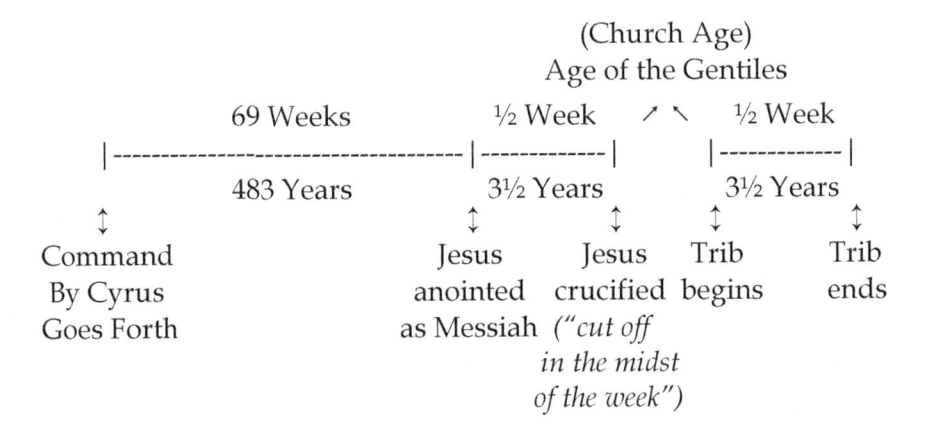

```
                                        (Church Age)
                                      Age of the Gentiles
              69 Weeks               ½ Week    ↗ ↘    ½ Week
     |---------------------------|-------------|   |-------------|
              483 Years              3½ Years              3½ Years
     ↕                               ↕         ↕      ↕          ↕
   Command                         Jesus     Jesus   Trib      Trib
   By Cyrus                       anointed  crucified begins   ends
   Goes Forth                    as Messiah ("cut off
                                            in the midst
                                            of the week")
```

To summarize this interpretation, there is but a three and one-half year period of end-time prophecy yet to be fulfilled when evaluating this passage in Daniel chapter nine. There is a Biblical rule that consistently applies here being that the best interpretation of Scripture is not what others say or think (which is mere speculation) but rather what other Scriptures have to say about it. The writers of

Scripture, especially in penning the New Testament, frequently used words, phrases, or conceptual ideas that cross referenced to the Old Testament Scriptures. Why? Well, at the time of their writing the New Testament books, the only existing Scriptures that they had were what we would call the Old Testament. Thus, humanly speaking, the referencing of the Old Testament Scriptures helped to validate their (New Testament) writings. Also, the Divine writer, being God the Holy Spirit, used the rule of two witnesses to validate these facts (see Mt. 18:16). Unfortunately, in the case of a seven year tribulation as is often the interpretation from this passage, one can find no other Scriptural reference to this same time period. On the other hand, there are numerous references to but a 3½ year time period left (Dan. 12:7; Rev. 12:6; 13:5). This necessitates the question of whether this passage in Daniel has been interpreted correctly. The above explanation not only has a Scriptural basis based on other Scriptures, but also has the luxury of fitting in throughout God's Word as one begins to "rightly divide the word of truth" (2 Tim. 2:15) with this interpretation in mind, to include fitting in with all the other major end-time passages (e.g., Revelation). The implications of this particular interpretation should only further raise numerous questions coming from those who have in the past embraced the various other end-time viewpoints. At the same time, it should also raise some serious concerns regarding the generally accepted "traditional" teachings. The bottom line here is that if Daniel 9:24-27 has been traditionally misinterpreted, and if the only character in this passage is Jesus the Messiah, then **to teach that the "prince" in this passage is the Antichrist is not only very dangerous, but it is borderline blasphemous**! Nevertheless, in response to the many additional questions that are assumed to therefore arise from this interpretation, many of them should, and in fact, will be answered in the remaining chapters that follow within this book.

Dennis Crump

- Part 3 -

"The End-Time Players"

Dennis Crump

Chapter 2

"Israel"

Many people really do want to know just who will be involved in this end-time event known as the tribulation. Some desire to know just because of a genuine interest that they might have in God's plans while others are just more fascinated with the sensationalism of the event and its details. Still others want to know because of sheer fear for their own well being. Regardless of the reason, the outcome won't change. God knows who will be involved and He has set it in their hearts to accomplish His will. The events will fall into place just as He has determined and that includes the individuals, nations, and peoples. One thing is for certain however, the nation of Israel, and specifically the city of Jerusalem, will be the focal point of all that will occur during this 3½ year tribulation period.

"Israel"
Scripturally Explained

When it comes to defining who is involved, Bible teachers agree on some players and disagree on others. In fact, there are a variety of viewpoints. The views are varied and range from everyone being involved, albeit global catastrophe, to the mention of just those with more extended roles such as a nation or an alliance of nations. What was once the predominant viewpoint of a revived Roman empire being the major player has now undergone reconsideration as various other interpretations have also arisen. People often wonder what the role of the United States will be in this scenario? To answer this, many Bible teachers make predictions while others speculate. People also desire to know if the Christians will be here to witness this terrible time? There have been three prevailing viewpoints to answer this question, each identifying their position by a label — the pre-tribber, the mid-tribber, or the post-tribber. These however all assume a seven-year tribulation. Yet with only a three and one-half year tribulation, as was taught in the previous chapter, the range of choices now narrows to only two potential viewpoints. One thing is for sure on this subject — Israel is a major player. Yet, even its extent of involvement can be debated. Certainly in the midst of all of this confusion it would be wise to ask, "What saith the Scriptures?"

Obviously, a good place to start is on common ground. Do the Scriptures teach that Israel will be involved in this tribulation? Without a doubt! And the words of Jesus, referring to the time of the tribulation, suffice, "Then let them which be in Judea (Israel) flee into the mountains" (Mt. 24:16). Certainly, Israel will be right there in the midst of this event. Unfortunately, this will not be a pleasant time for this people, for Jeremiah refers to it as "the time of Jacob's trouble" (Jer. 30:7). But why Israel and why will it be such trouble for them?

It is important to note again that this period of three and one-half years relates back to Daniel's prayer as recorded in the book of Daniel (Dan. 9:2). Desolations were determined upon Israel and Daniel inquired about this, seeking to know the length of this judgment. Daniel refers back to the book of Jeremiah as to why Israel was being judged (with "perpetual desolations"). In this book, Jeremiah relates how God, provoked by Israel to anger, accordingly pronounces His verdict (Jer. 25:3-11). What Israel failed to do was hearken unto God, obey Him, follow Him as their God, and thereby possess and dwell in the cherished land that God had purposely reserved for them. The result: No Promised Land to come for them. Rather, the land that they had would be perpetually desolate — for seventy weeks of years, or until the end of the tribulation. At that point, in humility, Israel will finally cry out to Jehovah God in repentance and acknowledge Jesus Christ as their Messiah (Mt. 23:39; Zech. 12-13; Rm. 11:26). In effect, this is why Israel is a part of the tribulation period. But does this (a lack of obedience) really explain why Israel will have it so bad during this period? Hardly.

Actually, God chose Israel as His people to work with and through whom to demonstrate Himself to the world. They were entrusted with the Gospel. The Gospel, though, was a Gospel of repentance during that time, associated with the Law of Moses and illustrating faith in a living God. However, Israel continually would not obey God and in turn, complicated and messed up the Law. As a result, they even served other gods. Thus, rather than these other nations turning to Israel's God, Israel instead turned to their gods. Ultimately, Israel was even credited with the deaths of its own prophets and the crucifixion of its Messiah (Mt. 23:31-37; Zech. 12:10). As the Bible puts it, "(Jesus) came unto His own, (but) His own received Him not" (Jn. 1:11). It is for this reason that blindness came upon Israel and the Gospel was made available to the Gentiles (Rm. 11). This was a mystery indeed and included within this mystery was the result that Israel would suffer!

Chapter 3

"Mystery Babylon"

Anything that is a mystery means that most people neither recognize it nor figure it out, especially without a great deal of investigation and/or evaluation. Believe it or not, there are some things that even God happens to categorize as mysterious. This does not mean that they are a mystery to God, yet to us they are! Although these mysteries are identified as such, they are not beyond figuring out. God honors those who diligently seek to know Him and His ways, to include even revealing to them the mysteries of Scripture. In fact, He has assisted those in this process who believe in Him by providing them with the Holy Spirit – the same One who inspired the Scriptures and who teaches Believers by revealing spiritual truth and understanding to them.

On the subject of the end times, although it is certainly true that the whole thing is a mystery, at the same time there is a specific end-time topic that is also a mystery. Not surprisingly, it is found in the book of Revelation, yet it is seldom the subject of various end-time discussions, debates, or teachings. Then again, this makes sense being that it is a mystery. What is amazing, however, is that the Apostle John actually spends two full chapters discussing it. In other words, basically ten percent of what he wrote about was this mysterious subject. Does this not surprise you? Although John devotes one-tenth of his time discussing just this one particular subject, it seems that we rarely, if at all, ever even touch on it. But then again ... it is a mystery.

So what is this mystery? He identifies it as "Babylon." That's right – Babylon! A city! The same one that today is located in Iraq, right? Sorry! Actually, that wouldn't be too much of a mystery, would it? Yet this particular Babylon we know is a mystery. God actually declared it as such! Unfortunately, it seems that few people have identified what this "Mystery Babylon" truly is referring to.

In chapter 17 of Revelation, John describes a woman that he saw in a vision. His description of her seems to show no mercy because he immediately labels her as a whore! By verse five he writes, under the inspiration of the Holy Spirit by the way, "And upon her forehead was a name written, **MYSTERY, BABYLON THE GREAT, THE MOTHER OF HARLOTS AND ABOMINATIONS OF THE EARTH.**" Sounds pretty flattering, wouldn't you say? But seriously, what is John really talking about here? And who is this woman? And of course, what is this mystery? Or better, WHY is it a mystery?

I have to admit, I once sided with the traditional viewpoint. That is, I used to believe that the Babylon here was the city of Rome. Oh by the way, it is a city! By the end of chapter eighteen, that becomes obvious and clear. Traditionally, it was believed that this was Rome because it was not only the central location of the empire that physically destroyed Jerusalem following Christ's time on earth, but also because it presently is the location of the Vatican. To be sure, many have concluded that the Catholic Church with its Papal system of religion is the true enemy of both God and Christianity. No longer, however, do I see this mysterious Babylon through the eyes of tradition.

I next began to believe that it was to be taken literally. That is I believed, as so many others do, that this Babylon was in fact the actual Babylon – the one in Iraq! There exists other viewpoints as well, such as it being symbolic of the world, or the world's system of today, or even that it is a representation of the system of religion. However, none of these viewpoints truly fit the full context of all forty-two verses from chapters seventeen and eighteen of Revelation in which John describes this mystery. That being said, the question begs to be asked, "Who is this Mystery Babylon?"

The answer, incidentally, is Jerusalem. **That's right, JERUSALEM!** The first time I heard that it was Jerusalem, I balked at it. Didn't give it a second thought. No way could it be the beloved city that is so dear to the Christian faith! Even more so, it was near and dear to God's heart. It didn't make any sense, I thought. So how could it be Jerusalem?

However, I began to think with my eyes and not just my emotions. In other words, I began to compare Scripture with Scripture and sought to rightly divide God's Word. The result – it fit like a glove! It really did. Folks, Jerusalem is the "Mother of all harlots and abominations of the earth." Jerusalem is the whore! Sure, it doesn't seem to make any sense. But do you realize the impact of this? In other words, it truly is a mystery! Even though it was already established that Israel would be a major player during the end-times, I bring this up because it begins to shed light on just how much they might have to do with God's reason for the tribulation, or the end-times as a whole. (I am sure it would shock you if you truly knew the answer, as I too am, of which we will increasingly discover as we continue further into this book.)

"Mystery Babylon"
Scripturally Explained

The seventeenth and eighteenth chapters of Revelation concern the fall of a great city, referred to as Babylon. Debate follows as to whether this is a literal or symbolic Babylon. But again, what saith the Scriptures? Neither!

Specifically, the Scriptures refer to it as "Mystery Babylon" (Rev. 17:5). This "Mystery Babylon" is none other than Jerusalem (in Israel) and, amazingly, depicts that horrific judgment (or wrath) that God assigns it. Though few realize this, these two chapters are full of clues that point to Jerusalem as this "Mystery Babylon," especially when compared with other Scripture(s):

1. 17:1 - "Whore" & 17:2 - "commits fornication" (because Israel went after the gods of other nations)
2. 17:3 - "Woman in the wilderness" (see Rev. 12:6)
3. 17:4 - "Arrayed in purple and scarlet colour, and decked with gold and precious stones and pearls" (Ex. 28:5-8; Jer. 4:30)
4. 17:5 - "Great City" (= Jerusalem – see Rev. 11:8)
5. 17:5 - "Mother of Harlots" (Is. 1:21; Ezk. 16:3,46; Gal. 4:25)
6. 17:5 - "Mother of Abominations of the Earth" (Ezk. 6:11; 7:1-27; 16:17; Num. 25:1; Jdgs. 2:17; Jer. 3:20; Hos. 1:2)
7. 17:6 - "drunk with blood of saints" and "the martyrs of Jesus" (Acts 26:10-11)
8. 18:2 - "Habitation of devils" (Jn. 8:44; Mt. 12:43-45)
9. 18:12-13 - The descriptions here mirror those in 2 Chronicles 2:4-8.
10. 18:21 - The "great millstone cast into the sea" (see Mt. 18:3-7) reflects the judgment on the teachers of the Law (Pharisees) who "offend" (deceive) God's children (Israel was often referred to by the word "children" — see Mt. 23:37).
11. 18:22 - This description can be cross-referenced with 1 Sam. 10:5; 2 Chr. 5:12; and Ps. 33:2; 81:3.

These present just a sampling of the clues referenced by other Scriptures. Of course, two major passages in chapter seventeen are excluded in this sample. However, upon further review, these two passages will only serve to strengthen the above conclusion, that Jerusalem is the identity of "Mystery Babylon." These passages (vs. 7-12 and vs. 16-17) are as follows, first:

> *vs. 7* - "And the angel said unto me, Wherefore didst thou marvel? I will tell thee the <u>mystery of the woman, and of the beast that carrieth her, which hath the seven heads and ten horns</u>."
>
> *vs. 8* - "The <u>beast</u> that thou sawest <u>was, and is not, and shall ascend out of the bottomless pit</u>, and go into perdition: and they that dwell on the earth shall wonder, whose names were not written in the book of life from the foundation of the world, when they behold <u>the beast that was, and is not, and yet is</u>."
>
> *vs. 9* - "And here is the mind which hath wisdom. The <u>seven heads are seven mountains</u>, on which the woman sitteth,"
>
> *vs. 10* - "And there are <u>seven kings: five are fallen, and one is, and the other is not yet come</u>; and when he cometh, he must continue a short space."
>
> *vs. 11* - "And the <u>beast</u> that was, and is not, even he is the <u>eighth</u>, and <u>is of the seven</u>, and goeth into perdition."
>
> *vs. 12* - "And <u>the ten horns which thou sawest are ten kings, which have received no kingdom as yet; but receive power as kings one hour with the beast</u>."

The second passage is:

> *vs. 16* - "And the <u>ten horns</u> which thou sawest upon the <u>beast</u>, these shall hate the whore, and shall make her desolate and naked, and shall eat her flesh, and burn her with fire."
>
> *vs. 17* - "For God hath put in their hearts to fulfill his will, and to agree, and give <u>their kingdom</u> unto the <u>beast</u>, until the words of God shall be fulfilled."

Obviously, upon reading these verses, it is understandable that both a discussion of and identification of the beast, the seven heads, and the ten horns are necessary. Amazingly, as you will see in the next few chapters, the interpretations of these passages point to Jerusalem as our "Mystery Babylon" while also unlocking many insights into the overall end-time picture.

Chapter 4

"The Beast: The Arab Empire!"

Certainly it is a mystery and yet, John the Revelator still proceeds to tell us about this "Mystery Babylon" — the city that encounters judgment and destruction. That it happens to be Jerusalem is especially mysterious! What this therefore means is that we need to look at Jerusalem to even begin to really understand how the end-time puzzle pieces truly fit together. Essentially, it is Israel in general and Jerusalem specifically that these end-time pieces revolve around. In fact, they are actually the cause for this tribulation. That's right! As a matter of fact, the Bible speaks of this tribulation as the "time of Jacob's trouble" (Jer. 30:7). In other words, the purpose for the tribulation is to discipline Israel, though out of God's love, in order to bring them to repentance and thereby eventually restore them! Don't forget, "God causes all things to work together for good to those who are called according to His purpose" (Rom. 8:28). God will fulfill His promises, and His promises for Israel are the provision of peace for Jerusalem, the Messiah for leadership, and a land flowing with milk and honey – or the Promised Land! But they must first encounter God's wrath and unfortunately, it won't be pleasant.

As a matter of fact, let me restate the last verse from the preceding chapter's discussion – "For God hath <u>put in their hearts to fulfill his will</u>, and to agree, and <u>give their kingdom unto the beast</u>, until the words of God shall be fulfilled (Rev. 17:17)." With this it is time for me to introduce to you the second major player of the end-time tribulation period – the BEAST! Just the very name "beast" conjures up a sense of dread and fear. However, the beast is not what most people think it is. Most think it is some person such as the antichrist world leader. But the beast is not a person. Rather, the beast is an empire. Specifically, it is the grouping together of a number of Arab countries from the Middle East. Essentially, God puts it in their heart to do His will, which is to become the tool used by God to discipline Israel. It won't be pretty, but it will be effective, yet they (the Arab empire) won't even realize that they are actually fulfilling the very will of God. Unfortunately, neither will Israel!

Nevertheless, one thing is certain. This Arab empire, in fulfilling its role as the tool of God to administer His wrath upon and discipline against Israel, will still fail in fully achieving its objective. This is because following their 3½ year tyranny of Israel, the Lord Jesus Christ will return to earth to deliver Israel and in turn, execute His wrath upon Israel's enemies (this Arab empire) in the battle of Armageddon, thereby ushering in a 1,000 year period of peace.

"The Beast: The Arab Empire!"
Scripturally Explained

Certainly, ideas such as the Second Coming of Jesus Christ, the wrath of God, the end of the world, the tribulation, and the Beast inspire numerous sensationalistic imaginations. Admittedly, some of these are probably true and accurate, even from a Biblical standpoint. Nevertheless, others have ventured into theoretical and speculative viewpoints, supported superficially by Scriptural references, yet lacking a basis that is able to be fully proven by other Scriptures. Some of these, in fact, have gained worldwide support over the centuries, are popularly taught, and appear to be very logical from an historical standpoint. Yet in spite of the notoriety of any interpretation, again, the question must be asked, "What saith the Scriptures?" The rule still applies: "The best interpreter of Scripture is other Scripture!" In the discussion of the end-time "Beast," this is the case as well.

The Beast of Revelation is, without a doubt, a remarkable entity. In chapter 11, he "ascends out of the bottomless pit" and makes war with, and even kills, the two witnesses (vs. 7). In chapter 13, he "rises up out of the sea" with seven heads and ten horns. He is far superior to any previous power, having derived his authority from the dragon himself. Greater still, he receives a deadly wound, only to be healed with all the world wondering after him, even worshiping him. He makes war with the saints, blasphemes against God, and even causes others to receive either his mark, his name, or the number (Six hundred threescore and six) of his name. Even at this point, the Beast has an impressive resume. Then in chapter 17 we see him again, this time carrying the woman, "Mystery Babylon," into destruction.

So who is this Beast? The most popular answer says it is the Antichrist, a national leader incarnated by the Devil himself. Other interpretations point to an alliance of countries, most notably the revival of the historic Roman Empire while still others give various other answers. But does the Bible give us an answer?

An often overlooked reality in understanding the Scriptures is that the writers of the New Testament books of the Bible often quoted or else alluded to Old Testament verses, phrases, words, or ideas in penning their God-inspired works. For example, in the book of Revelation alone, the Apostle John makes reference to more than 500 Old Testament verses or parts thereof. It is this realization alone that gives one confidence to assume that to accurately interpret Scripture, onr would be wise to begin by referencing other verifying Scriptures. In the case of Revelation, the Old Testament book of Daniel is the most vital key to opening up its understanding. John draws on numerous references from this book in the unique recording of His revelational experiences. Ironically, it is this very book of Daniel that also mirrors (or vice versa, for that matter) John's discussion of the Beast, the Seven Heads, and the Ten Horns in Revelation. As a matter of fact, in the case of the Beast, it could hardly be any clearer.

In Daniel chapter 7, Daniel records an incredible prophetic vision he experiences. In this vision, he observes "four great beasts" (vs. 4). The first was like a lion, the second like a bear, and the third was like a leopard. The fourth, however, was much different than the others. It was "dreadful and terrible, and strong exceedingly" (vs. 7). In fact, it was even described as having "ten horns" (vs. 7).

The interpretation of this vision and these creatures would be very difficult if it were not for Daniel giving us the interpretation himself in the very same chapter. In verse 17, Daniel gives us a positive identification of the four creatures when he says, "These great beasts, which are four, <u>are four kings</u>, which shall arise out of the earth." But then he gets even more specific with an often overlooked passage in verses 23 and 24 stating, "Thus he said, The fourth beast shall be the fourth <u>KINGDOM</u> (emphasis mine) upon the earth, which shall be diverse from all kingdoms, and shall devour the whole earth, and shall tread it down, and break it in pieces. And the ten horns out of this kingdom are ten kings that shall arise..." Now fortunately, for our sake's, he did not leave the interpretation up to ourselves. It is very clear that the beast here is no less than a kingdom. Daniel did state at first that the beast was a king, but then made it very clear that the beast as a king was not to be interpreted apart from the beast as a kingdom! Why is this so important?

The reason is because when it comes to the book of Revelation, the beast in both chapters 13 & 17 are mirror images of this one in Daniel (ten horns – Dan. 7:7,24; Rev. 13:1; 17:7,12). As a matter of fact, Revelation 17:12 even restates Daniel 7:24, "And the ten horns which thou sawest are ten kings." This alone should prove inconclusively that the beasts of both Daniel and Revelation are one and the same. This being the case then, "Who is this beast?" Unfortunately, when it comes to answering this question, many conclude again that it is the Antichrist. After all, the beast in Revelation 13 "speaks" (vs. 5), "opens his mouth" (vs. 6), and even receives a deadly wound, only to be healed of it later (vs. 3). Are these descriptions characteristic of a kingdom? Or rather of a person? Actually, they are both. In the case of a kingdom, this would be true only if the author happened to be using the literary skill known as "personification," that is, giving to some object or thing qualities or characteristics normally associated with a human being. In this case and in light of the above conclusions, this would certainly be true regarding this particular beast. So the question again is, "Who is this beast?" Or better, "<u>What kingdom</u> are we talking about?" To answer this, it is time to take a look at another passage of Scripture seldom discussed – one which both introduces and identifies for us the subject of "the 10 horns!"

Chapter 5

"The 10 Horns"

Imagine, if you will, things heating up in the Middle East. As they do, various countries unite with one purpose in mind. Their aim – to eliminate Israel! Not the land itself, but rather the people. That is, they collectively unite in purpose – a miracle in and of itself – though they still may be at odds with one another. Could this happen? Actually, it will. The Bible declares it so! Somehow...

Of course, I am speaking of an alliance of nations with one intent. Amazingly, these nations are continuously at odds with one another. They seem to never get along with each other. And yet one objective draws them together – the elimination of the Jews! Of whom am I referring to? The answer is the Arabs. Maybe not all of them, but definitely some of them. And it is revealed in Scripture.

Amazingly, Psalm 83 is a chapter without any historical fulfillment ever being recorded. Why? Because it is prophetic. It has yet to be fulfilled. And yet to the Church, it is a chapter that exists in relative obscurity. Very little is said about it and it is rarely taught on. Why? Primarily because few know how to handle it. For example, it speaks mostly about an alliance of peoples — each of whom in Biblical times were neighbors of the land of Israel. Incidentally, you will discover that those same peoples, when placed on a map of today, unmistakably occupy present day Arab nations. Who are they? The Psalmist lists (from his day) ten different peoples in verses six through eight – Edom, the Ishmaelites, Moab, the Hagarenes, Gebal, Ammon, Amalek, the Philistines, Tyre, and Assur. Today, these same peoples occupy portions of Jordan, Saudi Arabia, Lebanon, Sinai, Palestine, and Syria. Admittedly, they don't correspond to an identical number (10) of present day nations, but that is only because again, the prophecy was written from the perspective of the writer (in his day). Nevertheless, it has yet to be fulfilled, and the Psalmist warns us that these people purpose together with one goal — the elimination of Israel. Personally, I find it very intriguing since it seems that they, the corresponding Arab nations of today, can't seem to agree on anything except when it comes to their intense hatred for the Jews, culminating in what seems to be complete annihilation.

To give you an example of this, I recently read in the newspaper, following the September 11th, 2001 World Trade Center attacks, an article regarding various terrorist organizations in the Middle East. Among those, these were listed with the following goals:

Al-Qa'eda: Led by Osama bin Laden and located throughout the Middle East. Its goal: "to eject non-Muslims from Muslim countries and overthrow U.S.-allied regimes in the Arab world."

Hamas: Located in Israel and the occupied territories of the West Bank and Gaza, its goal is to "replace Israel with an Islamic Palestinian state."

Hezbollah (Islamic Jihad) (Jihad means "holy war"): Located in Lebanon, its goal is to "increase its political power in Lebanon and to oppose the Middle East peace process (between Israel and Palestine & others)."

Palestine Liberation Front: Located in Iraq, its goal is "an independent Palestinian state" and therefore Israel is an enemy.

Popular Front for the Liberation of Palestine: Located in Syria, Lebanon, Israel and the occupied territories, its goal is "an independent Palestinian state" and therefore again, Israel is an enemy.

Popular Front for the Liberation of Palestine – General Command: Located in Syria and Lebanon, its goal also is "an independent Palestinian state" and therefore once again, Israel is an enemy.

I don't know if this sounds an alarm for you, but let me remind you that these entities are not just regular organizations, but rather **they are TERRORIST organizations!** Could it be that God has already put it into the hearts of these people to bring about the fulfillment of His sovereign and holy will? Unfortunately, for Israel it is inevitably the case. The prophet Daniel told of this end-time scenario, "The fourth beast shall be the fourth kingdom upon earth (the other three were before Christ), which shall be diverse from all kingdoms, and shall devour the whole earth (land), and shall tread it down, and break it in pieces. And the ten horns out of this kingdom are ten kings that shall arise" (Dan. 7:23-24). From the Psalmist we then learn what their goal is, "They (the ten kingdoms) have taken crafty counsel against thy people (Israel), and consulted against thy hidden ones. They have said, come, and **let us cut them off from being a nation; that the name of Israel may be no more in remembrance**" (Ps. 83:3-4).

Strangely, very little is said by our Bible teachers when it comes to the fate of Israel at the hands of their Arab neighbors. And yet, it is quite clear in Scripture the role that they have. The ten horns certainly are players during this tribulation period, and yet they are not alone. As we will see in chapter 6, the plot thickens as with the introduction of the "seven heads."

"The 10 Horns"
Scripturally Explained

What does the Bible really say about the "10 horns"? Both Daniel (7:24) and John (Rev. 17:12) indicate that the "beast" (or Arab empire) is comprised of this unusual characteristic. Nevertheless, there is a slight difference in each one's description. Whereas Daniel tells us that "the ten horns out of this kingdom (beast) are ten kings that <u>shall arise</u>," John tells us that the ten have yet to receive (or form) a kingdom, "the ten horns which thou sawest are ten kings, <u>which have received no kingdom as yet</u>." Actually, there really isn't a discrepancy here for each takes into account the matter of time from the perspective of the author. In the case of what Daniel writes, the statement is a present tense description of this future end-time beast. With John however, what is recorded is a future tense statement from a present day vision. This being the case, we know that if one could find a prophetic Scripture which referenced 10 kings forming a kingdom (especially against Israel), then we would further be able to accurately identify this end-time beast. But is this possible? As a matter of fact, it is!

Once again, it is an often overlooked Scriptural passage which gives us the answer. In this case, the passage is one that is deemed prophetic because it has yet to be historically fulfilled, though it seldom is discussed or adequately explained. The passage is found in the book of Psalms. In chapter 83, we have a prophetic account of eighteen verses in the form of a prayer. This prayer regards the oppressors — an alliance of 10 peoples representing past nations, lands, countries, or descendants — of God's people, or the nation of Israel. Thus, what we have is an outline of 10 kings aligning together with one intent — the destruction of Israel. Observe what it says:

> vs. 2 - "For, lo, thine enemies make a tumult: and <u>they that hate thee</u> have lifted up the head."
> vs. 3 - "<u>They have taken crafty counsel against thy people</u>, and consulted against thy hidden ones."
> vs. 4 - "They have said, Come, and <u>let us cut them off from being a nation; that the name of Israel may be no more in remembrance</u>."

Wake Up Church: The End is Nigh!

vs. 5 - "For <u>they have consulted together with one consent:</u> <u>they are confederate against thee</u>:

vs. 6 - "*The tabernacles of Edom, and the Ishmaelites; of Moab, and the Hagarenes;"*

vs. 7 - "*Gebal, and Ammon, and Amalek; the Philistines with the inhabitants of Tyre;"*

vs. 8 - "*Assur also is joined with them: they have holpen the children of Lot."*

In this passage, ten names of former historical peoples are listed which consent together with the aim of eliminating the nation of Israel from existence. These ten are of Arab descent and on a map, currently exist in the area we refer to as the Middle East. Ironically, the locations of these ten back then even today still exist on Arab soil. As listed, these former ten are represented today as follows:

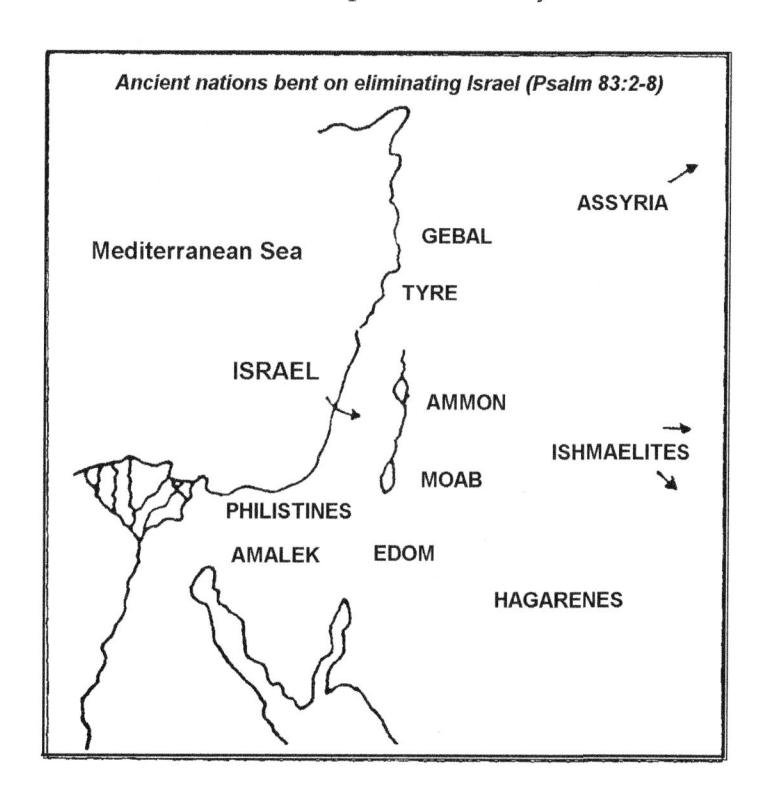

Ancient nations bent on eliminating Israel (Psalm 83:2-8)

- Mediterranean Sea
- ASSYRIA
- GEBAL
- TYRE
- ISRAEL
- AMMON
- ISHMAELITES
- MOAB
- PHILISTINES
- AMALEK
- EDOM
- HAGARENES

1. Edom = Southern Jordan
2. Ishmaelites = Northern & Western Saudi Arabia (Persian Gulf area)
3. Moab = Central Jordan
4. Hagarenes = Central Saudi Arabia (Hagar's descendants)
5. Gebal = Northern Lebanon
6. Ammon = Northern Jordan (present Capital)
7. Amalek = Northern Sinai
8. Philistines = Palestine, Gaza Strip
9. Tyre = Southern Lebanon
10. Assur (Assyria) = Syria

Again, each of the above names would today be found in Arab territories. Admittedly, these former ten do not represent 10 distinct kingdoms or nations of today. However, in Biblical prophecy, what is recorded is often related to the historical frame of reference of the author. The fulfillment may or may not be an alliance of exactly 10 present day kingdoms or nations. Nevertheless, that this points to a future Arab empire is irrefutable. As a matter of fact, it is worth noting that the Scriptures are chock-full of end-time prophetic references that likewise refer to present day Arab peoples. For example, just a casual trace through the books of Isaiah, Jeremiah, Ezekiel, Joel, Obadiah, etc., reveal as much as entire chapters devoted to identifying these people along with their end-time roles – e.g., they identify Egypt, the Philistines, Babylon, Tyre, Persia, Assyria, Edom, etc. — all of Arab relations. Even more so, you will find that within both the books of Daniel and Revelation are numerous passages devoted to revealing the identity of the beast as an Arab Empire.

Chapter 6

"The 7 Heads"

Poor Israel! At least that is the feeling I have towards them when I think of them. And yet I also think of just how incredible they are. I mean, here is a nation that has amazingly survived throughout history against incredible odds, numerous foes, and dire circumstances. Currently, they are one tiny little island of a country surrounded by neighboring countries of whom few get along with them in any sort of way. Talk about being vulnerable! If these neighboring countries all agreed to unite and turn on them, Israel would be completely trapped. And yet they have survived, thrived, and even strongly been able to stand up and defend themselves. It really is quite amazing. Yet tragically, they once were the objects of ruthless ethnic cleansing, as in the horrible Nazi-led holocaust of World War 2. Thousands upon thousands mercilessly lost their lives. And yet as a whole they continued to survive. As a matter of fact, shortly thereafter, in 1948, after having begun to return to their homeland following the Great Britain sponsored Balfour Declaration of 1917, they were able to reestablish themselves as a nation. Prior to that, the Jews were in desolation. That is, they were spread out all over the world, without a country, for hundreds of years. This was known as the Diaspora. Any other people, under these same circumstances, would have seen their nation die out, completely disappearing from civilization. But not the Jews. Not only have they survived, but they even have rebounded. It really is incredible. Fact is, THEY are incredible!

Still, I do pity them. Today they seem to continue to endure such tragic circumstances such as being the victim of numerous Hamas or Islamic Jihad led suicide bombings. The Palestinians want peace, but they want it <u>their</u> way! They use violence and terrorism to accomplish their goals. Israel, on the other hand, wants peace too. But they have been pushed back into a corner. To get security and safety, they must sacrifice land – something they already have done. But how much are they to give, and at what price? The stakes have increased and the hour is nigh upon us. The final issue at stake is really the key to it all — the city of <u>Jerusalem</u>! This is essentially the last item on the negotiating table. And yet it really is not up for negotiation, at least to Israel. So what in the end will give? Amazingly, the Scriptures tell us this regarding God's divine plan for Jerusalem in these last days, **"Behold, I will make Jerusalem a cup of trembling <u>unto all the people round about</u>, <u>when they shall be in the siege</u> both against Judah (Israel) and against Jerusalem. And in that day will <u>I make Jerusalem a burdensome stone for all people</u>: <u>all that burden themselves with it</u> shall be cut in pieces, though all the people of the earth (land) be gathered together against it (Zech. 12:2-3)."** In other words, God has ordained that the enemies of Israel (or Jerusalem) will suffer greatly, but this is NOT referring to the whole world. Presently, the people that surround Israel are Arabs and they are the ones intent on both possessing Jerusalem and eliminating Israel. And for that they, too, will eventually suffer. But Israel, of course, will suffer first. And so again, for this I feel deeply for Israel and the Jewish people. And yet this type of predicament, from an historical standpoint, is really not too unusual for them.

A number of times throughout their history the people of Israel have greatly suffered. Most people know the story of Moses, when God spoke to him from a burning bush and gave him an assignment. Israel was held in captivity back then by Pharoah and the Egyptians, so God used Moses to free the Israelites from their tyranny. This story seems to reflect a pattern in their history — an enemy rises, directs itself against Israel, and destroys either its city or temple and/or takes captive the people. Eventually, they cry out to God and in His divine timing, He provides a way of escape. This is a pattern in their history. Thus, they have encountered many enemies. Ironically, the vast majority of their enemies have come from one general location on earth - the Middle East! Certainly Germany during the holocaust was an exception. And so was Rome, under which the emperor Nero in the first century destroyed both the Temple and the City. But in most cases, the enemy resided in the Middle East.

This very point is made much clearer when evaluating the end-time passages of Scripture. Specifically, in the passage of Revelation regarding "Mystery Babylon," which has been identified as Jerusalem, you will find that the "beast," or Arab empire, is certainly unique. For not only is it described as having "ten horns," it also is said to consist of "seven heads." Ouch! Definitely a monster, wouldn't you say? So, just what are these "seven heads"? The answer is that they are enemies of both the nation of Israel and its city Jerusalem.

You have probably heard of Nebuchadnezzar. He was the leader of the Babylonian empire. Though before the time of Christ, he nevertheless directed an attack on Israel, even taking them captive. Then there was the Medo-Persian empire. Its leaders were both Darius and Cyrus. They too orchestrated an attack on Israel, likewise taking them captive. Of course, you've probably heard of Alexander the Great. He was the leader of the Grecian empire, which also captured Israel. But then there are two additional enemies that few people have heard of. They are Ptolemy and Antiochus. Ptolemy was the leader of the Ptolemaic empire and Antiochus the Seleucid empire, known in Scripture respectively as the "King of the South" and the "King of the North." That, by the way, totals five named enemies that have tormented Israel. Then there was a sixth enemy, of which I mentioned earlier. It was the Roman empire. Although Rome is not in the Middle East, they did however at that time control a portion of the Middle East. Thus, their empire extended into that area. In particular, they controlled Israel with their rule, eventually even destroying Jerusalem and its Temple. This, of course, took place around the time of Christ. With the addition of Rome, this now totals six empires that have tormented Israel, and yet there remains one last empire.

The final empire that will torment Israel is the aforementioned Arab empire. It is the seventh one and of course, it also resides in the Middle East. Collectively, these seven empires represent the "seven heads" of Revelation. Incidentally, it goes without saying that if there are seven <u>kingdoms</u> represented here, then there also should be seven <u>kings</u>, for each kingdom or empire must at least have someone who is considered to lead them. Thus, these "seven kings" will be the next subject discussed, when we get to chapter 7.

"The 7 Heads"
Scripturally Explained

If we return to take another look at chapter 17 of Revelation, we see a unique characteristic of the Beast — that it has 7 heads (vs. 7). Mysterious as this Beast is, not only does it have 10 horns, but now 7 heads as well. As we have already seen, the 10 horns represent 10 Arab peoples and thus, point towards an Arab origin for this Beast. But what about these heads — what do they mean? Interestingly enough, we get a very clear explanation in this same chapter, "The seven heads <u>are seven mountains</u>" (vs. 9). Most interpreters at this point, with the literal or topographical nature of mountains in mind, quickly identify this (the 7 mountains) as indicating Rome. Unfortunately it is difficult, at best, to make this connection unless you consider "hills" to qualify as "mountains." Thus, without an obvious answer, what might this unique characteristic really represent? We have already identified the Beast as an Arab empire. However, even this particular empire lacks a city with the condition of truly having 7 mountains surrounding it, thereby qualifying it as this "Mystery Babylon" city. Or does it really?

That the heads here are likened unto mountains is clearly stated. But does the Bible have more to say about "mountains" than the obvious understanding of which we all have — being large rock formations on the earth's crust? Certainly, the Bible's use of the term "mountains" includes these (e.g., Mt. Moriah, Zion, Ararat, Carmel, etc.). However, the word "mountain," as used in Scripture, also carries another meaning - not a literal one, but rather a symbolic one. And herein lies the secret that unlocks this mystery, its impact being that it once again points to the Arab empire as our Beast.

Quite often, the word "mountain" in Scripture is used to symbolize a "kingdom" (see Jer. 51:25 & Zech. 4:7). As a matter of fact, Jesus even alluded to this very idea when speaking, <u>from the base of a mountain</u>, about the **Kingdom** of Heaven (thus, referred to as the "Sermon on the <u>Mount</u>" - Mt. 5-7). Even the devil, Satan, in tempting the Lord to take over all the **kingdoms** of the land, chose "an exceeding high <u>mountain</u>" as the location from which to do so (Mt. 4:8-11). Bearing this in mind, might we therefore find a reference to the "seven heads" that also points to this Arab empire as the Beast?

Ironically, once again we find ourselves in Daniel chapter 7. Remember the dream Daniel had which involved the "four great beasts" (vs. 3)? As was stated previously, it was the interpretation of this dream which revealed that the "beast" was a kingdom (vs. 23). Likewise, it indicating that the ten horns were ten kingdoms (vs. 24). Incidentally, a careful analysis of these four beasts also provides for us the answer of what our "seven heads" represent. Notice for example that in Daniel 7:4, the first beast is a lion. Then in verse 5, we see that the second beast is a bear. Each of these two creatures have but one head (this of course is implied). Then in verse 6, we see that our third beast is referred to as a leopard, but in this case it is described as having not one, but four heads. At this point that totals six heads. Finally the fourth beast, as described in verse 7, again has but one head. Adding all of these heads together gives you a grand total of <u>seven heads</u> and collectively, these seven heads reveal the origin of the "beast" — again, that territory controlled today by the Arab peoples! In other words, what the first three beasts (lion, bear, and leopard) historically represented were the three kingdoms known respectively as the Babylonian, Medo-Persian, and Grecian empires. When consulting a map, you will notice that these empires governed territory the likes of which today we would characterize as the Middle East, which certainly includes Israel. Of course, the fourth beast was prophetic in nature and therefore depicts that end-time kingdom simply referred to as the "beast." Thus, to stay consistent with the pattern revealed by these other three beasts, this fourth kingdom would also have to derive itself from Middle Eastern territory.

Incidentally, you will notice that the beast in Revelation 13:1 is said to have risen up "<u>out of the sea</u>, having seven heads and ten horns." Likewise, we see that Daniel states the same thing, indicating that these "four great beasts <u>came up from the sea</u>" (Dan. 7:3). In other words, as strange as it may seem, both writers indicate that this "beast" originates from the "sea" — or do they really? Actually, we discover that Daniel 7:17 provides for us the correct interpretation of the sea's meaning with this symbolic explanation, "These great beasts, which are four, are four kings, <u>which shall arise out of the EARTH (land)</u>." In other words, the "sea" from which the "beast" shall arise is really symbolic, meaning that it will arise from the land of that particular region. Once again, it is plain to see here that this "beast" is actually the Arab empire that develops from (or arises out of) the land that is commonly known as the Middle East. That these four beasts collectively have seven heads is truly a strange and unique characteristic. Yet, it also is a remarkably telling characteristic for it once again helps us to identify the origin of this "beast" by revealing, through a divine and consistent historical pattern, that it is none other than the aforementioned Arab empire.

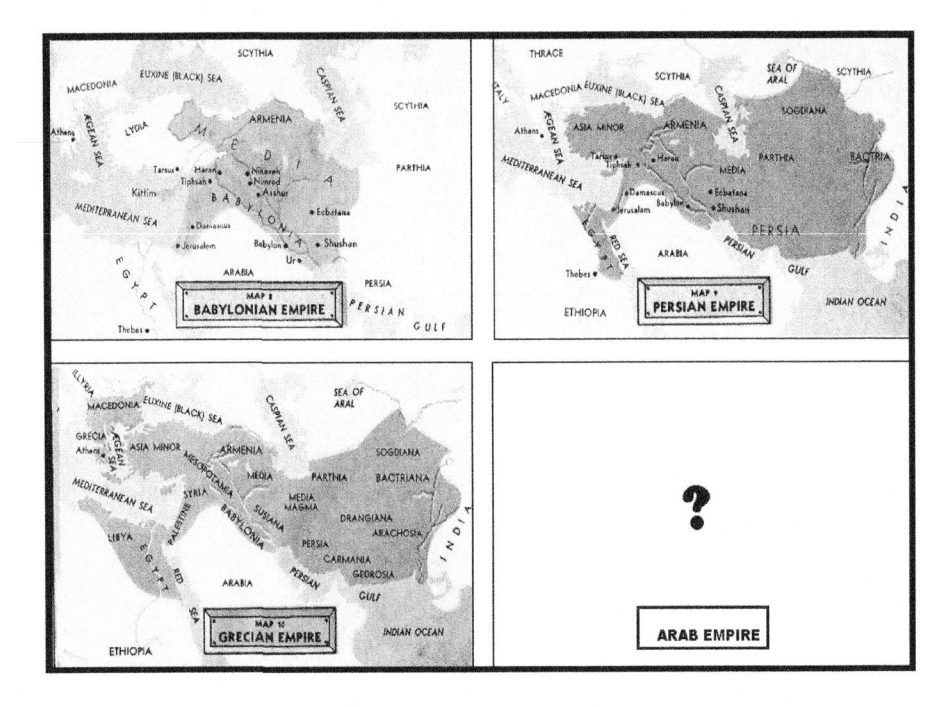

Although I have explained, utilizing Daniel's vision in Daniel 7, the identity of the first three heads (the Babylonian, Medo-Persian, and Grecian "kingdoms" or empires) along with the seventh head (the Arab "kingdom" or empire), there remains yet an explanation for the fourth, fifth, and sixth "kingdoms" or empires. These I will explain in more detail in later chapters of this book. But first I want to share, in even greater detail, a very peculiar characteristic regarding the seventh of these heads. For this we must continue on in the next chapter in which I discuss the meaning of "The 7 Kings."

Chapter 7

"The 7 Kings"

What if I told you that Israel, during the 3½ year tribulation period, was to be oppressed by not just this one Arab empire, but also by another empire as well. Would you believe it? And what if I added that not only would there be two empires that oppress her, but also that BOTH would be Arab. Would you believe that? But that doesn't make any sense, you say. How can there be two Arab empires? Yet that is exactly what is going to happen. Certainly it seems confusing — that is, until further explanation is provided.

I admit, it doesn't sound logical. But God has again ordained this as part of His plan. And with this explanation, you will see it makes sense. So, what is this explanation? Well, let me first give the scenario, which goes something like this. The Arab countries, because of their common descent, are basically viewed as one entity, or as Scripture labels them, one kingdom. And this is no surprise. They have a common purpose - the destruction of Israel and the takeover of Jerusalem - and they are forever linked as common blood descendants of one another. Additionally, they live in the same basic area - the Middle East - and let's not forget that they even share the same faith, generally speaking - Islam. And so they can, on the one hand, be considered as one empire or kingdom. On the other hand, they also are very different. Each Arab country is unique and very much its own entity. As a matter of fact, the above mentioned characteristics are quite often where the similarities end. History has proven that the many different Arab countries have often been in conflict with each other, even at war. And yet there is one thing that they do agree on - their intense hatred for the Jews! But it will be their differences which actually split them when it comes to the end-time tribulation. Essentially, there will be two very different Arab alliances (or kingdoms) during this 3½ year period. And yet they will have one common goal — to obtain Jerusalem — and not only will they be intent on getting it, but they will in fact succeed! And thus strangely, as I would agree, it is these two Arab kingdoms which over all help to formulate this one end-time "Beast." Or to be more accurate, it is really the reverse. That is, this one end-time "Beast" subdivides and therefore actually helps to formulate these two Arab kingdoms, which incidentally will exist as oppressors of Israel during this tribulation period.

"The 7 Kings" Scripturally Explained

If we return to Revelation 17, we see that verses 10 and 11 continue to describe the "seven heads" with the following strange explanation, "And there are <u>seven kings</u>: five are fallen, and one is, and the other is not yet come; and when he cometh, he must continue a short space. <u>And the beast that was, and is not, even he is the eighth, and is of the seven</u>, and goeth into perdition." This sounds very strange indeed, don't you think? And yet, might we be able to find a Biblical interpretation for this passage? Actually, the answer is yes.

Remembering that the identity of the "beast" is to be understood as a kingdom, specifically, as an Arab empire, we can again see the connection to it here in this passage. That the "beast" in verse 11 is numbered the eighth, especially after the seven prior to it in verse 10 are referred to already as kings, should only serve to further establish that this "beast" is actually a kingdom, rather than a person. Yet this too seems to often be overlooked.

At any rate, we will find that in this context, these seven, or rather eight kings (and therefore eight kingdoms) are best understood through their connection with our "Mystery Babylon," which we know is Israel. Specifically, as we have already seen from Scripture, these kings which make up the "beast" are referring to various Gentile oppressors of this nation. Remember though that the Apostle John recorded the book of Revelation in the 1st Century. It is an historical fact that in that day there happened to be one kingdom already in existence that was oppressing Israel – or as most people know, it was the Roman empire. Accordingly, we can identify it in this passage. In verse 10, it is referred to as the kingdom that "is." In other words, the Roman empire "is" the kingdom that is oppressing Israel at the time of John's writing Revelation. Now regarding those five that "are fallen," Israel happened to have been previously oppressed (again, as viewed from the time John was writing = 1st Century) by the following empires, mentioned here with their leaders: (1) the Babylonian empire with Nebuchadnezzar (Dan. 2:1, 37-38), (2) the Medo-Persian empire with both Darius the Mede and

Cyrus the Persian (Dan. 1:21; 6:28; 10:1), (3) the Grecian empire with Alexander the Great (Dan. 8:5), (4) the Ptolemaic empire with Ptolemy (Dan. 11:5), and (5) the Seleucid empire with Antiochus (Dan. 11:21-39). Again, since these five empires historically existed prior to the time of John's writing Revelation, they accordingly are depicted as those that "are fallen." Sequentially then, the "beast" or Arab empire is the only one that is left (since it was a "future" kingdom to John) and is thus "the other (that) is <u>not yet come</u>."

Of course, John then complicates matters by telling us that this one future kingdom will actually become two by stating that it is "the eighth, and is (also) of the seven." Obviously, he indicates that there is a connection with or relationship between these seventh and eighth kings. Incidentally, this unusual detail is validated even more so by Daniel 7:23-24, "The fourth beast shall be the fourth kingdom upon the earth (referring to the Beast or Arab [the seventh] empire), which shall be diverse from all kingdoms, and shall devour the whole earth (land), and shall tread it down, and break it in pieces. And the ten horns out of <u>this kingdom</u> (referring to the seventh one) are ten kings that shall arise: and <u>another</u> (he now introduces the eighth kingdom) shall rise after them; and he shall be diverse from the first." Amazingly, you can see from this reference that even Daniel foretold that the last oppressive kingdom of Israel would subdivide into yet "another" one. In other words, Daniel confirms this truth by providing the second witness in Scripture related to this unique characteristic.

Now, even though we see that this Arab empire, which will oppress Israel in the last days, is to actually consist of two separate alliances, we nevertheless are not done regarding our discussion of this "beast." For one, there is still another popular passage in Daniel that, although often understood by others as referring to a different end-time oppressor of Israel, nevertheless when properly interpreted reveals how again, it is the Arabs that make up this empire. This, of course, will be the subject of our next chapter as we investigate the end-time meaning of Daniel's record of Nebuchadnezzar's dream and the subsequent image that he would have constructed and eventually worshiped.

Chapter 8

"Nebuchadnezzar's Image"

There is a King who has greatly influenced Americans for years with his infamous message given during the 1960's. The title of his sermon was, "I Have a Dream!" Of course, the King that I am referring to is none other than the inspirational civil rights leader, Martin Luther King, Jr.. Incidentally, there is another King whose dream will also greatly influence the world over, though the influence that will come from this dream has yet to occur. Instead, it will be for sometime in the near future. But one thing is for certain, they both had dreams of great influence. Unfortunately, this is where the similarities end, for this other King's dream is not one that is inspirational. Rather it is dreadful, for it in effect warns others of impending judgment and devastation. This dream is not from the 60's, but instead took place over 2,500 years ago. Finally, the King of this dream was not the man's name, but rather his position. So then, who is it that I am referring to? Of course, I am speaking of Nebuchadnezzar, the King of Babylon. And we find the record of this dream in the pages of Scripture as recorded by the Prophet Daniel. Interestingly enough, this dream happens to also be something of a mystery!

While Nebuchadnezzar was in power, his kingdom covered much of what today would be the Middle East. Unfortunately for Israel, they too were captives of this Babylonian empire. As a result, the King seemed to revel in his accomplishments and status. But God was not impressed. So one night, unbeknownst to Nebuchadnezzar, He gave him a dream. And it greatly troubled the King. So much so that he beckoned his court to pretty much accomplish the impossible. That is, they were to produce someone who could first tell him exactly what the dream was (the King hadn't told anybody his dream) and then second, an even more critical demand and yet impossible feat, they were to tell the King the dream's meaning! Talk about impossible odds. To make matters worse, if one attempted this and was found wrong, it would cost him his life. On top of that, if no one at all could be found to interpret this dream, then it would cost the King's entire court their very lives! Phew! I am sure glad that I was not one of those men. However, as is always the case in situations where the stakes are seemingly impossible, God would once again show Himself to be strong and mighty.

As God would have it, one man ended up stepping forward – the Prophet Daniel! His response, "As for the <u>mystery</u> about which the king has inquired, neither wise men, conjurers, magicians, nor diviners are able to declare it to the king. However, there is a God in heaven who reveals mysteries, and He has made known to King Nebuchadnezzar <u>what will take place in the latter days</u>. This was your dream and the visions in your mind while on your bed (Dan. 2:27-28 NASV)." By the grace of God, Daniel was given one chance and when he stood up to the plate, he hit a home run, for he went on to tell both the dream and its interpretation, resulting in three significant outcomes. First, the lives of the King's court were all spared. Second, Daniel was exalted to prominence in the kingdom as ruler over Babylon and third, the King would charge that the main component of his dream be made into a golden statuesque replica to be set up for worship by all within his kingdom. But of course, what was the dream, you ask?

Essentially, Nebuchadnezzar saw a statue of a man made up of four parts – a head of gold, a chest of silver, a mid-section of brass, and legs and feet of iron and clay. They each represented a kingdom. Their common characteristic was that they oppressed the nation of Israel. Who were these kingdoms? The first was the Babylonian empire led by Nebuchadnezzar himself. The second was the Medo-Persian empire led by both Darius and Cyrus. The third was the Grecian empire led by Alexander the Great and the fourth was one that would take place in the future just before the return of Jesus Christ. Of course, we have established that this would be the empire that is developing even now – that is, the Arab empire. Incidentally, as was discussed in the previous chapter of this book, even Daniel suggests how this future tyrant of Israel would also subdivide into two parts. But this wasn't the complete interpretation of the dream, for one other detail not mentioned was that a far superior kingdom would follow the rise of this fourth one. But this kingdom would not torment Israel. Rather, it would instead crush their enemies and in turn, set itself up as a kingdom of peace on the earth for a long, long time. Of course, I am speaking of Christ's return to take vengeance upon Israel's oppressors and to usher in His Kingdom – a Kingdom of heaven on earth!

"Nebuchadnezzar's Image"
Scripturally Explained

A very key passage in end-time prophecy is found in chapter two of Daniel. It regards the dream of Nebuchadnezzar and portrays a "great image" (vs. 31). Fortunately, the dream (vs. 31-35) is interpreted within this very same chapter (vs. 36-45). Unfortunately, the interpretation that is provided within this passage needs also to be interpreted.

Revealed within the interpretation is that the image reflects four kingdoms — the first at that time already in existence with the next three prophetic or future. The first is depicted as a "head of gold" (vs. 38) and was the Babylonian Kingdom headed by Nebuchadnezzar himself. The second is to follow thereafter and is depicted as having "breast and arms of silver" (vs. 32). This was the historical Medo-Persian empire headed by both Darius and Cyrus. The third kingdom (vs. 39) is the "belly and thighs of brass" (vs. 32). This too is historical and was fulfilled by Alexander the Great and his Grecian empire. Thus, we come to the fourth kingdom.

The fourth kingdom was depicted by the "legs of iron (and) feet part of iron and clay" (vs. 33). The descriptive nature of this kingdom is of one yet to be fulfilled, pending the return of Christ with His Kingdom.

The Prophet Daniel records this passage as follows:

> vs. 40 - "And the fourth kingdom shall be strong as iron: forasmuch as iron breaketh in pieces and subdueth all things: and as iron that breaketh all these, shall it break in pieces and bruise."
>
> vs. 41 - "And whereas thou sawest the feet and toes, part of potters' clay, and part of iron, <u>the kingdom shall be divided</u>; but there shall be in it of the strength of the iron, forasmuch as thou sawest the iron mixed with miry clay."
>
> vs. 42 - "And as the toes of the feet were part of iron, and part of clay, so the kingdom shall be partly strong, and partly broken."
>
> vs. 43 - "And whereas thou sawest iron mixed with miry clay, they shall mingle themselves with the seed of

men: but they shall not cleave one to another, even as iron is not mixed with clay."

vs. 44 - "And in the days of these kings shall the God of heaven set up a kingdom, which shall never be destroyed: and the kingdom shall not be left to other people, but it shall break in pieces and consume all these kingdoms, and it shall stand for ever."

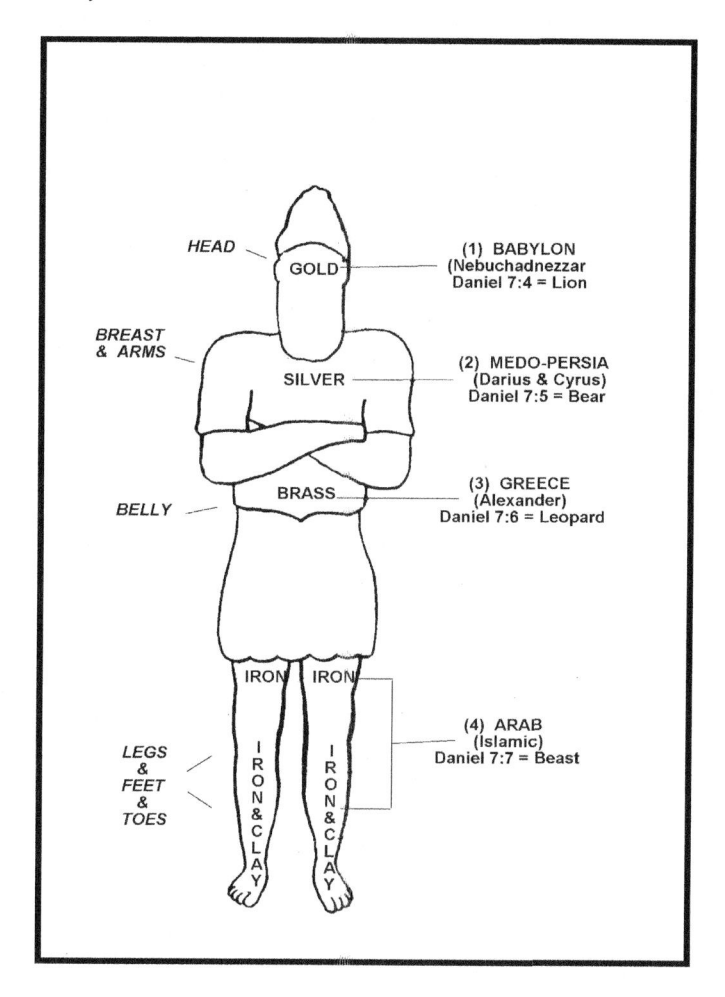

```
HEAD — GOLD                    (1) BABYLON
                               (Nebuchadnezzar)
                               Daniel 7:4 = Lion

BREAST
& ARMS — SILVER                (2) MEDO-PERSIA
                               (Darius & Cyrus)
                               Daniel 7:5 = Bear

BELLY — BRASS                  (3) GREECE
                               (Alexander)
                               Daniel 7:6 = Leopard

         IRON   IRON
LEGS                           (4) ARAB
&        IRON   IRON           (Islamic)
FEET      &      &             Daniel 7:7 = Beast
&        CLAY   CLAY
TOES
```

That this kingdom would precede the return of Christ makes clear its identity — that being the Arab empire. Unfortunately, this is often mistaken due to the other or traditional teaching of its identity being the once Roman empire now being revived. However, we have already in the preceding chapters of this book logically set forth its true identity. Yet certainly, we can still let the Scriptures do the speaking for themselves.

First of all, if we were to look for a pattern (the Bible often silently speaks through the use of consistent patterns), we would find an obvious one by looking at a geographic map. By observing the historical location of the first three kingdoms and the extent of their jurisdiction, we would see that all three comprise of the same basic area we know today as the Middle East, again including Israel! Thus, staying consistent with this pattern, would it not be wise to conclude that the fourth and future kingdom would also originate from this region? This being the case, what people other than the Jews dwell in the Middle East? That's right, it is predominantly the Arabs (again see map in chapter on "The 7 Heads").

Second, notice the word "mingle" in verse 43. Contextually, it is a word used to refer to the actions on the part of a particular group of people. Believe it or not, this word for what they do is also the word "arab" in the original Hebrew text of which Daniel was written in. Now, is this an accident, a coincidence, or a Divine clue? As a matter of fact, even more interesting is the region of land that they inhabit. It is said in chapter seven of Daniel regarding this fourth kingdom that it "shall devour the whole __earth__, and shall tread it down, and break it in pieces (Dan. 7:23)." Yet even though our translated version of this verse indicates that the "whole earth" would be controlled by this kingdom, this really is not the case. The word used in the original Hebrew text was the word "ara." Again, notice that it closely resembles the word "arab." However, although this word means either earth or land, nevertheless it is best translated as land because it does not refer to the whole earth, such as in "planet" earth. When denoting the "planet" earth, as in Genesis 1:1, "In the beginning God created the heaven and the earth," the word "erets" is used. Thus, "ara" means "land" and as such, communicates an entirely different picture altogether. In other words, it points more specifically to the immediate land from within that region — the region of the Middle East. This would further explain other passages in which "ara" is used for "earth," though it should be translated "land," such as in Daniel 7:17, "These great beasts, which are four, are four kings, which shall arise out of the earth." Obviously, this means that they will originate from within that region of __land__, not that they would ascend from inside of the planet earth! By the way, notice also that in this verse, this characteristic is true of all four of these kingdoms, which is consistent with a map. Again, if you look at the map in the chapter on "The 7 Heads" you will find that each of these kingdoms controlled pretty much the same area of which is predominately what we know as the Middle East of today! Likewise, this explains an apparent contradiction or error found in another verse, Daniel 2:39, "And after these shall arise another kingdom inferior to thee, and another third kingdom of brass, which shall bear rule over <u>all the earth (ara)</u>." This is a reference to the third kingdom, or Alexander the Great's Grecian empire. Of course, we all know that Alexander did NOT rule over the whole entire earth. But he did in fact rule over all the land – that is, the land of the Middle East (again see map). So the point is, it really does make a difference in the understanding of these passages if we are able to establish the correct intent of the words used. But again, what is even more amazing is the very word ("ara") itself. As was already pointed out, notice how it is spelled and how closely it resembles the word "Arab!" Again, is this merely a coincidence or a divine clue?

Most importantly, however, is the allusion to the image's anatomy — the legs, feet, and toes. Let me explain by going in reverse order. First, the toes are obvious. There are ten of them and they symbolize the exact same thing as the "ten horns" of the "beast" do, which we discussed earlier. That is, we again see a direct reference to the alliance of the ten Arab peoples of Psalm 83:4-8. But the passage in Daniel says also that "the kingdom shall be divided" (Dan. 2:41), hence the two feet and legs. In fact, it says of these two that whereas one "shall be partly strong, (the other is) partly broken" (vs. 42). Does the Bible validate this characteristic? Remember, in speaking of the seven kings (or kingdoms) of Revelation 17:10, the Scriptures actually characterized the seventh one as subdividing into an eighth kingdom (Rev. 17:11). Or as Daniel put it, the eighth would "(a)rise after them; and he shall be diverse from the first, and he shall subdue three kings" (Dan. 7:24). Doesn't this seem to sound like one is "partly strong" (subduing three kings) while the other is "partly broken" (being subdued)?

Yet even more convincing than this is the identification of who these two "divided" kingdoms are. Can we possibly find an explanation for these within the pages of Scripture? Once again, the answer is a resounding "Yes!" and it is this issue that is the subject of our next chapter on "The King of the North vs. the King of the South."

Chapter 9

"The King of the North
vs.
The King of the South"

At some point in the near future, there will be a movement by a grouping of various peoples from the southern portions of the Middle East. What will they do? Actually, they will rise up and attack a grouping of various peoples from the northern portions of the Middle East. Who might these peoples from the southern parts be? Essentially, it could consist of any of a number of countries, but the primary ones that might be stirred up are Egypt and/or Saudi Arabia. Incidentally, this "southern" grouping could also include the United States and/or any other United Nations' counterparts, not because they are from there, but rather because they (the U.S.) could be <u>aligned</u> with them (the "southern" group). This, incidentally, would be similar to what took place during the Gulf War. The United States defended Kuwait (from the south) against Iraq (from the north). With the United States' participation in its war against terrorism, a similar scenario is very likely. But what about the northern peoples? Who might these be? There are quite a few that could unite such as Syria, Iran, Iraq, Afghanistan, Pakistan, Lebanon, and Palestine. If I was to guess as to who would be the key ones initiating this activity, I would look for Palestine to take the initiative with support coming out of Iraq first, and then possibly Afghanistan and/or Syria. At any rate, the response that those from the north will take will be a counter reaction to being attacked and incidentally, it seems that their reaction will be successful. In fact, Egypt somehow will suffer greatly in this process. Why? Probably because of their political policy of being at peace with both Israel and the United States. This does not bode well for them. In addition, Libya and Ethiopia will also yield to the power of this northern alliance. Yet even though these northern armies will be greatly successful in their efforts, it seems that the country of Jordan will be spared, probably because it tends to be more neutral in its affairs with Israel. But the country that will suffer the most in this whole process will be, you guessed it, the nation of Israel! And its suffering will be great!

In so many words, the aforementioned scenario is taken right out of the pages of Scripture. Believe it or not, it is a composite description of what will happen just prior to and right on into the period of time known as the tribulation – those 3½ years of great loss for Israel called "the time of Jacob's (Israel's) trouble" (Jer. 30:7). The Prophet Daniel basically foretold this above scenario in verses 40 through 43 of his eleventh chapter. Fortunately, it does not continue forever for eventually, Israel will cry out to God and even acknowledge Jesus as their Messiah. Thus, He will come to their rescue, at last avenging her of her enemies in the battle of Armageddon. Accordingly, this will usher in the period of Christ's rule here on earth known as the Millennium – a thousand year period of peace on earth! Unfortunately, this trial for Israel must first take place.

As was explained earlier, the Arab empire, or the "Beast," will be the future oppressor of Israel. Yet it was also mentioned that this empire would actually subdivide, or break off into two distinct alliances. These two groups are Biblically known as the Northern and Southern Kingdoms, headed, of course, by the King of the North and the King of the South. That they torment Israel would not be the first time. Actually, prior to Jesus Christ's first coming to earth, these two kingdoms were quite active in their efforts against Israel and considerably successful as well, especially in their ruthless treatment of the nation. Consequently, they too are identified as genuine enemies and because of this, they are included in the list of kingdoms that have oppressed Israel which we discussed in the previous chapters. This, if you remember, was the list derived from Revelation 17 in the topic known as "The 7 Heads" which was depicted to mean seven different kingdoms that have troubled Israel. As a result, this completes our list of the seven enemy kingdoms as follows: (1) Babylon, (2) Medo-Persia, (3) Greece, (4) Southern Kingdom, (5) Northern Kingdom, (6) Rome, and (7) the Arabs. Of course, as was also indicated earlier was how this future Arab empire would actually further split into two distinct kingdoms. This therefore would correspond to the above mentioned Northern and Southern Kingdoms of the future. But as far as these Northern and Southern Kingdoms of the past, they were actually known respectively as the

Seleucid and Ptolemaic empires. These Kingdoms preceded Christ's first coming to earth and were ruled respectively by the Generals Antiochus and Ptolemy. Incidentally, although this "7 Heads" characteristic of the "beast" is both complex and confusing, at least now we can see how once again Bible prophecy is fulfilled.

"The King of the North vs. The King of the South"
Scripturally Explained

In Daniel chapter 11, a very familiar end-time passage is given in verses 40 through 45:

> vs. 40 - "And at the time of the end shall the king of the south push at him: and the <u>king of the north</u> shall come against him like a whirlwind, with chariots, and with horsemen, and with many ships; and he shall enter into the countries, and shall overflow and pass over."
>
> vs. 41 - "<u>He shall enter also into the glorious land, and many countries shall be overthrown: but these shall escape out of his hand, even Edom, and Moab, and the chief of the children of Ammon</u>."
>
> vs. 42 - "He shall stretch forth his hand also upon the countries: and <u>the land of Egypt shall not escape</u>."
>
> vs. 43 - "But he shall have power over the treasures of gold and of silver, and over all the precious things of Egypt; and <u>the Libyans and the Ethiopians shall be at his steps</u>."
>
> vs. 44 - "But tidings out of the east and out of the north shall trouble him: therefore he shall go forth with great fury to destroy, and utterly to make away many."
>
> vs. 45 - "And he shall plant the tabernacles of his palace between the seas in the glorious holy mountain; <u>yet he shall come to his end</u>, and none shall help him."

In this passage, there is essentially a movement of two empires against one another. In the process of this activity, it says that they in turn pass through the land of Israel (the "glorious land" - vs. 41). These two empires are termed the "king of the north" and the "king of the south." Who these kings are or where they come from is not evident. What is evident, however, is that some Arab and/or Moslem peoples become indirectly involved — Edom, Moab, Ammon, Egypt, Libya, and Ethiopia. Bearing in mind the already stated origin of this "beast" while also unlocking the interpretation of the "kings of the north and south" makes the previous (and already puzzling) prophetic passages all the more clearer.

With respect to the "king of the north," most people, due to the influence of traditional teaching, will emphatically state that it is to be Russia, or specifically the Soviet Union. But again, what does the Bible?

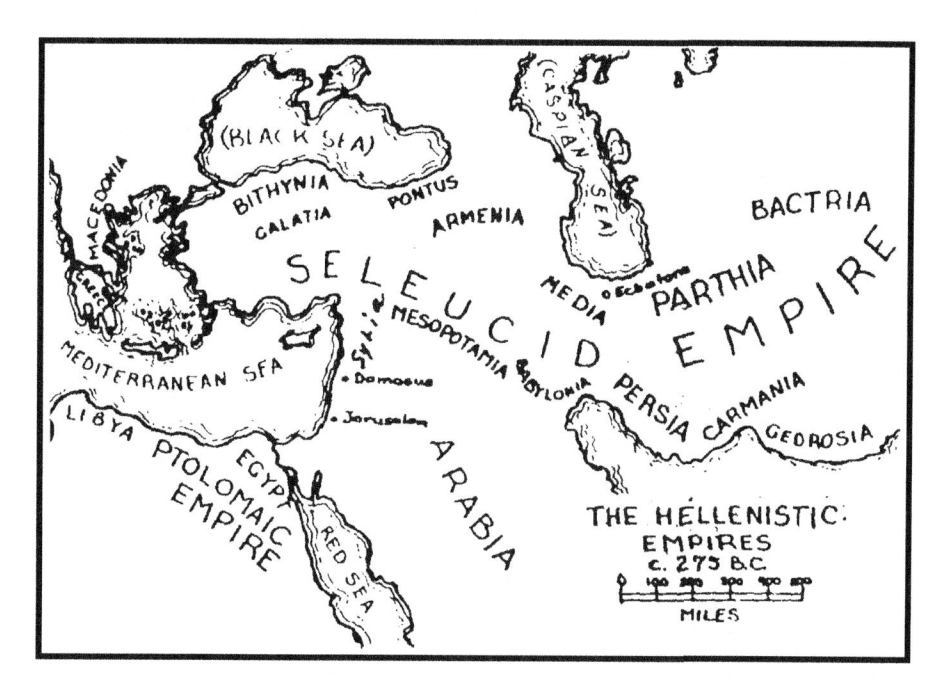

THE HELLENISTIC EMPIRES c. 275 B.C.

To fully understand its identity, one must evaluate this king in its proper context. The entire chapter (Daniel 11) reveals an amazing pattern which, when taken to its logical extreme, identifies this "king of the north." In fact, it also identifies the "king of the south." In other words, seven times earlier in this chapter (prior to verses 40 to 45) Daniel makes a reference to the "king of the north." To be sure, he previously mentions the "king of the south" seven times as well. It is important to note for this discussion that the first part of this chapter has already been historically fulfilled. As a result of the historical fulfillment, their origins can thus be properly identified. In other words, when the "king of the north" was mentioned, his origin was known as the historic Seleucid empire. In addition, the "king of the south" was a reference to the historic Ptolemaic empire. This is confirmed, by the way, by a casual reference to most any Bible Atlas with which you can identify their locations. What makes this point so interesting is what is revealed from the map. That is, the area covered by the Seleucid empire is none other than the likes of modern day Syria, Turkey, Iran, Iraq, Lebanon, Afghanistan, and Palestine, for example. Likewise, the area covered by the Ptolemaic empire basically includes Egypt, Kuwait, Saudi Arabia, Libya, and Ethiopia. In each case, the present day locations of these former empires directly associate with what today are either Arab and/or Moslem peoples. Thus, with this pattern in mind, would we not be wise to expect that both the <u>future</u> kings of the north and south would also originate from these very same geographic locations? I believe so and yet, even if we don't use this pattern to identify who they might be, we still find many other Biblical references that confirm these kings' identities as such.

For example, in Zephaniah 2:13, Assyria (Syria), and thus its king, is connected with the north, "And he (the Lord) will stretch out his hand against <u>the north, and destroy Assyria</u>." Then, as far as the king of the south is concerned, you probably noticed already that in Daniel 11, Egypt was mentioned twice in connection with it (vs. 8 & 43). That these countries would be considered as these identities makes even more sense when you consider them from Israel's defensive standpoint. For on the part of Israel, whenever they were attacked by the Seleucids (Northern Kingdom), the attack would come against Israel from its north, primarily because of the strategic set up of the land. The land to Israel's north was one of the more vulnerable locations that they had to deal with. Thus from Israel's standpoint, especially in that day with the lack of world maps and satellite pictures, they were in effect being attacked by someone coming from "the north." This was even true when they were attacked by Babylon (see Jer. 1:13-16) which was located to Israel's east, yet they would be attacked from the north and as a result, were considered part of the northern kingdom. Egypt, on the other hand, was actually more west of Israel than south. But again, to attack Israel by land required an approach which had them coming more directly from the south. Thus, they were given the name "king of the south."

Incidentally, you will find that both the Syrian and Egyptian roles during the end-times are specifically discussed in other parts of the Scriptures as well. For example, judgment on Syria is pronounced in

Isaiah 17 and, in the case of Egypt, you find its future hostility towards Israel referenced in both Zechariah 14:18-19 and Joel 3:18-19, while the future judgment that is also pronounced against it is referenced in Isaiah 19-20.

At any rate, it would serve to look more closely at this future King of the North because, after all, he does the most damage and ultimately invades Israel. Believe it or not, it seems that the Bible provides some clues as to whom this "king" (or leader) might be. And if you are at all like me, you too will be truly amazed as we take a closer look at a character to whom Daniel refers to as the "little horn," the subject of our next chapter.

Chapter 10

"The Little Horn" (Yasser Arafat?)

During the last decade or so, a couple of ruthless men have arisen from within the Middle East only to capture a great deal of media attention in the process. Why? Well for one, certainly because of their roles and their objectives but probably more so, because of their horrific ways of treating their foes. They have sought annihilation and complete destruction of those whom they have come up against. In addition, they have utilized various means of which seem to morally conflict with those of us from the western world.

In 1991, the first character really captured the spotlight with his unilateral decision to go in and capture land belonging to their neighboring country to the south. Of course, I am speaking of Iraq's Saddam Hussein, with his ill-fated attempt to take over Kuwait. Why was this so shocking to most of us? Probably because it just seemed beyond our imagination that a person would all of a sudden go into another country and then, all of a sudden, just decide that it belonged to him. But as we soon discovered, this was just the nature of this human being. Not that it transpired this way, but it seemed almost as if he one day was looking through a history book, noticed that the land belonging to Kuwait was actually once Iraq's, and as a result got up and ordered his military to go and get it back! Never mind political negotiation. Never mind professional conduct. Never mind common sense or even consideration of other people. He decided he wanted it and therefore decided to go and take it back! And that was the nature of this person that the world in general all of a sudden found themselves having to deal with. This was besides the fact that he was a cruel dictator and menace to society. As a result, and yet not surprisingly, many people soon began to question whether this man was the antichrist! Was Saddam Hussein the leader who would soon rule the entire world, they wondered?

On September 11th of 2001, the second character stole the world's spotlight. As New York City's World Trade Centers came tumbling down and as countless lives were unmercifully taken, one man stood tall as the mastermind behind this and other formerly dreaded terrorist attacks – the exiled Saudi and wealthy Osama bin Laden. As news agencies began to reveal his biographical sketch, it was clear that this man alone had surpassed the evil conduct of many others before even though, and more importantly, he continued to keep his targets in the dreaded clutches of fear as the possibility for further attacks loomed. Would this man continue? Or would he be captured, or even be killed? And how far reaching did his network, al-Qa'eda, really extend? Could he possibly be a Biblical character reserved for the end of times? These and other related questions dominated our minds as we awaited the outcome of this new war against terrorism.

Whether or not Saddam Hussein and/or Osama bin Laden are end-time characters remains to be seen. Personally, I don't know. Certainly it would have to be considered a possibility. Actually, I would even go so far as to say that somehow they both play a part in the overall big picture, which probably is not much of a stretch for me to say. Nevertheless, there is a character unmentioned that I do believe is worth even greater attention regarding a possible end-time role. The role, incidentally, is that of the "little horn," as introduced to us by the Prophet Daniel, a character seldom even mentioned in most end-time discussions. Rather, too often the discussions center on the subjects of the Beast, Antichrist, and Man of Sin, to name a few, of which quite often are considered by some to be the same individual. But rarely will you hear someone bring up the subject of the "little horn." And yet, I am convinced that this character is worthy of more concern than most any other of these end-time subjects. In fact, by the end of this chapter, I believe you too will conclude the same. But why? Could it be that we really are ignorant when it comes to much of what is really recorded within the Scriptures? Or could it be that we are limited to some degree by what our "teachers" actually choose to teach on? Or maybe we have misunderstood the nature of some of these end-time characters, along with their true identities and actual roles? Actually, I think that the answer is related to all of these questions. In other words, the answer is basically yes to each of these. And for that reason we know very little about this "little horn." With this being the case, we accordingly will be even less concerned with the actual identity of this character. Nevertheless, it is this subject that I believe is very key in both the unraveling of and the understanding of the overall end-time scenario with its many events.

For example, what if I told you that right now, today, there is an individual that has majorly been in the news for almost a decade, of whom is probably this "little horn!" And what if I told you that he has pulled on us the very same thing the Bible depicts him as doing. And more importantly, what if I told you that his chief coup yet remains — the capture of and subsequent control of the city of Jerusalem! Unfortunately, this is the Biblical destiny for this character. Of course, I am referring to none other than, or as the title of this chapter suggests, the person of Yasser Arafat, the infamous Palestinian leader. Is he an important character regarding the end-times, or even this character of the "little horn?" To put it mildly, I not only believe that he very well may be this "little horn," but I also believe that this character of the "little horn" is probably the single most important character that influences the outcome of these end-time events! But why?

As was previously mentioned, Daniel 11 records an end time scenario in which the southern kingdom rises up and challenges the northern kingdom. However, the northern kingdom relents and even responds - rather aggressively, I might add. Remember now, these two kingdoms are depicted as being alliances within the Middle East and consisting of Arab (or even Muslim) peoples. But not only does this northern kingdom respond against the southern kingdom, we discover that it even reacts against another country — a move of which becomes probably the most critical of moves — at the onset of the tribulation period. In other words, I am referring to their coming against the nation of Israel - specifically against the city of Jerusalem! This move is critical because of what Jesus forewarned us with in Luke 21:20, "<u>when ye shall see Jerusalem compassed with armies, then know that the desolation thereof is nigh!</u>" As a matter of fact, John informs us in Revelation 11:2 that upon this occurring, "<u>the holy city shall they tread under foot (for) forty and two months</u>." In other words, this marks the beginning of the 3½ year tribulation period. But even if this is to happen because of the "little horn," the question still remains, "Could this character really be Yasser Arafat?"

The Bible has spoken in prophetic language in the past regarding various important characters. For example, take Jesus. There were many major prophecies regarding Him as being the Messiah, or the

Son of God, as well as many minor ones. Yet, the probability of just a few of those prophecies being fulfilled by a single man was extremely slight, let alone many of these being fulfilled. Actually, God intended it to be that way. He was exact in His divine plans and He therefore removed all possibility for error. This, in fact, was a pattern He set in Scripture regarding prophecy. Of course, to us we only realize this in hindsight. Nevertheless we should be mindful of this as we consider the future, and this can be seen also with regards to this "little horn." For example, the Bible outlines many unique characteristics regarding this individual within the book of Daniel – 78 to be exact. These details range from being rather specific to being somewhat general. Still, they are provided specifically for a reason. God intended them to be provided as part of His plan and as a result, they are recorded to help give us insight and wisdom in the attempt of seeking to know His ways. In the case of Yasser Arafat potentially fulfilling the role of this "little horn," it is important to note that **well over 50 of these characteristics and details have already been fulfilled by him!** Does this make Yasser Arafat a Biblical Character? Only time will tell, but it sure seems that the handwriting is on the wall!

Though I will provide greater detail supporting this possibility in the explanation portion of this chapter, let me at least at this point state a few things regarding him to pique your curiosity. First of all, have you ever noticed his headgear, called a kaffiyeh? What does it look like? It looks as though he has a **LITTLE HORN**, wouldn't you say! Not that this alone is a distinctive that nails him down as the little horn, but I just think that it is a truly remarkable characteristic, especially in light of its uniqueness, that is, that it seems that he is the only one to wear his headdress that way — ANYWHERE! Where else can you find another like it?

Yasser Arafat – The "Little Horn?"

Second, do you at all recall who it was that was a recipient of the world renowned 1993 Nobel Peace Prize? After meeting to shake hands with the then Israeli Prime Minister Shimon Peres on the White House lawn on September 13, 1993 – a first of its kind – and after the signing of the Declaration of Principles between Israel and the Palestine Liberation Organization (PLO), the world it seemed was more than happy to present this prize to Palestinian Leader Yasser Arafat. Of course, a very interesting point here is that Daniel indicates of this "little horn" that "by peace he shall destroy many" (Dan. 7:25). Additionally, he adds that "he shall come in peaceably, and obtain the kingdom (control of the northern kingdom?) by flatteries" and "he shall enter peaceably even upon the fattest places of the province (the Promised Land); and he shall do that which his fathers have not done, nor his fathers' fathers (obtain control of Jerusalem?)" (Dan. 11:21, 24). Incidentally, this is even more compelling when you consider what the Apostle Paul forewarned us

Wake Up Church: The End is Nigh!

with, "For when they shall say, <u>Peace and safety (security); then sudden destruction cometh upon them (Israel?)</u>, as travail upon a woman with child; and they shall not escape" (1 Thess. 5:3). Does this not sound like a genuine description of the current state of affairs in the Middle East as well as its predictable future? It does to me!

A third characteristic of noteworthiness, as recorded by Daniel, is as follows, "Through his <u>cunning</u> he shall cause <u>deceit</u> to prosper under his hand" (Dan. 8:25). In other words, Daniel is saying that the "little horn" will lie himself all the way to the top! Sad how prosperity is achieved sometimes, isn't it? But then again, we know that the "god of this world," or Satan, is described as being "the father of all lies" (John 8:44), so why wouldn't this character achieve this high (or low!) calling through this same type of conduct? As far as Yasser Arafat goes, can this policy of lying be descriptive of him? Or rather, is he known to be one who talks out of both sides of his mouth? Without a doubt! Unfortunately, due to the way the news is covered and how things are portrayed, many might be totally unaware of just how "cunning" he really is at this. For example, in this past year of the "uprising" (called "intifada"), or since September of 2000, as Israel has encountered numerous terrorist attacks against it, their response has frequently been to go into Palestinian occupied territories to track down and attack these so-called terrorists. And yet it is Arafat who decries Israel as the aggressor and violator of the peace agreements for their doing so. However, few people really know what the agreements say, nor do they care, when in fact it is the Palestinians who are in violation. Israel has the jurisdictional right to enter into autonomous land areas to track and pursue criminals whereas Arafat has the responsibility to stop these terrorists. Yet isn't it cunning how he is able to swing the popular opinion of others to believe that it is the Palestinians who are the victims while Israel is the "bully!" Another disturbing reality is just how often he is quoted in the media as saying something politically appropriate with respect to the state of events between them and Israel. This is because afterwards, in addressing his own people (whether directly with him speaking or indirectly through an official representive), it is frequently in a manner that is offensive, hostile, and even threatening of Israel while also being in direct violation of the peace agreements! But then again, this is his policy, he is skilled at it, and it is how he gained his voice in this world. The fact is, it very well may be due to it being a fulfillment of prophecy as well!

Accordingly, it would serve us well to reflect a bit on the Palestinians' history as well as their true objectives. Actually, this will be done in the next chapter when we discuss the PLO charter. But first I would like to provide even greater detail and explanation regarding this "little horn," especially in light of its fulfillment possibly being Palestine's Yasser Arafat.

"The Little Horn" (Yasser Arafat?)
Scripturally Explained

Before I go into further detail, I would first like to express a great deal of appreciation to one Marvin Byers. Though I have never personally met him, I owe all credit to him on this issue of the "little horn" possibly being Yasser Arafat. For a more complete presentation on this subject, obtain his book, "Yasser Arafat – A Biblical Character?" He definitely presents a very compelling argument regarding Arafat as this character. The explanations I provide are generally derived from his work. However, I would like to present my explanation utilizing another author's writings. Colin Deal is not only a dear friend of mine, but is also a very respected teacher on the subject of the end-times. He authors a monthly newsletter entitled the "End Time News" and he, too, derived much of his thought on this subject from Mr. Byers. The following is from Deal's August 1996 Edition of his newsletter in which he cites Byers' work:

Who is this man, known as Yasser Arafat? His name at birth was Rahman Abdul Rauf Arafat al-Qudwa al Husseini. "Arafat" is the name of the sacred mountain near Mecca where Mohammed experienced a spiritual transformation in his life. His family called him Rahman, but his boyhood teacher and first verifiable homosexual partner, Majid Halaby, gave him the name Yasser. So his last name calls to mind the very spiritual source of Islam and his first calls to mind Sodomy!

HE IS A LITTLE HORN

"I considered the horns, and, behold, there came up among them another little horn" (Dan. 7:8a).

Why is this horn called "little?" Yasser Arafat can indeed be called "little" for several reasons. First, he is physically little. He's only five feet four inches tall. Second, he is politically little. Even Arafat knows that he was rescued from political oblivion by Israel's decision to make peace with him. Third, he is territorially little. Even after Israel has finished giving him all the West Bank, and he has established his rule or "kingdom" over it, the new Palestinian State will be the smallest Arab country on earth. Fourth, he is financially little. Although Arafat himself is wealthy, when he has finished establishing his new government over the Palestinians, it will be the poorest of all the Moslem nations. Last, he is morally little. It could be argued that he is the most morally bankrupt of all the Islamic leaders on earth.

HE COMES UP AFTER THE TEN HORNS

> "The ten horns are ten kings, who shall arise from this kingdom. And another shall rise after them..." (Dan. 7:24a).

He does not receive a kingdom at the same time they do. Today, all the other Islamic nations around Israel are already independent. Yasser Arafat has not yet succeeded in establishing an independent Palestinian state within the Holy Land. Some Israelis suspect that Arafat, in flagrant violation of the Oslo agreements, will soon make a unilateral declaration of Palestinian independence. In the autonomous areas, he is already beginning to issue passports, stamps, and independent Palestinian currency. It has been correctly stated in the Israeli press that regarding the emergence of a Palestinian state, it is no longer a question of if but when.

HE HAS EYES LIKE THE EYES OF A MAN

> "And there, in this horn, were eyes like the eyes of a man" (Dan. 7:8c).

Those who have personally known Arafat have been greatly impressed by his eyes just as Daniel was. Many things have been said about his eyes, including these comments: "His eyes were hypnotic and they could stop you cold."[i] "When he looked at one, (he) seemed to peer into one's deepest interior recesses."[ii] "He had two ways of looking at you with his large eyes – very softly, like a man looking at a woman... or blankly, as though his eyes were going right through you."[iii] He did not speak with his voice so much as with his body – his hands, his eyes."[iv] It has also been said of his eyes that they "bore holes into you."[v]

HE HAS A MOUTH SPEAKING GREAT THINGS

"and, behold, in this horn were eyes like the eyes of man, and a mouth speaking great things" (Dan. 7:8d).

Since signing the 1993 peace accord, Arafat is now referred to as an international statesman. Just after Arafat signed the Israeli-PLO peace accord in Cairo on May 4, 1994, he immediately began to proclaim, "Jericho and Gaza first, and then on to Jerusalem."[vi] He openly declared that Jerusalem would soon be the capital of a Palestinian state.

HE SHALL BE DIFFERENT FROM THE OTHER HORNS

"The ten horns are ten kings who shall arise from this kingdom. And another shall rise after them; he shall be different from the first ones" (Dan. 7:24a).

There are several ways in which Arafat is different from the ten horns, as well as from most other world leaders. One of those differences is unmistakable. In any photograph where he appears with any group of world leaders, including Islamic leaders, his difference from them is remarkable and causes him to stand out immediately. Even if all the leaders in the photograph are Arab and are all wearing a kaffiyeh, the Arab headdress, Arafat still stands out. First, he ties his kaffiyeh differently from all other Arabs, forming a little horn on the top. Another difference is that he dresses in military fatigues that are often rumpled while the other leaders are all dressed in their finest clothes. Furthermore, he is almost always unshaved with a three or four day beard. And he always wears his pistol at his side. Even when he addressed the UN in 1974, he refused to surrender it. It has been said that "Arafat is extremely careful about his careless appearance," so that "he stands out immediately, attracting attention."[vii]

HE SHALL SPEAK AGAINST THE MOST HIGH

"He shall speak words against the Most High" (Dan. 7:25a)

Although this description of the little horn may not yet be fulfilled in its entirety, Yasser Arafat does mock the God of the Jews and also the God of the Christians – the same God. A saying that he continues to endorse is, "On Saturday we will kill the Jews, and on Sunday we will kill the Christians." This slogan often appears in Arabic on PLO flags.[viii] Possibly the most publicized example of this took place during the visit to Israel of Archbishop Desmond Tutu of South Africa. He is another well-known Nobel Peace Prize laureate. In 1989, he visited Israel, where he publicly denounced the Jews. Behind him, the PLO flag was flying with this slogan written on it.

The "Dome of the Rock," called the Mosque of Omar, is built on the site of the Jewish temple, and the al-Aksa Mosque is built on Solomon's Porch where Jesus taught. The Moslems point to the fact that those two mosques are built over two of the most important Jewish and Christian sites as proof that the god of Islam is greater than the God of the Jews and also greater than the God of the Christians. These are strong words spoken against the God of the universe!

HE SHALL CHANGE THE SACRED SEASONS AND LAW

"and (he) shall attempt to change the sacred seasons and the law" (Dan. 7:25c NRSV).

This passage speaks of the religious times and religious laws. The religious laws and seasons that the little horn will change could well refer to those of his own religion. In Yasser Arafat, there has already been a fulfillment of this prophetic revelation of the little horn both regarding a change of religious law and change of sacred seasons or times. In accordance with the laws of the Islamic Arab League the mufti of Jerusalem is to be appointed by King Hussein of Jordan.[ix] The title "mufti" refers to the top Islamic religious leader who is in charge of any Islamic holy site or mosque.

Shortly after Arafat signed the initial peace agreement with Israel in September 1993, the mufti of Jerusalem just happened to die. To demonstrate his authority over Jerusalem, Arafat immediately named the next mufti, and announced that the appointment of the mufti whom King Hussein had chosen was void. Arafat "extracted a declaration from the foreign ministers of the Arab League to the effect that the PLO has the sole right to rule in eastern Jerusalem."[x] He also announced that "henceforth the PLO would be responsible for the Moslem Council and the Wakf" (the religious body in charge of Moslem affairs), thus changing the religious status quo in Jerusalem.[xi] Arafat had succeeded in changing the Islamic religious law over Jerusalem and the West Bank!

Next, Arafat and his mufti proceeded to change the timing of Islam's most important "sacred season," or religious holy day. The ninth month of the Islamic calendar is Ramadan. During this entire month, Moslems fast during the day and feast at night. The first day of the month, and therefore the first day of their fasting and feasting, is determined by the first appearance of the moon. The religious authorities in Mecca are traditionally responsible for announcing when the new moon of Ramadan first appears. Arafat and mufti changed all that in 1995. Arafat declared, "For the first time in the history of the Palestinian nation, we announce... to the Arab and Islamic world the witnessing of the new Ramadan moon from the Aksa Mosque (in Jerusalem) under the Palestinian Authority."[xii] The Moslems of Palestine duly obeyed their new leader and began the feast one day sooner than Jordanian Moslems. Arafat had succeeded in making his first change in the timing of a "sacred season!"

HE COMES OUT OF ALEXANDER'S FORMER KINGDOM

"And out of one of (the four horns) came a little horn"
(Dan. 8:9a).

Geographically, there is no question about Arafat's credentials regarding this aspect of the little horn. He definitely was born and raised in the Middle East, which was part of the four kingdoms into which Alexander the Great's kingdom was divided.

HE GROWS GREAT TOWARD THE SOUTH, EAST AND THE GLORIOUS LAND

"(he) grew exceedingly great toward the south, toward the east, and toward the Glorious Land" (Dan. 8:9b).

Yasser Arafat has already fulfilled this revelation of the little horn in at least two ways. His growth toward greatness has followed this south, east, Glorious Land sequence at least twice. His growth first began when he was sent south – by his father, from Gaza to Cairo. He returned to Egypt to study at the University of Cairo. That's when he joined the

Palestine Students' Federation and ultimately became its leader. His work of hatred against the Jews finally earned him the respect of the Egyptian government, where he was enlisted in the army and trained in explosives,[xiii] which are his specialty to this day! After Egypt, he went east – first to Kuwait and then to Jordan. In Kuwait, along with others, he founded the terrorist group known as Fatah, which was later incorporated into the PLO. After Kuwait, where he reportedly became wealthy in a construction company that he began, he moved his Fatah terrorists into Jordan. In 1970, he and his cohorts were expelled from Jordan in a very bloody conflict with the armies of King Hussein. If Arafat is in fact the little horn, we should assume that from Jordan in the east, his next step would be the "Glorious Land." This is precisely what happened, though it is not immediately obvious. From Jordan he moved into Lebanon. Though Israel does not yet possess Lebanon, from the beginning it was included by the Lord in the Holy Land.

Arafat has followed this south, east, Glorious Land sequence again in the last few years since the Oslo accord. After Arafat was expelled from Lebanon by the Israelis in 1982, he moved his headquarters to Tunis. In the Oslo accord, Israel agreed to give him territory within the Holy Land on which he is now founding his Palestinian government. The sequence in which he has taken possession of this land has been the south, east, Glorious Land sequence.

THROUGH PEACE HE DESTROYS MANY

"by peace (the little horn) shall destroy many" (Dan. 8:25c).

"Peace for us means the destruction of Israel."[xiv] These are the words of Yasser Arafat. They were not invented by this author to prove that Arafat is the little horn! The Apostle Paul reveals that when Israel declares, "Peace and safety," then "sudden destruction will come upon them" (1 Thess. 5:3). This word "safety" in the Greek can also be translated as "security from enemies"[xv] – Israel's longing. This is also what the Hebrew word translated as "peace" means in this detail that Daniel gives us about the little horn. Quietness and tranquility is what Rabin and Peres thought had come to Israel through their peace agreement. Rabin promised that now we will have "a time without worries, nights without anxiety, the end of death." Peres added: "This agreement has inaugurated a new, violence-free era."[xvi]

If we combine Daniel's revelation with Paul's revelation, we discover how this "destruction" referred to by Paul will come upon Israel at the precise time they are seeking peace and security. It will come through the little horn. The little horn uses the "security" of a fictitious peace as an occasion to destroy many. Yasser Arafat has already begun to fulfill this prophetic word with precision. As mentioned previously, immediately after he had signed the peace accord, twice as many Israelis began dying as a result of terrorist attacks than at any other time in the nation's modern history.[xvii] Arafat's plan calls for the rate of Jewish murders to increase from dozens to thousands until the Jews are exterminated!

Can Israel pretend they never heard what Arafat said in the interview he gave live on Jordanian TV, transmitted from the US on the very day he first signed a peace agreement with Israel? As we already mentioned, he explained, "We take any and every territory that we can of Palestine, and establish a sovereignty there, and we use it as a spring board to take more." Arafat continues to shout before Moslem audiences, "With blood and spirit we shall redeem thee, O Palestine." Everyone knows that his definition of "Palestine" includes the entire Jewish state. The Israeli government makes excuses for him, saying that he is just playing to the crowd, but one day, when thousands of Israelis are dying, they will have to admit that this game was deadly serious and that he was also speaking truth that they were unwilling to hear! Then, even the unbelieving Israeli politicians will understand why Daniel said that "by peace (the little horn) shall destroy many."

A PRINCE OF THE COVENANT SHALL BE DESTROYED BEFORE HIM

"Then an overwhelming army will be swept away before him; both it and a prince of the covenant will be destroyed" (Dan. 11:22 NIV).

The Hebrew word "prince" can mean "prince, captain, chief, or general."

Both Israelis and non-Israelis frequently declare that Rabin died for peace. This is simply not the real reason Rabin died. If we analyze what is being said, it is actually just one more direct attack against the people of Israel. As a result of Rabin's peace initiative, the nation ended up totally and almost equally divided. About half the population endorsed his peace plan and the other half remained strongly opposed to his plan as long as it involved giving away the land that God had promised Israel. The feelings ran so deeply that a group of ultra-orthodox rabbis got together and pronounced a seldom-used powerful curse against Rabin in front of his house in September 1995.[xviii] One report reads, "According to several news accounts, (a rabbi) organized a minion of supporters outside Rabin's residence... on the eve of last Yom Kippur and invoked the 'angels of destruction... to kill (Rabin)... for handing over the land of Israel to our enemies.'"[xix] The report goes on to say, "The curse was to have been effective within about 30 days. Rabin was murdered 33 days later."[xx]

Jews throughout the world were reading a certain Hebrew text the week Rabin was murdered. Since before the time of Christ, orthodox Jews throughout the world have had the custom of all reading the same designated portions of Scripture each week. To understand the "coincidence," we must understand several details about written Hebrew. First, there are not any written vowels; all the written letters are consonants. Second, there are no capital letters or punctuation. Third, in the original Bible there were no spaces between one word and the next. The text was just one continuous string of consonants. Rabbis added spaces for the convenience of the Hebrew reader. Fourth, many times there is more than one possible way to divide the consonants into words in a given passage. Many Rabbis believe that all of the possible ways to divide a passage into separate words reveal truth as long as the divisions form legitimate words with a logical meaning.

The passage that worldwide Jewry was reading during the week that Rabin was assassinated included Genesis 15:17-18 where God made a covenant with Abraham promising to give the land of Canaan to his descendants forever. In that very passage, if the Hebrew is divided differently from the way it appears in the modern Hebrew Bible, the following message appears: "Fire, fire, evil for Rabin." The word "fire" here is used in Hebrew today in the same way it is used in English on the firing range when soldiers are commanded: "Ready, aim, fire." Yitzhak Rabin was assassinated when Amir fired two bullets.

(End quote from Colin Deal's End Time Newsletter.)

Do the above explanations sound pretty convincing? Maybe not, but I would think that serious consideration has to at least be given to the possibility of Yasser Arafat being this "little horn." Again, the explanations provided in Marvin Byers' book, considerably more exhaustive than what's provided here, give an even more compelling argument. Of course, I want to thank both Marvin Byers and Colin Deal for their excellent works on this subject and I would strongly encourage you to see Byers' book for a more thorough presentation — a verse by verse breakdown regarding Daniel's "little horn" and Arafat's possible fulfillment of it. Next, I would like to examine a bit of history regarding both the PLO (now Palestinian Authority) and the Hamas militant terrorist group, as well as what they truly stand for.

Chapter 11

"The PLO & Hamas"

Believe it or not, the greatest enemy of the State of Israel since it became a nation in 1948 has been the Palestinian leader, Chairman Yasser Arafat. Fact is, he has attacked Israel for a longer period of time, more frequently, and has killed more Jews than any other person in the whole world. Actually, his work against them began even while a teenager, some 50 years ago. Along with his hate-filled father and some others, he set out to destroy the Jews. In turn, he organized a group of terrorists (known today as the Fatah) of which later was incorporated into the Palestine Liberation Organization (PLO) upon his seizing its control. This organization would sponsor terrorism while also strategizing its goals of gaining the Holy Land, capturing Jerusalem, and eliminating Zionism. With the signing of the peace accord in 1993, Arafat gained a strategic foothold into the very land from which he could further these objectives while still utilizing this same means of terrorist activities, thereby able to launch even greater attacks against Israel. This new standing of being, in effect, a "nation within a nation" provided him this unique and advantageous position. Thus, he was determined to utilize it to its fullest advantage.

Ironically, his aim of restoring the Palestinian people back to its homeland has been one of the most creative and cunning lies imagined. As the saying goes, if you say something long enough people will begin to believe it, even if it isn't true. In this case, that would become an incredible reality. Preying upon emotions, Arafat has effectively managed to sound the mantra of the so-called plight of the "Palestinian people." Unfortunately, the truth is that there really has never been such a thing as a "Palestinian people!" Amazingly, this fact has been drowned out and therefore has disappeared into the great sea of lies, helped out no less by the work and voices of the international news mediums. The Arabs claim that Israel came into the land of "Palestine" and took it away from the "Palestinians" who had been living there for thousands of years. The truth, however, is that the Arab states not only invented this new race called the "Palestinians," but they also sent into this region multitudes of new "citizens" for the express purpose of opposing the State of Israel in the Middle East. Essentially, this has been going on since early in the Twentieth Century as the Jews began to return to their homeland, thereby increasing the concern of the surrounding Arab peoples. Thus, this actual creation of a people would eventually be replaced by the lie regarding their so-called plight of hundreds of years. If this is untrue, then what really is the truth regarding this people, and what are their true objectives?

To gain a better understanding regarding the "Palestinians," it would help to first take a look into their charter, "The Palestinian National Covenant." Known also as the PLO Charter, this covenant was adopted in 1964 and later revised in 1968. From it, you will see that their objectives involve a land void of Jews, inhabited by Palestinians, established with Palestinian statehood, and having Jerusalem as its capital. The language within this Charter is very explicit, making no doubt their true aims. How this language seems to be overlooked by Israel and the rest of the world during the peace negotiations makes no sense to me. It is almost like a "spell" has been cast over them. But then again, this too is remarkably in character with these "Palestinians." After all, the acronym "PLO" in the Hebrew is a word which actually means "sorcerers!"

That terrorism is the main tactic used to help achieve their objectives should by now be quite obvious. Accordingly, one such organization mandating considerable attention is the terrorist group known as Hamas. Although it is not directly under Arafat's control, it nevertheless is a weapon within his arsenal. As former Israeli Prime Minister Benjamin Netanyahu declared regarding the PLO and Hamas, "(they) are operating hand in glove."[xxi] Although Arafat denies a connection with Hamas publicly, he nevertheless includes them as part of his true aims, as evidenced by his declaration that, "The Islamists are part of the PLO... They are not against the PLO; they are in the PLO."[xxii] As a matter of fact, the Hamas Covenant goes so far as to say that, "The PLO, one of the movements closest to the Islamic Resistance Movement, **is father**, brother, kinsman, and friend."[xxiii] Thus, with Arafat's leadership role in the PLO, it makes sense that the PLO would be considered the "father" of the Hamas. Likewise, Arafat was involved in its "birth!" Thus, we can learn even more regarding the intentions of this people by examining the written manifesto of this Hamas organization. From it, we will discover their true aims are both the ethnic cleansing of the Jewish people along with the Arab control of the city of Jerusalem! A more thorough examination of both the PLO Charter and the Hamas' Manifesto is what is provided next in the explanation portion of this chapter.

"The PLO & Hamas"
Explained

Yasser Arafat's lifelong goal is to annihilate Israel. Normally, that would alarm you, especially if you were Israel. However, it seems that for some time, this was of no critical concern to them, or to anyone else for that matter. Oh, it used to be alright. After the signing of the peace accord in Cairo, Egypt, it was promised by Arafat that he would eliminate the rhetoric which confirmed this goal. In other words, he would adjust the language found in "The Palestinian National Covenant." This covenant espoused the goals as first adopted by the Palestine Liberation Organization in 1964 and later revised in 1968. Known also as the PLO Charter, it clearly stated how its objective was to rid the land of all traces of "Zionism," a term denoting people of Jewish heritage. However, these written goals, even if altered on paper, would not necessarily reflect a true change in practice. Fact is, Arafat has not only reneged on this commitment, but he has even declared publicly that he would not change this Charter. However, if pressured by Israel to do so, he also stated that it would then result in a confrontation! But what does this Charter actually say and what really is the PLO?

To most, the PLO (now referred to as the Palestine Authority) was formed to ultimately win back the land. Arafat himself declared that "the PLO is the sole legitimate representative of the Palestinian people."[xxiv] Yet the real truth has been that from its inception, the PLO was formed to eliminate the Jews from the Middle East by killing them all! This is clearly understood when examining the PLO Charter. Consider, for example, the following statements:

Article 3: "The Palestinian Arab people possesses the <u>legal right</u> to its homeland, and when the liberation of its homeland is <u>completed</u> it will exercise self-determination <u>solely according to its own will and choice.</u>" Notice that this so-called "legal" right is one that exists only in their minds. No one else recognizes it. Also, notice that in their minds, the liberation of their homeland, which means the replacement of Israel, is already deemed a done deal. Of course, that this is within the realm of their free will and choice is not to be taken lightly.

Article 6: "__Jews__ who were living permanently in Palestine until the beginning of the Zionist invasion __will be considered Palestinians.__" Does this seem like an arrogant statement to you? They actually think that a Jew is really a Palestinian just because he (the Jew) was living there (on this land which the Palestinians claim as theirs) prior to Israel becoming a nation!

Article 8: "...the Palestinian masses, whether in the homeland or in places of exile...comprise one national front which acts __to restore Palestine and liberate it through armed struggle.__" Notice the means they have already prepared to use — armed struggle — in order to achieve their objective - getting Israel's land. Obviously, they are not a civil people.

Article 9: "__Armed struggle__ is the only way to liberate Palestine and is therefore a __strategy__ and not tactics." Sounds to me like they are very intentional in how they plan on getting just exactly what they want - using terrorism and war to get the land of Israel!

Article 11: "The Palestinian Arab people...must... __resist__ any plan that tends to disintegrate or weaken it." The resolve of these people is clearly seen in this statement and only serves to reinforce their absolute will, which is not a good sign for Israel.

Article 13: "Arab unity and the __liberation of Palestine__ are two complimentary aims. Each one paves the way for realization of the other. Arab unity leads to the liberation of Palestine, and the liberation of Palestine leads to Arab unity. Working for both goes hand in hand." Obviously, they appeal to the principle that unity increases strength and that there is greater strength in numbers. Thus, their goal of getting Israel must be shared by other Arab nations, which is already occurring.

Article 14: "The __destiny__ of the Arab nation, indeed the very Arab existence, depends upon the destiny of the Palestine issue." I guess you could say that they (the Arabs) have put all of their marbles into one basket! Amazingly, this is belief is already being shared by many of the other Arab peoples.

Article 15: "The liberation of Palestine, from an Arab viewpoint, is __a national duty to repulse the Zionist__, imperialist invasion from the great Arab homeland and to __purge the Zionist presence from Palestine.__ Its full responsibilities fall upon the Arab nation, peoples and governments, with the Palestine Arab people at their head. For this purpose, the Arab nation __must__ mobilize its military, human, material and spiritual capabilities to participate actively with the people of Palestine." Can it be any clearer what their intentions are? Obviously, their goals extend beyond just obtaining a nation. They want to rid the land of the Israelis! And a call to the rest of the Arab world to share in this objective has been already made. Will Israel really be able to survive such an attack against them?

Article 16: *"<u>The liberation of Palestine</u>, from a spiritual viewpoint, will prepare an atmosphere of tranquility and peace for the Holy Land, in the shade of which all the holy places will be safeguarded, and freedom of worship and visitation to all will be guaranteed, without distinction or discrimination of race, color, language or religion. For this reason, the people of Palestine looks to the support of all the spiritual forces in the world."* This actually sounds like a very civil and noble objective, in that the guarantee of freedom and the atmosphere of security and peace would result. However, the prerequisite is of chief concern, which is the "liberation" of Palestine. What, to them, would that mean? Obviously, it means first, to obtain the land and second, to eliminate the Jews. Then, and only then, will this objective be fulfilled. Unfortunately, and especially in this case, we know that the end here can not justify the means!

Article 18: *"The liberation of Palestine, from an international viewpoint is a <u>defensive act</u> necessitated by the requirements of <u>self-defense</u>."* Sometimes it is very difficult to detain one who, after being bullied one too many times, suddenly snaps and goes into a rage. The conditioning of the people there in Palestine (or throughout the Arab nation) has been such that they are convinced that they have been victims far too long and that the time for redemption is now — essentially a do or die situation!

Article 19: *"The partitioning of Palestine in 1947 <u>and the establishment of Israel (in 1948) is fundamentally null and void</u>, whatever time has elapsed, because it was contrary to the wish of the people of Palestine and its natural right to its homeland, and contradicts the principles embodied in the Charter of the United Nations, the first of which is the right of self-determination."* Oh, okay. If you say so! Have you ever heard that ridiculous statement, "If I can't see it, it doesn't exist?" In other words, the person determines reality for themselves or they become the judge of what for them is reality. This seems to apply here. They have decided not that Israel exists inappropriately, but rather that they DO NOT EXIST AT ALL! I guess that that is what they mean when they say that the establishment of Israel as a nation is "null and void."

Article 20: "The Balfour Declaration (by Great Britain in 1917 which allowed Jews to begin to return back to the land), the Mandate Document, and what has been based upon them are considered <u>null and void</u>. The claim of a historical or spiritual tie between Jews and Palestine does not tally with historical realities nor with the constituents of statehood in their true sense. Judaism, in its character as a religion of revelation, is not a nationality with an independent existence. Likewise, the Jews are not one people with an independent personality. <u>They are rather citizens of the states to which they belong</u>." In other words, they once again decide what is reality. In this case, it is their belief that there is no nation of Israel at all. Rather, the Israelis are to be considered as citizens of Palestine, since they are living on the land which the Palestinians claim as theirs! Now even if this were to be true, I can't imagine that this would mean that the Israelis, as Palestinian citizens, would be welcome ones. Hence, the Palestinians' desire to rid the land of the Israelis.

Article 22: "<u>Zionism</u> is a political movement organically related to world <u>imperialism</u> and <u>hostile</u> to all movements of liberation and progress in the world. It is a <u>racist and fanatical</u> movement in its formation; aggressive, expansionist and colonialist in its aims; and <u>Fascist and Nazi</u> in its means. Israel is the tool of the Zionist movement and a human and geographical base for world imperialism. It is a concentration and jumping-off point for imperialism in the heart of the Arab homeland, to strike at the hopes of the Arab nation for liberation, unity and progress.

<u>Israel is a constant threat to peace in the Middle East and the entire world. Since the liberation of Palestine will liquidate the Zionist and imperialist presence and bring about the stabilization of peace in the Middle East</u>, the people of Palestine looks to the support of all liberal men of the world and all the forces of good progress and peace; and implores all of them, regardless of their different leanings and orientations, to offer all help and support to the people of Palestine in its just and legal struggle to liberate its homeland." Is this not the most amazing thing you've ever read? Does "the pot calling the kettle black" come to mind? Or how about the man who

sees a speck in another's eye while being unaware of the log in his own. I mean, really! To compare Zionism with imperialism, racism and fanaticism is extreme. But Fascism and Naziism? Actually, it is kind of funny to think of a country, ever so small in its true size and like a tiny island completely surrounded by Arabs and/or Moslems, as being imperialistic! Boy, are they (Israel) dominating (ha, ha)! And then, a people (Israel) who suffered greatly at the hands of the Fascist and Naziist holocaust is themselves being called the same (Israel being called Fascist and Naziist)? As a matter of fact, in this age of "political correctness," it truly is shocking that this type of language is not only not reprimanded, but is actually tolerated. Even more so, it seems it is even allowed, or at least it is ignored by the so-called media types as they continue to bury much of what really seems to occur.

Article 23: "The demands of security and peace and the requirements of truth and justice oblige all states that preserve friendly relations among peoples and maintain the loyalty of citizens to their homelands <u>to consider Zionism an illegitimate movement and to prohibit its existence and activity</u>." Again, how does one get away with communicating such harsh and offensive language like this without incurring any consequences? Certainly, their disdain for the Jews is at the fore of their greatest aims.

Article 28: "The Palestinian Arab people insists upon the originality and independence of its national revolution and <u>rejects every manner of interference</u>, guardianship and subordination." Not only are they bent on achieving their own objectives, but they now also address their feelings towards anyone who disagrees with and/or opposes them!

Obviously, from just this sampling of what is driving this force, you can see that the Palestinians are certainly a people to be reckoned with, especially if you are a Jew. Not that their size is threatening, but certainly their passion is, and especially their goals. This PLO Charter clearly states the Palestinians' embittered intent and because of it, you can be sure that during these end-times, it once again is just so true how God really does put into the hearts of people the very bidding of His will, as they help fulfill Israel's experience of tribulation. Incidentally, there is another force to be reckoned with, or an organization of terrorists that has outlined its true objectives, of which also closely resembles those of the PLO charter. This terrorist

Wake Up Church: The End is Nigh!

group is known as Hamas, and is likewise extremely dangerous to the Jews.

HAMAS

Obviously, the overall goal of the Palestinians is to rid the land of the Jews, achieve the status of statehood, and obtain Jerusalem for its capital. Certainly, Yasser Arafat stands as the key figure, not only politically, but in every move this people makes. And this includes organizations such as the terrorist group Hamas. Not that Arafat controls the Hamas, but that there is a correlation that exists between these two entities in what really takes place. And this group too is definitely one to be reckoned with. But what really is this group and what are their aims?

The Hamas is a terrorist organization that is located primarily in both the Gaza Strip and the West Bank. An outgrowth of the Palestinian branch of the Muslim Brotherhood, this group was officially formed in 1987. They number, if you include the sympathizers with the hard-core members, into the tens of thousands. In practice, the Hamas have used both political and violent means to pursue their goal. And what is their goal? It is to establish an Islamic Palestinian state in the place of Israel!

One of their most dangerous and yet hideous means of terrorism is the suicide bomber. This, by the way, is Hamas' claim to fame. Some of their more memorable attacks of late have been the suicide bombing on June 1, 2001 outside of a discotheque in Tel Aviv that killed 21 and the August 9, 2001 suicide bombing of a pizza restaurant in Jerusalem that killed 18. However, their most recent and infamous attack occurred on the Jewish Sabbath, December 2nd of 2001. In a couple of suicide bombings, most notably one in an outdoor mall in Jerusalem, they killed 26 people and injured close to 200. This has resulted in the decision of Israel to not only have to defend itself militarily, but also to join in its own war against terrorism. What will be the result of this? Only time will tell, but it sure seems that things are heating up, even approaching the dreaded boiling point. The Hamas, and especially these suicide bombers, can be thanked for this. Of course, Hamas doesn't just do suicide bombings. They also target Israeli citizens and their military facilities and posts.

Though they officially formed in 1987, the Hamas began its evolution in 1978 from a non-profit organization called *Mujam'a* which began in Gaza. This group was founded by Sheikh Ahmed Yassin after the start of the *intifada,* or "uprising," against Israeli rule in the West Bank and Gaza Strip. The ideology of the Hamas contends that the soil of all that is Palestine is a Wakf, meaning "Muslim holy property," and therefore belongs to the Muslims forever.

According to *B'NAI B'RITH*, the Hamas have a written manifesto called the **"Ten Principles Of Faith,"** which includes the following:

1. Hamas swears to conduct a <u>holy war</u> over Palestine <u>against the Jews</u> until Allah's victory is achieved.
2. The land must be cleansed of the filth and evil of the <u>tyrannical</u> conquerors.
3. Under the wings of Islam it is possible to have peaceful coexistence with other religious groups. But <u>without Islamic rule over the Dome of the Rock</u>, there can only be hatred, controversy, corruption, and repression.
4. By command of the Prophet (Muhammad), <u>Muslims must fight the Jews and kill them</u> wherever they are.
5. Hamas strives to set up an entity wherein Allah is the highest purpose – the Koran is its law.
6. Palestine is a holy Islamic entity until the end of time. Therefore, it is <u>non-negotiable</u> and no one can give up any part of it.
7. It is a personal, religious commandment for every Muslim to engage in the <u>jihad</u> (or holy war) until the land is redeemed.
8. Hamas opposes any kind of international talks or <u>negotiations</u> as well as <u>any possible peace arrangement</u>. Sovereignty over the land is strictly a religious matter and conducting negotiation over it means giving up some measure of control by (Islam's) believers.
9. The Jews control the media and the world financial institutions. By means of revolution and war, and organizations such as Masons, Communists, Capitalists, Zionists, Rotary, Lions, B'Nai B'rith, and the like, they undermine human society as a whole in order to destroy it. <u>By their evil corruption they try to gain domination of</u>

> <u>the world</u> *by such institutions as the United Nations and its Security Council. More details of their iniquity can be found in the Protocols of the Elders of Zion.*
> 10. *Hamas opposes any secular state the PLO would seek to create in Palestine, since by definition it would be anti-Islamic. On the other hand, if the PLO would adopt Islam and follow its flag, then all of (the Hamas') members would become freedom fighters who would <u>light the fire to consume the enemy</u>.*

Again, you can see some very strong language here clearly stating its end desire for Israel – its elimination! Unfortunately, whether it takes place at the hands of the Hamas, or any other organization for that matter, this nevertheless is something that is decreed by God in His prophetic Word. That much we can be assured of and yet, it too will only be for a season. The Messiah, or Yeshua, will come shortly thereafter to redeem the land (Israel) and restore the people. Until then, you could say that Israel's neighbors act as though they originated from the **"abyss"** — which they did, by the way, of which I will explain in the next chapter.

Dennis Crump

Chapter 12

"The Origin of the Beast: The Bottomless Pit (or Abyss)!"

If you were to be asked what you think of when you hear the term "bottomless pit," what would come to mind? Or how about the word "abyss?" Each of these terms for most people generally conjure up similar images. In most cases, what comes to mind is the place we refer to as "hell!" As a matter of fact, these terms usually bring about thoughts of the devil, or Satan, believing that these are additional names for the place where he resides. For example, to most people it is believed that the devil resides in hell and that this awful place goes by other names as well, to include both the "bottomless pit" and the "abyss." And this is, in a general sense, true. Nevertheless, the wealth of Scripture does not always limit itself to what is believed to be true by the masses!

Having established already that the coming "beast" is the Arab/Moslem empire, it serves us well to evaluate another of its characteristics. Specifically, its origin. John the Revelator describes this "beast" as ascending "out of the bottomless pit" (Rev. 17:8). Of course, this begs the question, "What does this mean?" In most circles of thought, it would mean "hell," primarily because of the thinking that the "beast" is either the Antichrist or else his world empire, thus meaning that the "bottomless pit" from which it originates would have to be "hell." However, this understanding of the "beast," as has been already explained, is inaccurate. Instead, the "beast" is the Arab/Moslem empire and with this being the case, it having an origin of "hell" would seem confusing. In other words, how can this empire be from "hell?" To some, this might seem like a very appropriate question. However, in this case it would really be a misleading question!

Though it is generally understood that "hell" is synonymous with both the "abyss" and "bottomless pit," Scripture does not necessarily indicate that. And if that is the case, then what do these terms really mean? As far as "hell" goes, it means what you understand it to mean – the future place reserved for the judgment of both unbelievers and fallen angels. This is not in question! But as far as the other two terms go, "abyss" and "bottomless pit," a closer look in Scripture is certainly necessary, primarily because we are told that this is the beast's origin.

As I just inferred, the "beast" is from both of these places. Actually, these two places — the "abyss" and the "bottomless pit" — are really one and the same. Specifically, the original Greek language uses just the single word "abussos," although with the many Bible translations now available, you will find that both words have been used in its translation depending upon the particular verse used. We already know from this particular passage in Revelation that the "bottomless pit" is the one used to translate "abussos" in describing the beast's origin. This, unfortunately, is what creates the confusion. In other words, it is this particular translation of "abussos" that is misleading! You see, it is not really a bottomless pit! It is, however, correct to call it the "abyss!"

What then is the "abyss?" Believe it or not, it actually means a place that is "out of the country!" That's right, "out of the country." In other words, the "beast," or Arab/Moslem empire, originates from somewhere "outside of the country!" And this is true if, in fact, you are standing in Israel - which is exactly what Jesus was doing when he spoke the very words that verified this. You got it, it was Jesus who provided us the true meaning of the word "abussos!" He was the one who revealed to us this understanding. And it actually makes a lot of sense!

If you recall, there was an incident recorded in the Gospel of Luke (8:26-34) in which Jesus encountered a man who was very demonized. The man was a recluse who struggled with self-mutilation and a fetish for ghoulish things. He loved to hang out in the graveyards. This man, upon meeting Jesus, experienced a tremendous deliverance. As Jesus was about to cast the demons out of him, the demon in charge, named "Legion," begged Jesus to not send them (the demons) to the "abyss!" Though most of us would think that this meant "hell," this is not what was recorded in another of the Gospels. Mark instead tells us that Legion, "besought him (Jesus) much that he would not send them away <u>out of the country</u>" (Mark 5:10). In other words, if you were in Israel, "out of the country" would mean the neighboring land outside of the land of Israel. Guess what that neighboring land is today? That's right -

Palestine, Jordan, Saudi Arabia, etc. – land that is governed today by Arab/Moslem peoples. And this makes sense now when you consider what John the Revelator was telling us when he said that the "beast" would ascend out of the "abyss." He was telling us that the "beast" empire would originate from the land immediately outside of that which is Israel – in other words, Arab soil! Amazingly, once again God's Word makes incredible sense!

"The Origin of the Beast: (or Bottomless Pit)"
Scripturally Explained

If we look again in Revelation 17, we see that in verse 8 John says of the "beast" that it "shall ascend <u>out of the bottomless pit</u>." This, believe it or not, actually is descriptive of the present day Arab lands. Unfortunately, as I already stated, "bottomless pit" is usually a term associated with the devil. But what is the Biblical meaning of "bottomless pit?" Think about it — if the earth is circular, can a pit really exist that is without a bottom? Or might there be a different meaning to this term altogether? Again, our answer must be found by looking first in the Scriptures?

The word from the original Greek used for "bottomless pit" is "abussos," from which we derive our word "abyss." Fortunately, this word is used elsewhere in Scripture. Actually, it is the Greek word "abussos" which is used elsewhere, although it is neither translated as "abyss" nor "bottomless pit." Rather, it is translated instead as the word "deep." The passage is in Luke 8:30-31 which reads, "And Jesus asked him, saying, What is thy name? And he said, Legion: because many devils were entered into him. And they (the demons) besought him (Jesus) that he would not command them to go out into the <u>deep</u> (abussos)." Certainly, the term "deep" conveys what could be thought of as a "pit" by the way it is used in this context. However, we are fortunate in that God has provided another Biblical author other than Luke who writes of this very same incident — only he records it a bit differently, yet providing for us the necessary understanding or interpretation.

In the gospel of Mark it is recorded as follows, "And he (Jesus) asked him (the demon), What is thy name? And he answered, saying, My name is Legion: for we are many. And he (Legion) besought him (Jesus) much that he would not send them (the demons) away <u>out of the country</u>" (Mk. 5:9-10). Fortunately for us, Mark's use here of "out of the country" provides for us the interpretation of the meaning of "abyss" - specifically meaning "out(side) of the country" of Israel. Returning back to Revelation 17:8, we now have a Scriptural explanation for the meaning of the "beast ascending out of the (abussos)." The "beast," or Arab/Moslem empire, will form itself from "out of country" — that is, outside of the boundaries of "Mystery Babylon," or Israel. This again makes perfect sense when you attempt to accurately fit this together with the rest of God's Word — or "rightly divide God's Word!" Reread Revelation 17:1-8 now and see so for yourself.

Again, God's Word amazingly can be relied upon to interpret itself for us, and sometimes it seems we only scratch the surface in applying this principle. In the next chapter, you will see another amazing reality that is so obvious in Scripture, and yet is so seldom even realized. For even though the bulk of Scripture used in discussions regarding the end-times is taken from Revelation, or the last book of the Bible, you will be surprised to know that the very basis for the end-times originates from Genesis, or the first book of the Bible.

Chapter 13

"The Family Feud: A <u>Land</u>mark Issue!"

Probably by now, you have noticed the tremendous amount of attention that I have placed on the role of the Arabs/Moslems in this end-time scenario. Likewise, you have seen that the nation of Israel also has a primary role. This emphasis, I am sure, has raised some questions for you, to include among others, "Who else is involved?," "What about the United States?," and "What about the rest of the world?" These questions are especially important to us here in the U.S., yet they won't be addressed specifically until later in this book. However, at this point I will at least say this — what God says in specific regarding who is involved does not necessarily mean that those unmentioned are not involved, even if in a general sense. In other words, we can know what we should know based upon that which God <u>DOES</u> tell us - and we know that He tells us that both Israel and the Arabs are involved. On the other hand, if He doesn't tell us something specifically, as is possibly the case regarding the roles of the United States and the rest of the world, does that mean that they won't be involved? Actually, you can't conclude that unless He specifically indicates that they <u>won't</u> be involved (which therefore means that they - the U.S. and the rest of the world — <u>could</u> be involved). Does this sound confusing? Well, as I just mentioned, I will address these additional questions more specifically in later chapters of this book. In the meantime, it is clear that at least two entities <u>ARE</u> involved, and those are the Israelis and the Arabs! But why?

It is this very question — Why? - of which in answering, a great deal of light can be shed on this entire subject that we call the "end-times!" As a matter of fact, it will totally put all that I have said up to this point into its proper perspective. Essentially, the end-time conflict can be referred to as "the Arabs vs. the Jews!" This is actually what it all boils down to! And by the way, it most definitely is Biblical.

Essentially, it is what I would call a "Family Feud!" (Not the television show, of course!)

Many people do not realize this, but in truth, the Jews and Arabs are actually related. That's right! Abraham is the original father, and they are all the children. One side went one way while the other side went the other way and ever since then, they have constantly been in contention with each other.

Essentially, it is a story interwoven throughout the Bible from as far back as Genesis, and it has continued on and will eventually climax in Revelation. It is both a "family feud" and a "spiritual war!" Thus, this war wages on and will necessitate the Divine intervention on the part of the Messiah, being Jesus Himself!

And this really is the story of the end-times!

Of course, if you are at all familiar with your Bible, it makes sense. Do you remember the story of Abraham? What was it about? Essentially, God honored his sincere belief in a "living God" and therefore chose to honor Abraham from that day forward on into eternity. He established Abraham as the one from whom all peoples would therefore be blessed by Him. He thus pronounced a blessing on his seed, indicating that his name would forever be remembered and that his heritage would multiply beyond number. Finally, He promised to his descendants that they would be given a very special piece of land that would be theirs for all of eternity. Of course, this land is known as the "Promised Land" - the land of Canaan — and is described as being so bountifully blessed that it is characterized as "a land flowing with milk and honey," meaning a very rich land indeed. This was the "covenant" that God made with Abraham and incidentally, it just so happens that God follows through with His promises! Unfortunately, there was one "related" problem.

Abraham had two sons. One started the Jewish race. The other started the Arab race. There was also another problem. Abraham had his children by way of two women. Through one of those women began the Jewish race while through the other began the Arabs. Does this sound confusing? Well guess what? It gets more complicated.

The Jewish son of Abraham, or Isaac, had two sons and thus, he too had a problem. One of those sons continued the Jewish race. The other began what was an additional, yet new (or 2nd), line of Arabs. Now, if this doesn't sound complex, let me add one more detail to make it all the more confusing.

Do you remember the second woman mentioned above that Abraham had a child with? She, by the way, was instrumental in beginning a third line within the Arab race. Her son, you could say, began the first line while she went on to establish the third line of Arabs (remember, it was Isaac's other son who started the second line).

I told you that it was complex (and probably confusing, too)!

At any rate, regardless of the complexity of it all, the real problem was in the promise that God made with Abraham (Not that it was a problem for or with God, mind you!), for the normal recipient of the promise would inherit it as a birthright, being the firstborn son. However, in this case, because of the various complexities, as already stated above, there was always room for debate regarding who was to be considered the legitimate firstborn. In these particular situations, God specifically identified the firstborn ahead of time (the firstborn spiritually) and yet the process did not materialize in what would be considered the normal means (the firstborn naturally). Thus, there arose an argument, and eventually, a conflict. This conflict would develop into an all out war at times, though the harbored anger and bitterness (of the Arabs) would continue on through generation upon generation. In fact, it continues on even today!

But don't forget – the major issue in this feud regards the right of ownership to the "promised" LAND!

Fortunately, there is an end in sight regarding this conflict. Unfortunately, prior to its end things will only get worse, culminating in a series of events that will last for a total of $3\frac{1}{2}$ years. This again is known as the "great tribulation."

My dear brothers and sisters, it is time to wake up and realize that the end-times are not about the whole world. Or at least, that is not the intended purpose God has for it. Rather, it is an issue involving land and as such, it results in a feud between two distant family relations – specifically, the Arabs vs. the Jews! Only time will tell as far as how involved "others" will get in this conflict. But you can be sure that their focus will be restricted, in a direct sense at least, to their primary focus and objective which is, of course, the seizing of (by the Arabs) or defending of (by the Jews) the Holy Land!

"The Family Feud: A <u>Land</u>mark Issue"
Scripturally Explained

Having identified the two major players involved in the end-time conflict (Arabs vs. Jews), the question certainly worth asking now is, "Why?" Once again, our answer lies within the pages of Scripture. Ironically, this conflict, though placed chronologically at the end, is really nothing new. Believe it or not, it was actually a conflict that existed way back in the beginning.

Remember the Old Testament? Actually, the word "testament" is synonymous with "covenant" which is largely what the Old Testament is about — the Old Covenant. This covenant was instituted by God with Abraham way back in the book of Genesis, or what is known as the "book of beginnings." In chapter 12, verse 2, God promised Abraham that through his seed all the families of the earth would be blessed (the ultimate fulfillment of this blessing is with Jesus Christ coming through that lineage). Then, God also promised to give the land of Canaan to the seed of Abraham (vs. 5-7). Ultimately, this promise of land would be intended to last forever (Gen. 13:15).

Unfortunately, Abraham's wife, Sarah, was beyond the age of childbearing and in turn, sought to help God out. Her plan was to offer Hagar, her Egyptian handmaid, as a surrogate mother. The result was a son, named Ishmael. Later, Sarah did have her own son, Isaac, which due to her jealousy, led to Hagar and Ishmael being "driven to the east (of Israel)" (Gen. 16:12 NAS). However, being true to His word, God in turn fully blessed the seed of Abraham by promising an exceedingly great multitude of descendants through not only Isaac, but through Ishmael as well (Gen. 16:10).

Eventually, Isaac would have twins who, ironically, would "struggle together (even) within her" (Gen. 25:22). The first born turned out to be Esau and yet, God broke the traditional practice of the natural firstborn receiving the birthright and instead promised the birthright (of the land) to the younger Jacob (spiritual firstborn) and, as a result, a perpetual struggle between the two and their descendants would ensue (Gen. 25:23). Jacob would later have his name changed to "Israel" and become the one from whom the nation of Israel, God's chosen people, would originate. From Esau, whose name means "the red child," would later evolve the Edomites. Collectively, from both the descendants of Ishmael and Esau, as well as from another one of Abraham's descendants, his nephew Lot (from whom we get both Moab and Ammon), would the formation of the Arabs come. However, as a result of these two lineages of people forming, so also would a unique feud develop and, unfortunately, even persist. The type of struggle? An internal family feud. The reason? The disparity regarding the birthright of a very valuable inheritance – the "Promised Land." The fuel for this feud – the very intense and deeply personal realization that this promise was <u>spiritually-based</u>, or one that was <u>from God</u>. Thus, the conclusion or result of this feud — an intense "Holy War," or as is known in the Islamic world – a "Jihad!"

"A FAMILY TREE"
(Jews vs. Arabs)

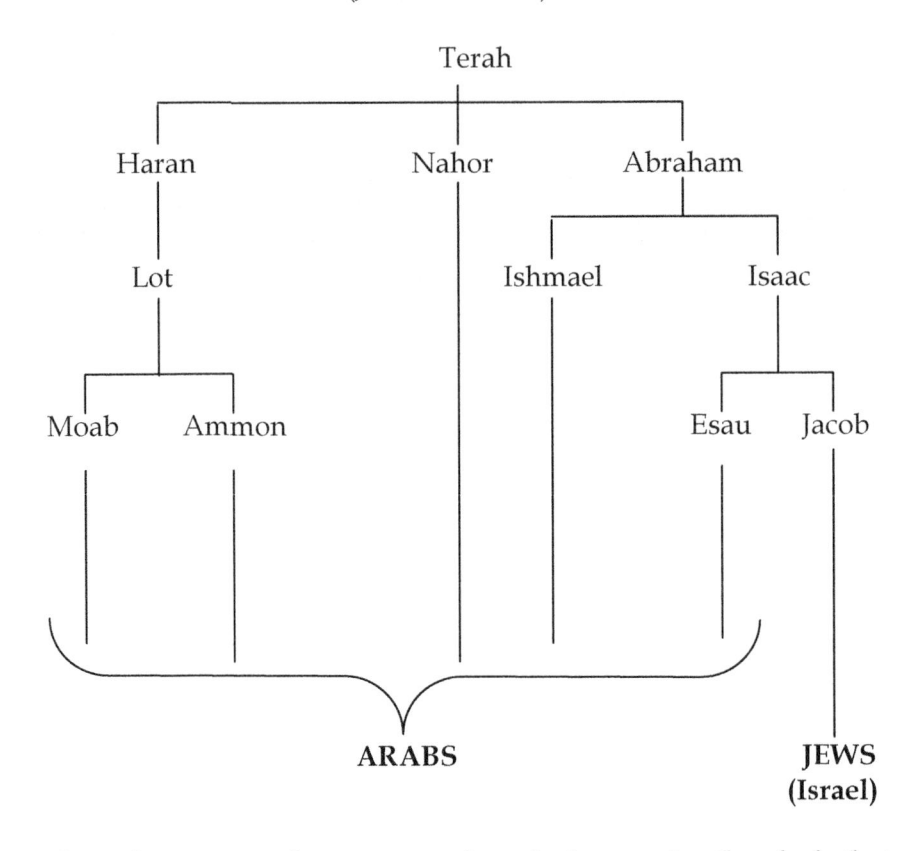

```
                    Terah
         ┌────────────┼────────────┐
       Haran        Nahor       Abraham
         │                    ┌─────┴─────┐
        Lot                Ishmael      Isaac
     ┌───┴───┐                        ┌───┴───┐
    Moab   Ammon                     Esau    Jacob
     └──────┴──────────────┴──────────┘       │
                        ARABS                JEWS
                                           (Israel)
```

In reference to the present day Arabs, again the fuel that continues In reference to the present day Arabs, again the fuel that continues to energize this conflict is primarily religiously based. The practicing religion of the great majority of Arabs is the Islamic faith. The god of Islam is Allah. Ironically, the "holy scriptures" of the Moslems is the Koran which has the parallel teaching that their god, Allah, was the one that promised to Abraham that the land would go to his descendants, only in this case it meant to Ishmael and Esau. Thus, from their perspective, the land where Israel is located rightfully belongs to them — it is their birthright and their "god" says so! Thus, to recapture "their" land is the ultimate goal – for it is their very right and duty! In fact, to eliminate Israel in the process is simply a matter of "divine justice." This being the case, it is important to realize that politics do not really play a part in this struggle because that is not what this is really about. It is not a political feud. Rather, it is a spiritual or religious feud – that is, it is a sacred, holy matter! Thus, to try to resolve this conflict politically is really an effort in futility.

Amazingly, this conflict has gone on now for over 4,000 years. Will it end? Not without the return of Christ. But what makes this feud so incredible, really, is that in speaking of the Arabs, they cannot even get along with each other, let alone with the Jews. Essentially then, though not being able to deal with each other, there is but one thing that they do have in common, or that they can agree on, and that is their incredible hate for the people of Israel. This, alone, is the tie that binds them together. All other things considered, it is chaos among them at best. But stay tuned and don't lose heart, for the end is rapidly approaching.

Chapter 14

"The Mark of the Beast"

Alright, now we are on to a subject that it seems everyone loves to talk about – the good ol' "mark of the beast!" But guess what? It is probably not what you think it is. If you think it is that computerized label that is to be worn, or the Uniform Product Code, you are wrong. In fact, if you think it is anything visible at all, again you are wrong. Fact is, it is something that is spiritual and is therefore invisible. Not exactly the answer you were looking for, is it. Well let me explain.

If you remember that the "beast" is representative of the Arab/Moslem empire, then it would make sense to assume that this "mark" is something that identifies itself in some connective way to the Arabs/Moslems. The idea of a "mark" is actually taken from the 13th chapter of the book of Revelation wherein John somewhat describes the control that this "beast" will have during its reign. John essentially reveals that this empire will require that people, for their very survival, "receive a <u>mark</u> in their right hand, or in their foreheads" (Rev. 13:16), else they won't be able to obtain food, necessities, etc.. This tends to be a very frightening passage for people because it conjures up all kinds of images of a worldwide holocaust, of dictatorial control and oppression, or of something along these lines.

Actually, this "mark" really won't be a worldwide phenomenon, but rather is something that is indicative of what will occur there in the Middle East. Likewise, this "mark" won't be generated by computers, but instead will reveal the spiritual allegiance necessary by individuals for their very survival. In particular, this "mark" will be identified with the Islamic religion, meaning that people there in the Middle East will be expected to be followers of Islam in order to participate in what will be a very controlled type of marketplace!

By the way, as of this writing there are already traces of this type of practice taking place in various places considered as Arab or Islamic controlled regions. Even Osama bin Laden, upon the first United States attacks levvied against Afghanistan, in a video taped statement declared that "These events have divided the whole world into <u>two sides</u>. The side of believers and the side of infidels, may God keep you (Moslems) away from them (infidels). <u>Every Muslim has to rush to make his religion victorious</u>. The winds of faith have come. The winds of change have come to eradicate oppression from the island of Muhammad, peace be upon him."[xxv] In other words, the American War against terrorism is really viewed by them as an attack against Islam, and every Muslim is being looked at to fulfill their duty of supporting the "Jihad." Bin Laden went on to say that, "neither America nor the people who live in it will dream of security <u>before we live it in Palestine</u>, and not before all the <u>infidel armies leave the land of Muhammad</u>."[xxvi] As a matter of fact, the Al-Qaeda terrorist organization's goal is to expel Westerners and non-Muslims from Muslim countries. In other words, what bin Laden is saying is aiming to prepare the people there to believe that the Middle East belongs to the Muslim peoples and that non-Muslims are no longer welcome – unless of course they were to convert to Islam! Incidentally, it is this conversion, evidenced by an allegiance to the Islamic faith, that depicts the actual meaning of this "mark of the beast!"

How can it be, you ask, that a "mark" represents allegiance to the Islamic faith? Consider, for a moment, what is revealed already in Scripture. For example, did you know that the New Testament believer in Jesus Christ has a "mark?" That's right! The Believer, upon salvation, is "marked" with the Holy Spirit. This is not something visible, at least to us humans, but it certainly is recognized within the spiritual realm by God and His angels. And what does this "mark" represent? Spiritual allegiance to Jesus Christ!

But what about this "mark" being applied to the right hand, or even forehead, you ask? Doesn't this refer to something physical or visible? Interestingly enough, this statement symbolically traces back to the Old Testament allegiance demonstrated by the Levitical Priests. While being commissioned for service, they would be anointed with oil on both their foreheads and right hands, an act that physically represented their "calling" and yet, spiritually, "marked" them in a unique and special way for this type of service!

As a matter of fact, this very gesture was later copied in a very real and tangible manner by some people in an attempt to somehow demonstrate to others that they were definitely "spiritual," thereby also increasing their religious commitment, though it essentially failed. This was not because of the act itself, however, but rather because of the very individuals doing the act – that is, they were essentially "frauds," or hypocrites. We know this because Jesus rebuked these people, due to this religious practice getting out of balance for them — it even misleading people regarding what He considered true spirituality to be. Specifically, it was the Pharisees (or religious leaders) who instituted this practice of placing Bible verses on their foreheads and hands in order to help encourage them while also demonstrating to others how religious they were. Unfortunately, these verses, called phylacteries, became an end in and of themselves, resulting in a group of people who tried to look religious while being far from it within their hearts. But again, this attempt to be religious was an outgrowth of a custom which originally, did in fact symbolically "mark" one for God's service.

The bottom line I guess is that God looks at the heart, and it is in the heart that one's true spiritual allegiance originates. In the case of the ill-fated "beast" empire, the allegiance that will be demanded will be towards "Allah," the god of Islam, and will therefore be evidenced by a devotion to the Islamic faith — the goal already of many within the Arab/Moslem communities of the Middle East. Although this teaching on the "mark of the beast" may be foreign to you, it nevertheless has a great deal of Scriptural merit and validity, which will be demonstrated next in the explanation portion of this chapter.

"The Mark of the Beast"
Scripturally Explained

As was communicated in the previous chapter, the conflict between the Jews and Arabs is really one of religion. To be sure, nothing can be more sensitive and provocational than to challenge one's religious beliefs. After all, it is so personal and therefore rubs at the very core of one's own soul. To do so can result in the most unpredictable of outcomes. Ultimately, life and death can be at stake for, in the most extreme cases, the eternal transcends the temporal, thus providing a supernatural motivation, if you will. As was previously demonstrated regarding this conflict over the "Promised Land," the challenge between these two peoples, at least indirectly, has long since been issued. Though this religious challenge has been mostly indirect so far, the Bible states that it will escalate and ultimately climax in a very direct showdown of great proportions in the end. In the case of these two, the Jews and Arabs, the Bible's prophetic account has resulted in one of the most intriguing, sensational, and yet, controversial subjects of all the end-time topics of discussion. Regarding this subject, mere speculation has been blown out of proportion. Yet within the Bible, we at least can be confident that the answers therein lie. What is this controversial subject that I am referring to? It is none other than that topic (or topics) known as the "mark of the beast" and his number (666) as recorded in the 13th chapter of the book of Revelation:

> *vs. 16 -* "*And he causeth all, both small and great, rich and poor, free and bond, to receive a <u>mark</u> in their right hand, or in their foreheads:*"
>
> *vs. 17 -* "*And that <u>no man might buy or sell, save he that had the mark, or the name</u> of the beast, <u>or the number</u> of his name.*"
>
> *vs. 18 -* "*Here is wisdom. Let him that hath understanding count the number of the beast: for it is the number of a man; and his number is Six hundred threescore and six.*"

It is from this very passage that many have attempted in the past to identify the "man" (Adolf Hitler, Ronald Reagan, Sadaam Hussein, the Pope, Mikhail Gorbachov, etc.). So too, in the age of computers and in this world of the credit card, many have also concluded that the use of some sort of "human" uniform product code would take place along with it being attached to every human being. Certainly, in simplistic terms, the technology of our day has surpassed human logic, almost knowing no bounds. Yet strangely, by both the seductiveness of power and the evils of our day, there has resulted some of the most vicious characters imaginable in just this 20th century. Yet, all speculation aside, few scholars, if any, seem to present an argument, when it comes to the subjects of the mark and/or the number of the beast, that is even remotely based upon or founded in Scripture. Has the Bible, when it comes to these issues, left us in the dark? Though you would be hard pressed to find from someone else at least one such genuine Scriptural explanation for either of these subjects, the answer nevertheless is no.

We can begin at least by going to the 13th chapter of Revelation. Interestingly enough, it is within this chapter that one finds a detailed discussion of the "beast," already identified in this book as the Arab/Moslem empire. Beginning in verses 1 and 2, in a description of this "beast," John records what seems to parallel some earlier verses already discussed. In verse 3 however, this "beast" suffers a deadly blow as John describes seeing "one of his heads as it were wounded to death." However, it then appears that "his deadly wound was healed." Now, remembering from Revelation 17:9 that <u>heads are symbolic of mountains, which likewise symbolize kingdoms</u>, we can therefore understand this verse. In effect, it is as if a kingdom from within this empire sort of dies, only to have it quickly rebound later. Interestingly enough, this may relate to an already historical and recent event (e.g., Iraq rebounding after the Gulf War and/or the Taliban rebounding after the war against terrorism), or it may relate to the combining of the 7th chapter of Daniel (where the 7 heads are referenced) with Revelation 17:11 which says, "And the beast that was, and is not, even <u>he is the eighth, and is of the seven</u>." Whichever it may be, the subsequent result is amazement on the part of the observers, "and all the world wondered after (had amazement regarding) the beast." Of course, the question to be asked at this point is, "Who are these observers?"

The answer to this question, though stated here as the "world," is not found by reading from the King James or any other version of the Bible. Rather, it is the original Greek which gives us the clue. The word translated here as "world" is from the Greek word "ge." Had this word been translated consistently in our Bibles, we would have a much clearer understanding. Unfortunately, this word has not been and thus, in this case, a translator's bias seems to appear. For you see, this word "ge" has also been translated as "land" a total of 42 other times within the King James Version. Though at times this word has carried the meaning of land (or earth) in a general sense, yet quite often it was used to actually refer to a specific region of land. In this sense, most of these times it was used in connection with the land known as Israel (the Promised Land or Land of Canaan), or the "ge" of Israel (Mt. 2:6,20,21; Jn. 3:22). Still other times, it simply implied Israel (Mt. 9:26; Lk. 4:25; Jn. 6:21). Thus, that this usage could be true of inferring Israel (or at most the Middle East) is, in this case, certainly possible while at the same time, it also fits contextually.

Continuing then in verse 4 of Revelation 13, we see the religious fervor and loyalty of the Moslem people in an implied sense as they "worship" their empire. Verses 5 and 6 then indicate that, in direct opposition (speaking blasphemies) to Jehovah (the Living God), these people operate for 42 months, or a total of 3½ years. It seems the description in this verse is kind of like the Old Testament account of Elijah's showdown with the prophets of Baal, only in this case it is reversed with them (the Muslims) challenging Israel's God as opposed to Israel's God challenging the prophets' god (back then it was Baal).

As we come to verse 7, we then see the Arabs/Muslims making war with and overcoming the Jews. In this verse the word "saints" is used, meaning "holy" people, which can, by the way, be interpreted to mean just the Jewish people (e.g., see Mt. 27:52). We then see that authority is given to the Arab/Moslem empire over "all kindreds, and tongues, and nations." Though initially seeming that this would refer to the whole entire world, we should realize that this very same phrase was used quite often by Daniel (which John happens to frequently reference in Revelation by the way) and in every such case, it was only referring to all the people within the jurisdiction of that specific empire being discussed. For example, this phrase was used specifically in describing the extent of Nebuchadnezzar's rule

(Dan. 2:38-39; 3:4,7; 4:1), yet we all know from history that he did not really rule over the whole entire world! At any rate, continuing in verses 8 through 10 we see that a warning is issued to the Jewish people while, at the same time, a description of some of the corresponding results of the Arabs'/Muslims' rule is given.

As John continues in verse 11, he introduces another entity that enters the picture, "And I beheld another beast coming up out of the earth." Unfortunately, this is not an individual working for the devil as some may have concluded. Rather, it is another mini-empire (remember "beast" means kingdom). John says of it, "he had two horns like a lamb." This again is a reference back to Daniel, "Then I lifted mine eyes, and saw...a ram (same as lamb) which had two horns" (Dan. 8:3). Daniel even tells us who this kingdom is in verse 20, "The ram which thou sawest having two horns are the kings of Media and Persia." At that time, this Medo-Persian empire consisted of what predominantly today would be considered the Middle East (see map in chapter on "The 7 Heads"). Incidentally, Daniel then tells us that this Medo-Persian empire would be overcome by an "he goat" (vs. 8) which, also being interpreted by Daniel, was Alexander the Great and his Grecian empire (vs. 21). Again, the Grecian empire also consisted predominantly of what today would be considered the land in the Middle East. In the case of this empire, Daniel indicates how it would spawn off into four individual empires (vs. 8 & 22). This too was historically fulfilled when Alexander's four generals, due to a power struggle, divvied up the kingdom upon Alexander's death. Of these four, two were of notable significance later in Scripture, specifically known as the Seleucid and Ptolemaic empires (headed up by the former Generals Seleucus and Ptolemy), in which they were referred to as the Kings of the North and South of chapter 11 in Daniel. Nevertheless, in this chapter Daniel indicates in verse 9 how "out of one of them came forth a little horn, which waxed exceeding great." This "little horn" would later be described as "a king of fierce countenance" standing up in the latter times (vs. 23). Cross-referencing to Daniel 11:40-45, we can interpret this king to be the "King of the North" which rules that region predominantly consisting today of Syria, Iraq, Iran, Afghanistan, etc.. Ironically, this "fierce king" was, in part, fulfilled by the historical Antiochus Epiphanes of Syria, though it will also require a future and complete fulfillment by another leader (the "little horn" — Dan. 8:19,24-25;

11:40-45). Nevertheless, what can be seen from this reference by John to Daniel 8 is that this second "beast" will originate once again out of this Middle East region of land. That this region is vastly Arab/Moslem dominated would explain my use of "mini-empire" to describe this <u>second</u> beast – they both are Arab/Moslem yet they are separate or unique in their roles!

Certainly, being from this same Arab-controlled land region, we know that there will be similarities in both religion and politics between these two "beasts." That the second is like-minded religiously (Moslem) and even politically is verified by verse 12, "And he exerciseth all the power of the first beast before him, and causeth the earth ("ge" = land [of Israel]) and them which dwell therein to worship (or pay allegiance to) the first beast, whose deadly wound was healed."

Verse 13 sounds again similar to Elijah's showdown with the prophets of Baal, but this time in a reverse form, "And he (the 2nd beast or mini-Arab empire) doeth great wonders, so that he maketh fire come down from heaven on the earth in the sight of men." You might wonder, "Will the fire be literal?" Or even, "Might it be symbolic of something like military missiles falling from the sky, or even nuclear chaos?" With respect to the idea of the fire from heaven being missiles, this would be pure speculation without any real Scriptural support. Could it be literal? Perhaps, but also remember that when used in Scripture, "fire" is often symbolic of judgment (1 Cor. 3:13; 2 Pt. 3:7). Judgment in this case certainly seems more plausible, especially when you consider the Arabs being used by God to render His judgment of "desolations" upon the people of Israel (Dan. 9:27; Mt. 23:38).

Continuing on in verse 14, near the end of the verse we see another amazing similarity to the book of Daniel, as the second "beast" causes the inhabitants of the "earth" ("ge" or "land") to "make an image to the (first) beast" (see Dan. 2:31; 3:1,4-7,15). That the image referred to in the book of Daniel, which came from Nebuchadnezzar's dream, is a representation of Gentile oppressors as well as Gentile supremacy over Israel is, in this case, a definite as well as it being another telling sign. For once again, we will see Israel suffer oppression and it will come at the hands of these Arab/Moslem "beasts."

Then in verse 15, we see that this second Arab/Moslem empire instills such new life into this image that a potential holocaust of martyrdom results for those who do not convert to their religion which, in this case, would be the Islamic faith. Bearing in mind both the past and present relationship between the Jews and Arabs as well as reports already of martyrdoms taking place among select Arab countries, does this not sound like something possible? Reports of this type of atrocity have already surfaced from Iraq, Iran, Syria, and even Afghanistan, as well as some other Arab/Moslem countries. Plus, with the city of Jerusalem being the location of an "Holy" site for both the Jews and Muslims, certainly anything could be possible.

At any rate, a detail worth noting at this point concerns this image. The word for "image" in the Greek means "likeness" and "involves the two ideas of representation and manifestation" (IMAGE, p. 246, Vine's Expository Dictionary of New Testament Words). In effect, the first "beast" becomes an image of the second, that is, it is in the likeness of or is a representation of this second "beast." How is this so? Remember that the first "beast" had a deadly wound (vs. 3,12). We are told, however, that this first "beast" also was revived (vs. 3,12). As a matter of fact, we are told that it was revived by the second "beast!" The end of verse 14 can appropriately be read, "it (the second "beast") deceiveth them...saying to them that dwell on the earth (in the land of the Middle East), that they should make (a representation of) the beast, which had the wound by a sword, and did live." This, in turn, would revive the wounded "beast." Now notice how verse 15 makes sense, "And he (the second "beast") had power (was able) to give life unto (revive) the image of the beast (the first "beast")." Even Revelation 17:8 now seems more plausible in its description of the (first) "beast" –"the beast that was, and is not, and yet is." Why? Because in reality it <u>was</u> (being the first "beast"), it <u>is not</u> (having had a deadly wound), and it <u>yet is</u> (as it becomes the "image" or representation of the first "beast"). Essentially, it is the same entity – an empire of Arab/Moslem control!

Of course, all of this (the interpretation of verses 1-15) was given just to bring us to the subject at hand — the "mark of the beast." In verse 16, the second "beast" now causes "all...to receive a mark in their right hand, or in their foreheads." That the "all" in this verse might be a reference to the "all" in verse 7, "all kindreds, and tongues, and nations," is not for certain, but is certainly worth noting. That would therefore mean that the "all" is limited to those within the realm of the beast's rule, yet this would also include Israel. At any rate, the real question to ask at this point is, "What is the mark?" Again, we will allow the Scriptures to do the talking.

By way of review, the very first mark we see in Scripture was back in Genesis 4:15 when "the Lord set a <u>mark</u> upon Cain." The word for mark in the original Hebrew is "oth" which happens to also be translated as "sign" and "token" in various other Scriptures. This same word "oth" is used (as "sign") very strikingly in Exodus 13:9, "And it shall be for a <u>sign</u> ("oth" or also "mark") unto thee <u>upon thine hand</u>, and for a memorial <u>between thine eyes (forehead)</u>, that the Lord's law may be in thy mouth." Then in Exodus 13:16 the same thing is said, only this time "oth" is translated "token," "And it shall be for a <u>token</u> upon thine hand, and for frontlets between thine eyes." Later, in both Deuteronomy 6:8 and 11:18, this sign ("oth") is used again in connection with the hand or forehead. That this "oth" or "mark" is used for the hand or forehead speaks significantly to us because the purpose in so doing was to remind the Jewish people of their faith. That the Lord's Law might be in their mouths was really supposed to reflect that it was already hidden within their hearts (Ps. 119:11; Mt. 15:1-20). Essentially, this practice was supposed to represent spiritual allegiance to God and the resultant worship from the heart. It even became a customary practice to put Scriptures on their hands or foreheads which was to, in turn, help them remember God's Holy Laws (Ex. 13:1-10,11-16; Deut. 6:4-9; 11:13-21). However, because they only wore God's Laws on their bodies (called "phylacteries") and not in their hearts, Jesus later would condemn them and this hypocritical practice (Mt. 23:5). Thus in connection with this verse (16) in Revelation's chapter 13, the interpretation should seem obvious. The Arab/Moslem empire will attempt to change, even by force, the Jewish people's allegiance from the Laws of God, with their worship of Jehovah, to the laws of Islam, with a worship of Allah – or to force them to convert, if you will. This forced conversion is very much the outcome of this required "mark of the beast," as is recorded in Scripture.

Chapter 15

"The Apostasy"

It would not be uncommon for you to have heard that there will be a great religious-type "falling away" just prior to the Lord's return. This is believed by most in Christian circles of thought, and with good reason. After all, it is Biblical. That should not really be in question. The Apostle Paul wrote, "Let no man deceive you by any means: for that day (the day of Christ) shall not come, except there come <u>a falling away first</u>" (1 Thess. 2:3). So this fact should be considered as an established one. However, what can be in question is just <u>what</u> this really may be – that is, what is this "falling away?" As a matter of fact, so also can the question be one of <u>when</u> – that is, when is (or even when was) this "falling away?" I will say this – most people when reading this verse automatically assume that this "falling away" is a description of an end-time event in which a great number of believers in Jesus Christ suddenly are found to be turning their backs on their faith in Him, most likely a result of persecution. Unfortunately, I do not think that this will be the case!

Persecution is a scary thing. Nobody wants it, and nobody wants to be the recipient of it. Without really experiencing it, we view it as being bad, wrong, evil, and of the devil. However, this can actually be quite the opposite. Take, for example, the early Church. They experienced persecution, and you know what they discovered? They found that the persecution did not defeat them. Rather, it only served to strengthen them as Believers! In fact, it even resulted in an outbreak of growth. Funny, but it almost causes you to conclude that the way to stir up a revival within the faith today is to somehow plan a persecution, if you will! Actually, it seems that this process is really one of the methods, from God's point-of-view, of how He increases the impact and growth of His Church. Of course, the point of all of this is that a "falling away" within the Body of Christ, due to an increase in persecution, is probably not a likelihood. If anything, persecution would probably strengthen the Church.

So then, if this is true, what really is this "falling away," as spoken of by the Apostle Paul? Actually, it should be known more properly as the "apostasy," the word derived from the original Greek word of "apostasia" that is used here in this verse. It is described as a "falling away" and is generally assumed by most students to be connected with the Christian faith. However, as was just mentioned, this is most likely not probable. Instead, although it is understood to be some type of religious struggle or decline, this does not necessarily mean it has to be a Christian one. Certainly, this religious struggle is assumed to be a great defection on the part of many within a particular religious persuasion. However, and in all likelihood, it probably will require a dual fulfillment. On this, let me explain.

One fulfillment of the "falling away" regards one that has already occurred. When? Some 2,000 years ago, in Christ's day that is. I am speaking, of course, of the "falling away" of those people in the days of Christ's first coming who were considered God's people, meaning the Israelites. Most people do not think of what happened to them in those terms, but that is exactly what took place. Actually, this is most clearly revealed when you read chapters 9 through 11 of Romans. Specifically, you catch a glimpse of this "falling away" while reading this text, although it is described in large part from the perspective of God. In other words, what you notice is that God, as a form of judgment, actually places a specific type of spirit over the Israelites which, as a consequence for their unfaithfulness to Him, blinds them so that they no longer realize the truth of God's ways or His intended purposes for them. Thus, as opposed to responding to God on the basis of faith, the people of Israel instead incurred a hardening of their hearts, thereby "falling" out of both fellowship with and favor with Him. Conversely, God at the same time opened up the opportunity to experiencing His Kingdom to the Gentiles which, upon responding to Him by faith, would now be the ones considered as "God's people." This change for Israel, specifically meaning the hardening of its heart and its turning from Christ, would then be the initial fulfillment of what is called the "falling away." For even though it took place some 2,000 years ago, it nevertheless is considered a part of the Bible's idea of what is called "the last days." Thus, this is the first fulfillment, and it obviously has already occurred.

The second fulfillment, however, has yet to take place and yet, it too is one that would not actually involve "Christians." Rather, this "falling away" again involves the Jewish people, although in this case it will actually be more of a religious defection for them during this tribulation period. In other words, it will not be one of choice, but will largely be due to extreme persecution and will therefore be the result of force. I am speaking, of course, about a forced conversion to the Islamic faith that the Arab/Moslem "beast" will require of those "infidels" (or non-Muslims) living in the Middle East, especially those in Israel, during this time of the tribulation. This persecution will first be evident, as has already been established in this book, by their aggressive and hostile capture of both the land of Israel and the city of Jerusalem. As a result of this persecution, the apostasy will actually be one of the few possible options for survival for the Jewish people. Others will choose to flee to the mountains and/or wilderness while still others will actually lose their lives. Nevertheless, this other option for the Jew, certainly of no better consequence, will be to convert to Islam and thereby deny Zionism. This, to be sure, is a sad reality. As you can see, it does however, provide the latter of a dual fulfillment to this Biblical idea of a "falling away." And sure enough, it once again corresponds to the workings of this latter day Arab/Moslem "beast" empire that is already formulating, even as we speak.

"The Apostasy"
Scripturally Explained

The Apostle Paul wrote as a precursor to the Lord's return, "Let no man deceive you by any means: for that day shall not come, except there come <u>a falling away first</u>" (2 Thess. 2:3). The Greek word used for "falling away" is "apostasia," from which we get the word "apostasy." By definition, it refers to "a defection, revolt, or apostasy" and "is used in the New Testament of <u>religious</u> apostasy" ("FALL" – p. 73, Vine's Expository Greek Dictionary). Thus, it does not necessarily involve the Christian faith and it seems, when you compare Scripture with Scripture, that this in fact is the case in the fulfillment of this verse as well.

As was indicated, a dual fulfillment of this "falling away" seems likely. The first "falling away" was God's judgment on the nation of Israel during Christ's first coming because "He came unto his own (the Jews), and his own received him not" (Jn. 1:11). He was their Messiah and they not only didn't recognize Him, but they in turn rejected Him. In fact, they even crucified Him! "Therefore let all <u>the house of Israel</u> know assuredly, that God hath made that same Jesus, <u>whom ye have crucified</u>, both Lord and Christ" (Acts 2:36). Thus, God's judgment resulted in a blinding of them spiritually, "Israel hath not obtained that which he seeketh for; ...and the rest were <u>blinded</u> (According as it is written, God hath given them the <u>spirit of slumber</u>, eyes that they should not see, and ears that they should not hear;) unto this day" (Rom. 11:7-8). This, of course, resulted in a great "falling away" on the part of the Jews, thereby providing the initial fulfillment of the apostasy (see also Hebrews 6:1-6 which few realize is actually a depiction of the Jews).

The latter fulfillment takes place again involving the Jews, but during the 3½ year tribulation period and in this case, comes at the hands of the end-time "beast" or Arab/Moslem empire. Recall in the chapter on "the Mark of the Beast," it was established that the "mark" was a symbolic representation of spiritual or religious allegiance to a particular faith or religion. In addition, it was shown that the Arab/Moslem empire that is forthcoming fulfills the role of the "beast." Thus in Revelation 13, in speaking of the "mark of the beast," remember what John wrote, "And he (the "beast") causeth all, both small and great, rich and poor, free and bond, to receive a <u>mark</u> in their right hand, or in their foreheads: And that no man might buy or sell, save he that had the <u>mark</u>, or the name of the beast, or the number of his name" (Rev. 13:16-17). Obviously, you can see that control of the land (the Middle East, to include Israel!) will include control of the marketplace. In that Israel will be under the control of this "beast" (Rev. 11:2), survival will depend upon them either fleeing to the wilderness and/or mountains (Lk. 21:21; Mt. 24:16) or upon submitting to one of a list of three stated conditions within this passage – either having "the mark of the beast, the name of the beast, or the number of his name." What is the "mark of the beast?" It is allegiance to the Islamic faith and therefore, if you are an Israelite, it would require a conversion to Islam. This, of course, would provide the second fulfillment for the "falling away." Incidentally, as far as the other two conditions from Revelation 13:17, the "name of the beast" is simply being an Arab (since the "beast" is the Arab empire), but as far as the "number of his name" goes, this will be the subject of our next chapter!

Chapter 16

"666"

Two chapters ago, I discussed the "mark of the beast." It was stated how the "mark" represented allegiance to the Islamic faith of that Arab/Moslem empire. It was also pointed out how the "name of the beast" is simply being identified with the Arabs. Finally, it was stated that I would discuss the "number of his name" in a later chapter. Of course, the number of the "beast" is 666 and this happens to be that chapter.

> "That no man might buy or sell, save he that had the mark, or the name of the beast, or the number of his name. Here is wisdom. Let him that hath understanding <u>count the number of the beast: for it is the number of a man; and his number is Six hundred threescore and six.</u>" (Rev. 13:17-18)

Although many interpretations have been given for the meaning to this verse, to be sure, most are merely speculative. For us to be honest in our search for the answer, it must be assumed that if there is one, it would be found within the pages of Scripture. That is, as opposed to guessing what the number might mean, there ought to be within the Bible some clues as to just what this number truly means. I, for one, believe God's Word is not silent on this subject. As a matter of fact, I have become fascinated as I have learned just what God did, in fact, say on this subject.

Let me first establish a few key points. The first is that we must realize that the number connects somehow to the "beast," which we already know is the Arab/Moslem empire. Fortunately, I think you will see that God's Word, in fact, does this very thing. The second point to know is that the number, although understood by you and I as one number, or 666, is also three numbers in the original language. That is, the Greek indicates that the number is three numbers – 600 and 60 and 6 – which can be understood as both the one number (666) as well as the three numbers (600, 60, and 6). Not to confuse the matter, but I think this only helps to reveal the fascinating depths of what God's Word really contains! These two points will serve to more clearly reveal what God has to say on this subject, for we already know that some extent of discovery is necessary to uncover His answer, or as He states, "Here is <u>wisdom</u>. Let him that hath <u>understanding</u> count (meaning "<u>calculate</u>") the number of the beast" (Rev. 13:18). So what does this number mean? Quite frankly, you will find that each number (600, 60, and 6) as well as the full number (666) once again point to the Arab/Moslem empire as being the identity of the "beast." And here's how.

When you go back into the Old Testament and do some research on these numbers, it is amazing to discover that they each connect back to the image that Nebuchadnezzar both dreamed about and later had constructed (for review, see chapter on "Nebuchadnezzar's Image"). If you recall, the image was first made, then required to be worshiped. But do you remember what the image represented? It was a symbolic portrayal of four empires of whom Israel was to be oppressed by. Of course, each of these empires, it was discovered, inhabited what was generally considered as the same region of land – the Middle East! Accordingly, the fourth one, being yet future, represented the aforementioned Arab/Moslem empire.

In addition, this image was to be constructed out of pure gold. In what would be considered an affront to the Israelites, the gold used not only came from Israel, but it was the very gold that once was identified with sacredness, holiness, and godliness. In other words, the gold was actually confiscated from their (Israel's) Temple! The very gold that was used in crafting the instruments of worship within their Temple became the same gold that would become this image of worship in Nebuchadnezzar's Kingdom. Or to state it another way, what was once used to assist in the worship of Jehovah God would now be used in the worship of Nebuchadnezzar. This, if you grasp the impact of it, is downright blasphemous! Nebuchadnezzar, <u>a man</u>, would attempt to put himself in the very position of the Almighty God! To me, this sheds light on that phrase in Revelation 13:18, "<u>for it is the number of a man</u>!"

As far as the numbers go, each one actually connects with this image as well. In particular, they each relate to the nomenclature of this image constructed. First of all, it originally cost **600** shekels of gold to purchase the site for which the Israelites' Temple would be built on. Again, the gold was later confiscated from this Temple and used instead in the construction of this image. Next, the heighth of this image upon completion happened to be **60** cubits high. Additionally, the width of this same image was **6** cubits wide. Lastly, the weight of the gold used in constructing this image was **666** talents. Amazingly, each number ties in with this image that was constructed in accordance with the dream given to Nebuchadnezzar by God. This image, of a man incidentally, was then replicated as a statuesque idol. In turn, Nebuchadnezzar mandated for all in his kingdom that they bow down to it and worship it. As was already stated, this image is a representation of various Gentile oppressors of the nation of Israel in which four are identified, each deriving itself from what is known today as the Middle East. Thus, in accordance with Scripture, this number "666" calculates as both the number of the beast and the number of a man!

"666"
Scripturally Explained

If we examine Revelation 13 again, we can now see that in an attempt to affect or enforce a conversion of faith to Islam (the meaning of the "mark of the beast"), the Arab/Moslem empire would thereby institute some sort of economic freeze against Israel, or quite possibly monitor transactions in the marketplace, "that no man might buy or sell, save he that had the mark, or the name of the beast, or the number of his name" (vs. 17). From this verse we can see that there are three conditions given here for one to personally avoid this type of economic sanctioning. That is, to participate economically, individuals must first have either the "mark of the beast" (now understood as the embracing of, due to a forced conversion, the Islamic faith), the "name of the beast" (this obviously being the citizenship of one of the Arab countries), or the "number of his name." So, what does this "number of his name" mean?

It is interesting to note that verse 18 begins with the statement, "Here is wisdom," because this very well may be the introduction to us of the first clue in interpreting this passage. After all, the wisest man to ever live other than Jesus, as recorded in Scripture, was Solomon (2 Chron. 1:10-12). Continuing on, we are then told to "count the number of the beast." Here, the word in the Greek for count is "psephizo" and is connected with the idea of one attempting "to consider or calculate." This would be similar to when Jesus, challenging others to count the cost of what it means to be one of His disciples, stated, "And whosoever doth not bear his cross, and come after me, cannot be my disciple. For which of you, intending to build a tower, sitteth not down first, and counteth (considers or calculates) the cost, whether he have sufficient to finish it?" (Luke 14:27-28). In other words, in attempting to determine the meaning of the "number of the beast," we should utilize the Scriptures and therefore "consider and calculate!"

As the passage in Revelation continues, it indicates to us regarding this number that "the number (is) of a man." In fact, the verse even gives us the very number, "Six hundred threescore and six." Again, it is interesting to note at this point a couple of things. First, the definite article "a" in the phrase "of a man" is omitted in the original Greek text, leaving us rather with this rendering, "for it is the number <u>of man</u>." Second, as far as the number itself is concerned, the rendering in the Greek has it appearing as only one number in effect (666), although it is comprised of three numbers in particular (600 and 60 and 6). Now, could these ever so slight details be important?

Returning back to the book of Daniel, we see the appearance of an image in chapters 2 and 3. This great image was that which originated in Nebuchadnezzar's dream and happened to be a representation of various Gentile oppressors of the nation of Israel. So impressed was he of this image in his dream that Nebuchadnezzar, in turn, had a statuesque replica of it made in gold. This golden image would then, as required by Nebuchadnezzar, be worshiped by all, to include even the captives of Israel, or else they were thrown into a fiery furnace.

Now, even more interesting than what this image represents is its unique composition which, in this case, happened to be gold. And yet even more interesting than its composition was its dimensions, "Nebuchadnezzar the king made an image of gold, whose height was <u>threescore</u> cubits, and the breadth thereof <u>six</u> cubits" (Dan. 3:1). Here, by way of its Scripturally recorded dimensions, we can see the use of both the numbers 60 and 6, with the resultant picture again connecting to this Gentile image which represented Israel's oppressors. But what about the number 600?

Once again, having seen what this image was made of — gold — could it be that we might be able to now even further identify the meaning of this beast's number? The answer, incidentally, is even more amazing still for the gold used to make this image, ironically, originated from the very center of Jewish worship — the Temple in Jerusalem. When Nebuchadnezzar besieged Jerusalem, he took also "part of the vessels of the house of God: which he carried into the land of Shinar (Babylon) to the house of his god; <u>and he brought the vessels into the treasure house of his god</u>" (Dan. 1:2). Remembering the connection between Solomon and wisdom, it serves to note that this Temple mentioned above happened to also be the very one built by Solomon (2 Kgs. 24:11-13). That this gold in the Temple, having formerly been used to assist the Jews in the true worship of God, would now be used in the construction of a god that the Jews would be forced to falsely worship, is indeed an amazing contrast. Yet even more amazing still is an interesting detail regarding the origin of this

Dennis Crump

Temple site. In particular, we find that King David, the very father of Solomon, had actually purchased this site, known as the threshing floor of Ornan, for "six hundred shekels of gold" (1 Chrn. 21:25). As incredible as that may be, an even more amazing detail is that this gold, used in the making of various ornaments and decorations within this Temple, turned out to weigh "six hundred threescore and six talents" (1 Kgs. 10:14).

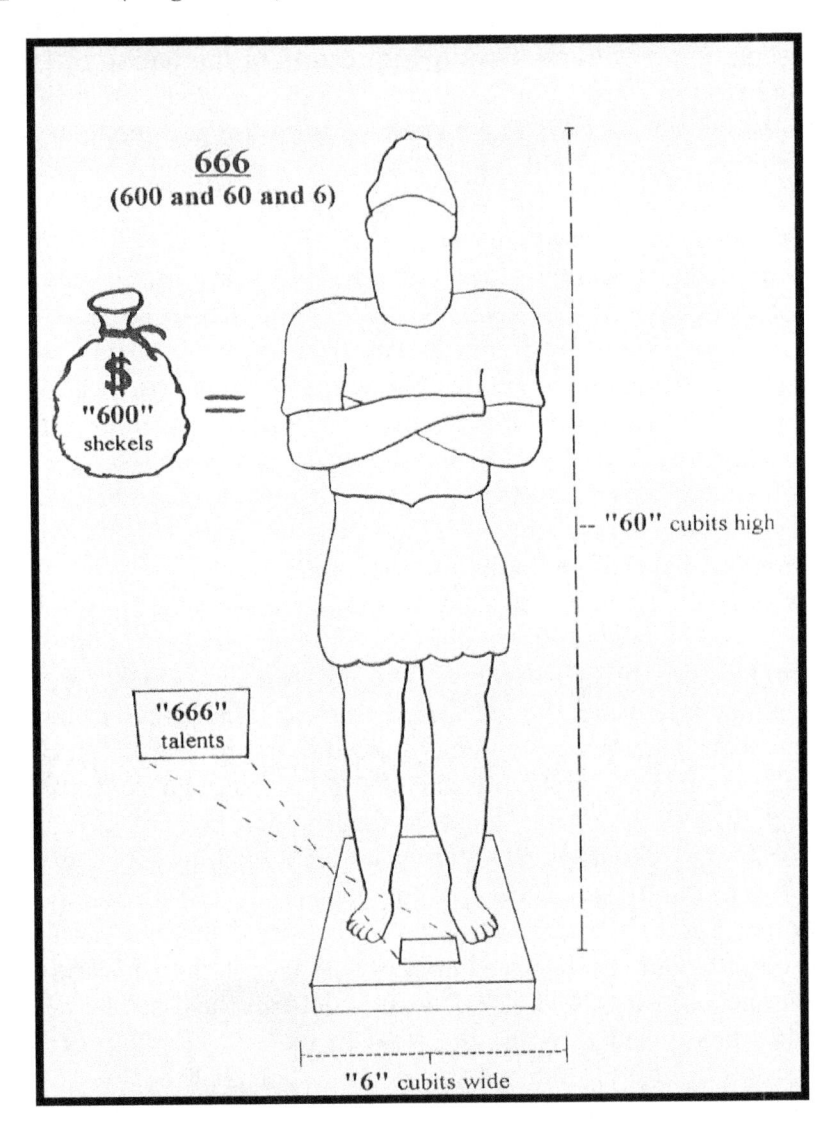

666
(600 and 60 and 6)

"600" shekels =

"666" talents

"60" cubits high

"6" cubits wide

Is it a mere coincidence that Nebuchadnezzar's image, representing Gentile oppressors of Israel from the Middle East and used to force false worship on the Jewish people, would be made of gold confiscated from the Jewish Temple? And is it even more coincidental that this same image would have dimensional characteristics such as being 6 cubits wide, 60 cubits high, valued at 600 shekels of gold, and weighing in at 666 talents of gold? Certainly, from a Scriptural standpoint, we have an amazing assortment of evidence here to help us "consider" ("count") the preceding explanation as representative of the "number of the beast?" In other words, the "number of his (the beast's) name" is merely another way to identify from Scripture who this beast is, which once again is the Arab/Moslem empire. To therefore put this into perspective, you could say that in order for one to avoid this economic sanctioning by the "beast," one would have to have the "number of the beast" which would mean that they would have to convert their religious allegiance to the Islamic faith. Incidentally, this again is indicative of the apostasy or "falling away," as was discussed earlier, that is to occur just prior to the return of Christ (2 Thess. 2:1-3).

Chapter 17

"The Antichrist?"

If all the subjects that relate to the end-times, probably the one that is the most popular regards the subject of the Antichrist. Who is he? Where will he come from? Just what will he really be able to do? I myself for many years was fascinated by this mysterious and yet dreadful character. I had heard that some individual would rise up during the tribulation, deceive the world with a message of peace, and then suddenly die. Amazingly, however, I was told that he would duplicate what Jesus Christ did by rising up also from the grave, in 3 days no less! And then I was told that he would do amazing and miraculous wonders, wooing many into following him. Not only would he suddenly turn evil and sinister, but he would even desecrate the Temple of God in Jerusalem by sacrificing a pig on the altar while also making himself out to be God. The evil work of this Antichrist would abound until the end of tribulation wherein the Lord Jesus Christ would return and defeat this evil character, thereby setting up His Kingdom of peace forevermore. For many years this, or something along these lines, was what I was taught.

On top of that, I had heard many names mentioned as possible candidates for being the future Antichrist — from evil characters such as Adolf Hitler and Saddam Hussein to good people such as Ronald Reagan and the Pope. Of course, there was even the belief that this future leader would be a relative unknown, conducting himself somewhere in relative obscurity, similar to the way Jesus Christ lived prior to the start of His ministry. At the appropriate time, it was believed, he would then suddenly appear out of nowhere to begin his final work of evil.

Unfortunately, none of these possibilities truly existed. They just weren't true. I must admit, I was similar to many other Believers, formulating my beliefs on a diet of hand-me-down teachings that I had been groomed on since my childhood. But the Bible communicates quite the opposite when you honestly examine what it has to say on the subject. When I wrestled through both a candid and yet thorough search of Scripture, I found myself faced with an understanding that certainly, although quite intriguing and fascinating, would not be considered popular.

The bottom line is this: There is no Antichrist! That's right – **NO ANTICHRIST**!

Actually, in terms of what we "think" the Antichrist to be, such as a fierce and horrific end-time world leader, this much is true. There is no such thing, and this really becomes clear when you allow yourself to honestly see just what God does and does not say on this subject in the Bible.

For example, what He does say is that the antichrist is a "<u>spirit</u>." In other words, the antichrist is a supernatural being that influences human beings towards a specific displeasing form of conduct in relationship to God. Another thing God tells us regarding the antichrist is that it was already in the world during the First Century, way back in the days of the early Church period. At the same time, God tells us that people were sometimes considered antichrists as well. That's right, not one person, but rather people (plural)! This was because these people conducted themselves in line with the very objective of those antichrist spirits, thus they were considered as antichrists as well, since they were of the same character as those spirits. Finally, God tells us that the antichrist is just that – an "anti" Christ, meaning one "opposed to" Christ. This, by the way, is a point that is really the whole secret to truly understanding this subject and yet, it also is the greatest cause of it being misunderstood. Let me explain.

There were two languages that were widely used in the time of Jesus – Greek and Hebrew. The Greek language was what the New Testament was written in, mostly because of God's intention to reach out to the Gentile peoples. The Hebrew language was what the Old Testament was written in of which, of course, was the native tongue of the Jewish people. To the average Jew, the Bible was solely the Old Testament, or the Septuagint. From the Old Testament, the Israelites, being God's people, were taught that God would be sending a King to them to forevermore deliver them – this being the long awaited "Messiah!" The term "Messiah" was a Hebrew term and certainly was one in which they were very familiar with. However, with the growing popularity of the Greek language in their culture, there obviously arose many new words to learn and use. One such word was the term "Christ" – a Greek term, by the way, which meant exactly the same thing as what the term "Messiah" meant in Hebrew. Thus, they were interchangeable until the writing of the Greek New Testament, at which point the term "Christ" became the one most commonly used. Of course, the point of all of this is to establish that the utilization of the word "antichrist" would be no different than if we were to use, say, "antimessiah!" In other words, it does NOT mean "the opposite of Messiah," but rather "something that is against the teachings regarding the Messiah." Thus, the antichrist spirit was the same thing as an antimessiah spirit which, by the way, was the very intent of these spirits – they opposed every effort of having the Jews (or anybody for that matter) understand that Jesus was the Messiah! This, incidentally, was exactly what occurred at the time of Jesus's first coming.

The Messiah was someone for whom the Jewish people awaited, being one who was to come only for them – meaning just the Jews! Of course, Jesus was this Messiah and when He came, they did not receive Him. As a matter of fact, they actually rejected Him, even to the point of crucifying Him. Why, we must ask, would the Jewish people, upon His coming, be so blind so as to not even recognize the very one for whom they so long and so fervently awaited for? Was it merely a coincidence, or was it possibly because God intended it so? Of course, the answer is that God had already planned it to be this way. The fact is, the Bible teaches us that Israel was actually made to be blind as a consequence for their stubbornness of heart. In other words, God was the One who planned this. The way He did this was to send a "spirit" over (or upon) them so as to blind them from seeing the truth. According to the book of Romans, this spirit was called a "spirit of slumber" — a spirit which blinded the Jewish people from recognizing that it was actually Jesus, the Carpenter from Nazareth, who was their long awaited Messiah. Incidentally, this "spirit of slumber," as Paul calls it, is this same "spirit of antichrist" that John introduces us to. Again, what it does is it blinds the Jewish people from realizing that Jesus was their Messiah. Of course, the way God "used" this spirit was to thereby utilize this situation to allow for the Gospel to be introduced to the Gentile (or non-Jewish) people. Nevertheless for the Jewish people, this spirit was a liar that ultimately deceived them. Again, we need to realize that this is what the Bible actually tells us regarding the subject of antichrist. Accordingly, this is a good point to mention what God does not say regarding the "antichrist."

Of most importance, God does NOT say that the antichrist will be coming in the near future. Rather, he (or it) already came. John does acknowledge to those of whom he was writing to (back then) that he was aware that they had heard that the antichrist was to be coming at some point (to be understood as coming for them, not as still coming for us!). But this was for back then, and he actually indicates to them that the antichrist was <u>already</u> in the world (thus, it would NOT come again!). Why could he say this? Because the Jews were already blinded! So when did they first hear of the antichrist, as John seems to suggest? Actually, it was years earlier by way of their reading the book of Romans (Romans was written much earlier than the books of First and Second John, which are the only books that discuss the "antichrist!"). Of course, it was referred to as the "spirit of slumber" in Romans, nevertheless its outcome was the same – the Jews would miss the Messiah (or Christ) upon His coming to them (the First Coming!).

Another thing that God does NOT say is that the antichrist is the same as either the "prince" in Daniel 9, the "beast" of Revelation, or the "man of sin" in 2 Thessalonians 2. Actually, there is only one Biblical author in all of Scripture who even ever mentions the term "antichrist," and that is the Apostle John. He discusses the "antichrist" in his first and second letters and, by the way, only mentions the word four times. The point is, nowhere else in all of Scripture will you find any other mention of the word. Not even in the book of Revelation which, by the way, John also wrote. Wouldn't he have mentioned it in Revelation if it (an antichrist) were still to come during the end-times? But this makes perfect sense. The antichrist is NOT a FUTURE world leader, but rather WAS and IS a spiritual presence and influence that befell the <u>Jewish</u> people – since they were the ones to whom the Messiah would come. Unfortunately, "He came unto His own (Jewish people), but His own received Him not" (Jn. 1:11). The reason being? This antichrist spirit caused them to neither acknowledge that Jesus was God's son nor that the Christ (Messiah) had come already in the flesh – two characteristics of this spirit that John very clearly states in his letters!

This is why, by the way, there is no end-time antichrist! Of course, this surely raises new questions for us, questions such as

"What about a world leader, will there still be one?" and "Who then will be in charge of the beast (Arab/Moslem empire)?" Again, there won't be a <u>world</u> leader because the tribulation is predominantly a Jewish judgment ("The time of <u>Jacob's</u> trouble" – Jer. 30:7) and because Israel's nemesis causing this tribulation is the Arab/Moslem empire. Of course, as we have already established, the leader of this Arab/Moslem empire with the most influence, from a Biblical concern, is the "little horn" (Dan. 7, 8, 11) which again may very well be Palestinian Leader Yasser Arafat. Only time will tell, of course, but certainly it seems that this end-time picture is rapidly taking shape.

"The Antichrist?"
Scripturally Explained

One of the most popular subjects of discussion, when it comes to end-time prophecy, revolves around the subject of the antichrist. "Who is he?" and "From where will he surface?" are the most popular questions. To speculate is dangerous, therefore we must allow the Word of God to do the interpreting for us on this intriguing and fascinating subject.

To be sure, the Bible has less to say on this subject than most people realize. In fact, the word is only mentioned a total of <u>four</u> times in Scripture. Even more amazing then that is the fact that it is only mentioned in <u>one</u> man's writings — the Apostle John. Three times John mentions the "antichrist" in his first letter and then once in his second. More amazing still is what he says, for if you evaluate these Scriptures, it becomes clear not only what the "antichrist" is, but also what it is not. These Scriptures (1 John 2:18, 22; 4:3; 2 John 7) indicate in very precise words that the antichrist is not a person, but rather a spirit, "this is that <u>spirit</u> of antichrist" (1 Jn. 4:3). This spirit is obviously a liar and he therefore causes people to deny two things: 1) That Jesus Christ is God's Son, meaning God is His Father, and 2) That the Christ, or Messiah (being Jesus), has already humanly appeared. First John 2:22 says, "Who is a <u>liar</u> but he that <u>denieth that Jesus is the Christ? He is antichrist, that denieth the Father and the Son</u>," while 1 John 4:3 states, "And every <u>spirit</u> that <u>confesseth not that Jesus Christ is come in the flesh is not of God: and this is that spirit of antichrist</u>."

Another interesting observation to note is that the antichrist is NOT someone or something that is waiting to appear in the end-times, but rather has appeared already as far back as of the First Century. The Scriptures make it very clear that the period of time immediately following Christ's first coming is already considered "the last time" and that this antichrist spirit was already in existence back then, "Little children, <u>it is the last time</u>: and as <u>ye have heard that antichrist shall come, even now are there many antichrists; whereby we know that it is the last time</u>" (1 Jn. 2:18). Ultimately, the work of this lying spirit is to deceive as many people (especially Jews) regarding the Messiah as possible, "<u>For many deceivers are</u>

entered into the world, who confess not that Jesus Christ is come in the flesh. This is a deceiver and an antichrist" (2 Jn. 7).

Of course, the greatest deception by this spirit was levied against the Jewish people in Christ's day. Paul wrote in Romans 11:7-8 of Israel, "What then? <u>Israel</u> hath not obtained that which he seeketh for; but the election (Gentile Believers) hath obtained it, and <u>the rest (Israel) were blinded</u> (According as it is written, God hath given them the <u>spirit of slumber</u>, eyes that they should not see, and ears that they should not hear;) unto this day." As a judgment, God allowed a certain spirit to blind them, thereby resulting in their being easily deceived. Fortunately for us, this paved the way for the Gospel to be extended to the Gentiles. Nevertheless for them (the Jews), it did result in what would definitely be considered unfortunate and dire circumstances for. This makes it all the more understandable why the Bible would command us to **"pray for the peace of Jerusalem"** (Ps. 122:6). They are certainly in great need of it!

Obviously, from these Scriptures, we can conclude that to interpret the antichrist as being some future human leader would be erroneous. Although this may be an unpopular interpretation, it nevertheless is Scripturally sound. Thus, we at least now know that there is one player that will not be involved in this end-time picture, and that of course is the "antichrist!"

Chapter 18

"The Locusts"

At this point, I would like to introduce one other "player" involved in the end-time picture that again, few people care to discuss. Actually, this is not really a different entity, but rather is just another term to reflect the same role previously identified that the Arabs are to have during this tribulation period. Of course, the term that I am referring to is the "locusts," mentioned in both the New Testament book of Revelation and the Old Testament book of Joel.

I remember the first real explanation that was given to me regarding these "locusts" of Revelation 9. I was told that they were symbolic of demons and that they would attack people during the tribulation. That alone was scary, but then I heard them described. I was told that they had heads like those of horses, long hair like that of women, vicious teeth like those of a lion, and yet they had faces like those of humans. Whew! Then there was their weapons. These creatures had fierce tails and they could painfully sting with them, much like that of a scorpion, thereby causing great pain and anguish even to the point of death, though not actually killing anyone. This is how they tormented people and it would last for a full five months. On top of that, there were hundreds of thousands of them, everywhere, thus making this an additional dreadful period to include as part of that already awful period called the tribulation. To say that it stirred up the emotion of fear was an understatement. But of course, that was what I was TOLD.

It really is amazing, and yet sad, when you realize just how often Biblical viewpoints are derived from hand-me-down teachings when in reality, they lack a true Scriptural basis. I am no less guilty in my own right, having far too often reproduced traditional viewpoints over and above what would truly be considered genuine Biblical doctrine. Nevertheless, at least I now realize the great tendency we all have of making this error. But don't get me wrong, I also find that many of the traditional teachings are rooted and grounded in Biblical truth. Yet, this is the point — all teaching is to be sifted through and through, allowing the truth of God's Word to ultimately be the best teacher of itself. Far too often, this is not the case. As a result, this process only lends itself to error, deception, and even sensationalism. Of course, I found this to be true as well in the case of my understanding of these "locusts," especially as I began to search God's Word on this subject.

Interestingly enough, these "locusts" were not, in fact, symbolic for demons, but rather were symbolic for people – believe it or not, Arabs! The Old Testament prophetic book of Joel actually reveals this. Essentially, Joel describes an end-time scenario in which an army, depicted as locusts, rises up against the land of Israel. This army, in turn, persecutes Israel, though they eventually receive their own judgment for doing so. The amazing reality, of course, is that this is one more confirmation that the end-times are about a Jewish-Arab conflict in the Middle East, wherein the land is the focal issue!

One of the more interesting realizations regarding these "locusts," as discovered in the book of Joel, is more than likely either an astounding coincidence (of which I doubt), or else an incredibly Divine clue. Unfortunately, it is not realized in the English language. Rather, it becomes apparent only upon reviewing the original Hebrew version of Joel. You see, the word that he uses for these locusts is "arbeh." Ironically, this is very similar to the word "Arab" and in fact, is only slightly different in the Hebrew language. Not that this proves that these "locusts" are a reference to Arabs, but it certainly is quite interesting. Actually, the proof is found more so in the similarities between these two accounts of "locusts" in both Revelation and Joel. Upon comparison, it seems that Joel provides the insight necessary to understand John's end-time "locusts" that are in Revelation. Being that this conflict (that Israel is to experience during the tribulation period) is with the Arabs, it makes this connection of the Arabs with these "locusts" all the more interesting. Thus, it certainly seems that the Jews and Arabs are major players. Nevertheless, the truth is that only time will ultimately tell for us who the real players will be. At any rate, and from what I can see in Scripture, what is currently taking place in the Middle East is not only a sign that the end is nigh, but also that it is time for the Church to truly wake up!

"The Locusts"
Scripturally Explained

To uncover the Bible's interpretation of these "locusts" of Revelation, we once again need to go back and reference one of the prophetic books of the Old Testament. Only this time, we find ourselves in the book of Joel. The prophet Joel speaks of a latter day invasion of the nation of Israel (1:15) by an army of locusts (1:4; 2:25). This army is identified as actually being a heathen nation (1:6; 2:17,25), therefore being an enemy of God's people (Israel). A careful reading of this book makes it very clear that these locusts are not to be understood literally as insects, but rather symbolically — in this case as an army of Gentile people that God uses to carry out His plan of judgment against Israel.

Of course, you will recall that we already identified the "beast that ascends from the bottomless pit" (Rev. 17:8) as an Arab empire. Amazingly, these locusts also ascend from the bottomless pit (Rev. 9:1-3), pointing to these same Arab peoples. But even more amazing is the Hebrew spelling of "locusts" — "arbeh" – which is basically the same Hebrew word for "Arab" except with an additional letter tacked on to its end. In effect, this word for "locusts" derives itself from the word for "Arabs." Incidentally, this might be coincidental or even intentional and yet, the truly convincing evidence for the identity of these "locusts" happens to more so be their characteristics as recorded within both the 9th chapter of Revelation and the three chapters of Joel. Notice, for example, the following similarities:

    Rev. 9:2 - "smoke of a great furnace" (see Joel 2:3)

    Rev. 9:3 - "unto them was given power" (see Joel 2:25)

    Rev. 9:4 - he shall hurt "only those men which have not the seal of God in their foreheads (Jews)" (compare with Joel 1:6-7)

    Rev. 9:5 - "they should not kill them, but they should torment" (see Joel 2:6,8)

    Rev. 9:5 - "five months" (see Joel 2:23 = this is the length of the dry season between the former and latter rains)

Rev. 9:6 - "men (shall) seek death, and shall not find it; and shall desire to die, and death shall flee from them" (compare with Joel 2:8)

Rev. 9:7 - "like unto horses prepared unto battle" (see Joel 2:4)

Rev. 9:8 - "their teeth were as the teeth of lions" (see Joel 1:6)

Rev. 9:9 - "the sound of their wings was as the sound of chariots of many horses running to battle" (compare with Joel 2:4-5)

Rev. 9:10 - "there were stings in their tails" (see Joel 2:8)

Obviously, when making a comparison of these Scriptures, we see that the Bible speaks both loud and clear regarding the identity of these future end-time "locusts" as the Arab armies. Incidentally, it is worth noting also that the context of the events as recorded in this book of Joel are actually best understood by having the proper interpretation of another New Testament Scripture which is so often misunderstood. This verse, by the way, is none other than that as recorded in 1 Thessalonians 5:2 which says that "the day of the Lord so cometh as a thief in the night." This is the subject of our next end-time topic which, by the way, begins a look for us at some of the more interesting and major end-time pieces that collectively make up this puzzle.

- Part 4 -

"The End-Time Pieces"

Chapter 19

"A Thief in the Night!"

"For yourselves know perfectly that <u>the day of the Lord so cometh as a thief in the night.</u>"
(1 Thessalonians 5:2)

If you were to be asked to share what you think this verse means, what would you say? This is an oft-quoted verse and most of us have shared the same thinking as to its meaning. To attempt to interpret it just from what it says is not difficult. Most of us have done that already. For some, it even reminds them of a popular movie in Christendom that originated back in the 70's – "<u>Thief in the Night!</u>" But I can assure you, there is more meaning to this verse than meets the eye. I found this out the hard way – I actually studied!

As I was growing up, this verse was understood to simply mean "always be ready!" I was told the Lord Jesus Christ could return at any moment. From this verse, I was taught that the analogy was simple – you would not know ahead of time if a thief came to rob your house at night and such would be the case with the return of the Lord. It would come as a surprise so you best be ready! This is basically what I was taught and chances are, the same is true for you.

And then I studied my Bible!

I do remember, however, thinking often, "Why is the Lord compared to a thief?" It seemed to me that if God was going to teach something important, as this was, that He would choose a much better thing to compare Christ with than a thief! That just didn't seem appropriate. But of course, I was a young Believer so it was not my place to question (which for some meant to challenge) what I was taught. I was left to believe that if God wanted to compare Himself to a thief, that was His choice and thus, okay.

It stayed this way for me for some time until one day, I began to really study my Bible. Believe me, I am not trying to emphasize myself in this, but rather the point that there are answers to be found that are seemingly hidden in the Bible. We just have to dig a little more. And it is amazing what you will find when you begin to do so.

Did you ever, like me, wonder why Jesus was <u>compared</u> to a thief? It really makes no sense at all. It seems we all know that a thief, in another passage, was <u>contrasted</u> with Jesus as quite the opposite. As a matter of fact, Jesus once said that "the <u>thief (Satan) cometh not, but for to steal, and to kill, and to destroy</u>: I am come that they might have life, and that they might have it more abundantly" (John 10:10). It certainly seems to me that a thief was a negative thing, being identified here as the devil. Then there was the time when Jesus was on the cross and He had a person on each side of Him, also on crosses. Guess what they were? That's right — thieves! Again, though one of these thieves would change and put his faith in Christ, they still were originally "negative" characters. Somehow, knowing all of this, it was very difficult for me to grasp the purpose God would have in using a thief to compare Christ with regarding His return and so, I decided to ask Him about this and accordingly, begin to do my research.

I'll never forget the day God turned the light on for me regarding this new search. If you recall in the previous chapter of this book, I shared how the "locusts" of Revelation were actually interpreted to be the Arabs' armies invading Israel during the tribulation period. I actually experienced this discovery one day while studying the word "locusts," which took me back to the Old Testament book of Joel. It was during this study that God opened my eyes in order to see His answer to my question regarding the "thief," and what I discovered was truly amazing. For one, the "thief" was NOT the Lord! Rather, the "thief" was, in fact, a negative term used to describe something bad, as you and I would normally associate it with. Thus with that understanding, it raised new questions as to just what it was that the Apostle Paul was really attempting to tell us in this passage he wrote in First Thessalonians.

Believe it or not, the Prophet Joel is the one from whose words Paul borrows to pen his verse. Essentially, "the day of the Lord coming as a thief in the night" is a reference to God's plan to use the Arab armies to judge the nation of Israel. In other words, the "day of the Lord" is basically a reference to that period God has chosen to begin this time of judgment. In addition, the "night" is essentially used as a much briefer way to describe the doom and gloom prescribed for Israel. Finally, the "thief" is a reference to the Arab armies who are found to suddenly be wreaking havoc on the Jewish people. Not only is this is the meaning of Paul's verse, but even he had this understanding while writing it. Don't forget, he also said to whom he was writing that <u>they already knew this</u> as well! If he, or anyone else for that matter, already knew this, then they had to have gotten their first knowledge of it from somewhere else. It just so happened that, as we also now know, it was from the book of Joel. By the way, Paul said that even we, as Believers, should know this and therefore not be surprised either, "<u>But ye, brethren, are not in darkness, that that day should overtake you as a thief</u>" (1 Thess. 5:4). I would guess then that this is really to be understood as good news for us, don't you think. Thus, all that is needed is for us Believers to discover what Paul and the early Believers already knew! This, incidentally, is where a look into the book of Joel will help us.

"A Thief in the Night!"
Scripturally Explained

Years ago, the Apostle Paul wrote, "<u>For you yourselves know perfectly that the day of the Lord so cometh as a thief in the night</u>" (1 Thess. 5:2). This verse is an incredibly popular verse when it comes to end-time discussions. On the one hand, it often strikes fear in the heart of the Believer whose conscience unfortunately might not be clear, knowing that they might not be ready for the Lord's return. On the other hand, it frequently brings confidence to the one who believes they are currently right with God, knowing that they are, in fact, ready for His return. And yet, it even will to some degree stir up curiosity within the unbeliever at times, as they consider whether or not this really could take place. But more importantly and from a theological standpoint, this verse has become foundational to the position known to many as the "Imminence Doctrine," which simply means that you never really know when Christ will return, except that it could take place on any day and at any time. This is believed by many regardless of what Paul wrote in the preceding verse concerning select events found within this same chapter, "But of the times and the seasons, brethren, <u>ye have no need that I write unto you</u>" (1 Thess. 5:1). Unfortunately, these verses are frequently understood erroneously and, even more unfortunate, they often result in Believers symbolically comparing the Lord Jesus Christ to, of all people, a THIEF! Fortunately, a closer look at this passage in First Thessalonians will reveal otherwise.

It is interesting to note that from the start of this passage, Paul makes it very clear that the idea of "the day of the Lord coming as a thief in the night" is not something he needs to write about AGAIN, for they ALREADY KNEW about it. Even more so, he makes it very clear in verse 4 that they are "<u>not in darkness</u>, that that day should overtake (them) as a thief." Rather, he instead reminds them that they "are all the <u>children of light</u>" in verse 5. Certainly, we can be sure that Paul knew something about this idea. Equally certain now, however, is that "the brethren" Paul was writing to also knew about this idea. The reason for this, of course, was because it happened to be introduced previously in Scripture. What is truly regrettable, however, is that so many Christians today are unaware of the origin

Dennis Crump

of this idea or verse. Can we possibly find within the Bible this idea's very origin? Of course, the answer is "yes" and to do so, we once again need to return to the book of Joel. With this return, we will now attempt to more properly understand the context of Joel's prophetic writings and in doing so, we will find that it will greatly enlighten us.

It is this Prophet Joel of whom, in Scripture, first introduces us to this phrase or idea of "the Day of the Lord coming as a thief in the night." You will recall that Joel spoke of a latter day invasion of Israel by locusts which are understood to be a Gentile army of heathen people (Arab armies). Ironically, it is in connection with this "locust invasion" that this idea is first introduced. In a less obvious manner than the Apostle Paul uses, Joel proceeds to introduce this phrase, only he does so in what would be considered three parts. Look first at Joel chapter 2, verse 1, "Blow ye the trumpet in Zion, and sound an alarm in my holy mountain: let all the inhabitants of the land tremble: for the day of the Lord cometh, for it is nigh at hand." Here we see from Joel's writings the introduction to us of the first part of this phrase, or the idea of "the day of the Lord coming."

Next, in a manner that steps out of chronological order, we are introduced to the third part of the phrase. In verse 2 of the same chapter, Joel continues with, "A day of darkness and of gloominess, a day of clouds and of thick darkness." In other words, it is from this description that the Apostle Paul would later choose the phrase "the night" in order to describe the state of non-readiness on the part of some of the people (the Jewish people) when this day of the Lord does, in fact, come.

Continuing on in verses 2 through 8 in the same chapter, Joel proceeds to even further describe this locust invasion. However, when he comes to verse 9, his description reads as such, "They shall run to and fro in the city; they shall run upon the wall, they shall climb up upon the houses; they shall enter in at the windows like a thief." Here we see the very reference from which Paul uses to complete the middle part of the phrase ("the day of the Lord cometh as a thief in the night").

Incidentally, Joel continues on in verse 10 with, "The earth shall quake before them; the heavens shall tremble: the sun and the moon shall be dark (a reference again depicting "night!"), and the stars shall withdraw their shining." It is at this point that (and in the next verse (vs. 11) too) Joel succinctly identifies just exactly which "day of the Lord" it was that he was referring to, "And the Lord shall utter his voice before his army, for his camp is very great: for he is strong that executeth his word: for the <u>day of the Lord</u> is <u>great and very terrible; and who can abide it</u>?" As you can see, the "day of the Lord" here is one that is definitely negative, for it is called "great and very terrible," even being one in which few "can abide it." Why? Because it is a day in which an army invasion takes place against a people (Israel) unprepared AND because it also is an event ordained by God Himself – thus, it is deemed the "day of the Lord!"

Now, which army is Joel referring to in this verse? Believe it or not, <u>it is the Lord's army</u>, but not His army of Saints who return with Him at His Second Coming (1 Thess. 3:13), for Joel goes on to give us the answer in verse 25, "And I will restore to you the years that the <u>locust</u> hath eaten..., <u>my great army which I sent among you</u>." Clearly, we see that this army, identified as the "locusts" (which we discussed in the previous chapter), is a reference to the Arab armies. Of course, it would serve to note that Joel later also clues us in on the timing of this locust invasion, in that it has a direct chronological connection to the return of our Lord. For example, notice verses 15 and 16 of chapter 3, "<u>The sun and the moon shall be darkened</u>, and <u>the stars shall withdraw their shining</u>. The <u>Lord also shall roar out of Zion</u>, and <u>utter his voice from Jerusalem; and the heavens and the earth shall quake</u>." From these verses, specifically the reference to the sun and moon being darkened (which if you recall, was also the case in Joel 2:10), it seems apparent that this locust invasion of Arab armies is closely associated with the Lord's return! This, to be sure, will certainly be found out in due time.

Chapter 20

"Peace & Safety"

By now, with all of this effort given to demonstrate the overwhelming evidence for who the major players will be (Israel and the Arab/Moslem empire) during the period known as the end-time 3½ year tribulation, you are probably wondering when will all of this begin to happen? That is, what is the starting point for the tribulation and just how close are we currently to it? These are critical questions and unfortunately, it seems many Believers have been trained to think that they shouldn't ask these questions. As a matter of fact, because they have been so ingrained with the notion that Christ could return at any moment and on any given day (the "Imminence Doctrine"), many are discouraged from even <u>seeking to know</u> the answers to these types of questions, even though God in His Word strongly encourages us to <u>seek to know</u> both Him and all of His ways.

For most Believers, the major event that they are looking for as the next end-time one is the so-called "rapture," or the sudden gathering of Believers into the clouds unto the Lord Jesus Christ. I will discuss this event in the next couple of chapters but for now, for one to merely be looking for this particular event is to deny the very "signs of the times" that are occurring even as we speak! Jesus even told us that we should be looking for these various signs. As a matter of fact, He even described them. Plus, He informed us that when they do occur, we would thereby know that the "end" is very near. Thus, I would take it that this is what we should be doing, looking to know and understand the time that we are in, since it was Jesus who actually instructed us to do so.

But just as Jesus provided us with some clues to help us understand the "end-times," so also did the Apostle Paul. As a matter of fact, he has provided us with a clue that not only should we be looking for it to happen, but we should also, at this point, probably be realizing that it already is upon us! As a matter of fact, it has actually been going on now for almost the entire last decade, right there in the Middle East. What is this clue that am I referring to?

Do you remember a few years back when the then President Bill Clinton brokered, on the White House lawn, the infamous meeting of and peaceful hand shaking between both the former Prime Minister of Israel, Shimon Peres, and the current Palestinian Leader, Yasser Arafat? This took place in 1993 and provided the foundation for the initial stages of negotiations for peace between Israel and the Palestine Authority. This peace process, with its various ebbs and flows, has been going on now for almost a decade and continues even today, though it seems at the time of this writing that it is only hanging on by a thread. Yet even so, that only further validates its Scriptural fulfillment in the context of prophecy. In other words, this peace process, which seems to mostly be a series of negotiations in which Israel trades to the Palestinians segments of its "land" for the so-called assurance of security (or "safety") for its people, is soon to fully unravel itself. In fact, the Apostle Paul assured us of this very thing in First Thessalonians 5:3, "For when they shall say, Peace and safety; then sudden destruction cometh upon them, as travail upon a woman with child; and they shall not escape." Just how close we are to this "destruction" commencing remains to be seen, but one thing is for certain, the signs are clearly indicating that it is time for us as a Church to begin to wake up, for the end is definitely nigh upon us.

"Peace & Safety"
Scripturally Explained

Certainly, an appropriate question at this point would be, "When will all this end-time stuff begin?" That is, is it possible to determine just how close we are to these end-time events? Amazingly, once again it is the Bible that gives us the very clues we need to work with regarding this question.

To begin with, we see that in His Olivet Discourse (Mt. 24) Jesus gave us some signs to look for which would indicate that the time of the end is very near (vs. 3-8). Upon reading these signs, it becomes evident that we are, even now, experiencing what He referred to symbolically as, "the beginning of sorrows" (vs. 8) – which refers to the beginning stages of a woman in labor. But just how far along are these so-called labor pains? And might we even conclude that the "woman" here referred to is but another reference to the nation of Israel?

Remember our earlier discussion of the "Day of the Lord coming as a thief in the night?" It was noted that this came from the Apostle Paul's writings, specifically in 1 Thessalonians 5:2. Recalling that the thief, in this passage, was a reference to the locust (or Arab) invasion of Israel, we now see here an amazing parallel given to us by Paul. Ironically, in the very next verse (vs. 3), Paul actually states, "For when they shall say, <u>Peace and safety</u>; then <u>sudden destruction</u> cometh upon them, as travail upon a <u>woman</u> with child; <u>and they shall not escape</u>." Obviously, Paul understands that the destruction upon the woman (which is in fact Israel according to Genesis 37:9-10 and Revelation 12:1) at the hands of this locust army (Arabs) will be directly preceded by a strong movement for peace and safety. Is it not ironic that we are witnessing, even now, the very negotiations for peace and safety (or security) among these same two parties? But the real question to determine at this point is whether or not we will actually see the genuine fulfillment of this peace and safety amongst these parties?

Chapter 21

"The Abomination of Desolation"

There is another sign that is given in Scripture, this one by Jesus, that once again few people really seem to notice or discuss and yet, it is one that is very key in the timetable of end-time events. So much so that it really can be considered as one that will be an obvious indicator as to the time in which we are in. As a result, it will also help to better identify just where these events lie on the so-called prophetic timeline. For so long, I too failed to notice this particular sign and then upon finally noticing it, I realized the very magnitude of it. In particular, I am speaking of a development in the Middle East that exists already in the early stages and that once again, involves both the Arabs and the Jews. To be more specific, it actually involves the city of Jerusalem which, by the way, is considered to be the final issue to haggle over in the peace process while, at the same time, it certainly is the most critical.

Currently, if you are at all even remotely aware of the state of affairs in the Middle East, you know about the struggle that persists between the Palestinians and Israelis. This struggle at times escalates while other times it seems to recede. Nevertheless, it doesn't seem to go away – and this is all while there is this ongoing process of negotiations passing over the table of peace. By now, you are probably aware that Israel has continuously placed its soldiers along its borders in order to protect its people – this due to the constant "uprising" wrought about by the Palestinian people, to include those horrible activities sponsored by the various terrorist groups such as the Hamas and Islamic Jihad. In fact, they are even now on occasion attacking back. "Israel must protect itself and will do so even by defending its very own self," is the typical mantra that is voiced. Of course, their position is that they are being provoked into doing so by the Palestinians. However, to hear the other side sounds very much like an echo. The Palestianians ironically claim that they are the ones being provoked, with Israel not respecting them through their (Israel's) various policies – for example, they argue that Israel keeps bringing their soldiers on to land that no longer belongs to them.

Thus, what you have is a constant argument! Who is right? Who is wrong? At this point, it is almost beyond proving and for that matter, it is probably beyond even redeeming! But then again, it may actually be happening intentionally – that is, being quite possibly ordained by God! So, what might be the eventual outcome of this situation?

Consider, for example, the strong unity of the Arabs/Moslems on what really is the only issue that they agree on – their intense hatred for the Jews! This attitude, and this alone, may very well be the flame that lights the fuse of the bomb that is ready to explode. I am speaking, of course, of an all out attack on Israel! Can it happen? You bet! Will it happen? I think so, and my position is based upon the clue given us by Jesus in the gospel of Luke, **"And <u>when ye shall see Jerusalem compassed with armies, then know that the desolation thereof is nigh.</u> Then let them which are in Judea flee to the mountains"** (Luke 21:20). This, I believe, is the single most important event to be looking for that takes place upon or immediately prior to the beginning of the 3½ year tribulation period. This we know because in Revelation we are told that **"<u>the holy city (Jerusalem) shall they (Israel's enemy) tread under forty and two months (3½ years)</u>"** (Rev. 11:2). In other words, with Jerusalem being in the hotbed of all that is to really take place over there in the Middle East, I would be looking for any type of gathering of Arab armies to take up Palestine's offense and thereby seize the Holy City! With Israel's armies being already active, the stage is set for a return act (or counter-reaction) on the part of the Arabs and, with the United States' war on terrorism already in progress, the stage is set and the time is ripe for them to now take advantage of this so-called "opportunity," if you want to call it that.

"The Abomination of Desolation"
Scripturally Explained

If we examine again His Olivet Discourse, we will see that Jesus gave us another telling sign regarding the end-times in Matthew 24:15, "When ye therefore shall see the <u>abomination of desolation</u>, spoken by Daniel the prophet, <u>stand in the holy place</u>, (whoso readeth, let him understand:)." This "holy place" referred to here is none other than the city of Jerusalem, within the land of Israel. As a result of this, Jesus indicates what these people should then do, "Then let them which be in Judaea (Israel) flee into the mountains" (vs. 16). Of course, this brings to mind the "abomination of desolation" of which Daniel also spoke, recorded in Daniel 9:26-27. If you remember, this (Daniel's) was a specific reference to the desolation that Israel would experience at the hands of the Arab peoples during the 3½ year tribulation — its cause and therefore its anticipated fulfillment was an abomination to God (incidentally, an "abomination" is something that "God hates or detests!"). This interpretation is further confirmed by Jesus' words, only in this case it from Luke's version of this same Olivet Discourse, "And when ye shall see <u>Jerusalem compassed with armies</u>, then know that the desolation thereof is nigh. <u>Then let them which are in Judaea flee to the mountains</u>" (Lk. 21:20-21). Could it really be any clearer regarding what Jesus is telling us? The word "compass" simply means "to surround or encircle" and implies the surrounding of Jerusalem by a predator-like enemy – the Arab armies. Again, does this currently sound like something inevitable from the Arabs? Interestingly enough, in its negotiations for peace, Israel continues to give up its land, in return asking for safety (or security) from the terrorist attacks, etc. in the process. But will Israel really obtain peace from their efforts? Not according to both Jesus' and Paul's words! Instead, they will find themselves surrounded by Arab armies, only to incur subsequent destruction. Admittedly, how to measure this encompassing of Arab armies is unclear. But one thing is for certain. When it happens, it will be fairly obvious, else the Jews would not know to at that time flee! And what, might we ask, are the prophetic ramifications of this "encompassing" around Israel by these Arab armies? Well, if you are perceptive, then according to Jesus' very own words, the occurrence of this one event will be that which ultimately triggers the start of the tribulation. That's right, this is the last Biblical event to occur just prior to or even beginning the period known as the great tribulation! Yet you ask, "But what about the rapture?" Of course in answer to this question we, once again, must take a serious look at what the Scriptures <u>really</u> have to say about it, of which we will now begin to do in the next few chapters of this book.

Chapter 22

"The Rapture"

Most people, especially believers in Christ, have by now heard of the "rapture." Even Hollywood, in a sense, has joined the fold. Movies such as "Left Behind" and the "Omega Code" have sparked considerable interest. So also has the "Left Behind" fictional book series. Incidentally the rapture, believe it or not, is really not even a Biblical term. Yet it does signify a Biblical event, an end-time one to be exact. Of more concern to people however, is not so much what it is, but rather when it will take place? Of all things, it is this issue that has actually created the controversy.

For those who don't know, the rapture is an event in which those who believe in Jesus Christ as their personal Lord and Savior will be taken up from the earth to go and forevermore be with the Him. In effect, they will be "caught up" into the clouds to meet the Lord in the air. For those Believers already dead, they will actually be raised up out of their graves and therefore precede those who are alive. The living will thus follow the dead, though they will then be united together. This will be an event that will be sudden, as in the "twinkling of an eye!" This, of course, is the traditional teaching regarding the rapture and to most, it is generally accepted as being the case. However, this also happens to be the point where most of the agreement on this subject ends.

As far as <u>when</u> this event takes place is another issue altogether. In general, there are three prevailing mindsets, each identified categorically as a particular position. For example, there are those who believe that the rapture will immediately precede the tribulation and therefore, these people are identified as "Pre-Tribbers." On the other hand, those who believe the rapture will immediately follow the tribulation are instead called "Post-Tribbers." Additionally, there are some who even believe that the rapture will occur in the middle of the tribulation, hence they are called "Mid-Tribbers." Of course, each of these positions presupposes one important thing — a seven year tribulation. What would be the case, by the way, in the event that there was only a 3½ year tribulation, as this book has established? This is a question which will be specifically answered in the next chapter of this book. In the meantime, the initial issue to address regarding the rapture is actually how it ties in with the end-time subject of the "wrath of God."

A large contingent of Believers embrace the teaching that Christians are not to experience God's wrath and therefore, they will be spared of it by way of the rapture. Accordingly, it is believed that this tribulation is actually the same thing as God's wrath. However, God's Word does not actually agree with this position. In other words, is the wrath of God something entirely different than the rapture? If so, would this make a difference in our understanding of the very purpose for this tribulation, to include its timing? Incidentally, I believe it is so. But first we need to examine God's Word to honestly answer these questions. Once again, I think you will find, as I too have, that God's answers do not always equate with our traditional teachings and yet, I think you will be both excited and amazed upon seeing what God really does have to say on this subject. Thus, in the next chapter on "The Wrath of God," we will let the Lord set the record straight.

"The Rapture"
Scripturally Explained

The subject of the rapture is another hotly debated event within the pool of controversial end-time topics. Simply put, the rapture is a Latin term for the event in which the living Christians are "caught up together with them (the risen dead) in the clouds to meet the Lord in the air" (1 Thess. 4:17). It is also described by Paul as "our gathering together unto him (the Lord Jesus Christ)" (2 Thess. 2:1). The timing of this event from a Scriptural standpoint is that it definitely will precede the Lord's return. However, by how much time it will precede His return is the question that poses the most controversy. Three doctrinal positions have developed in the process of trying to answer this question, known as the Pre-, Mid-, and Post-Tribulation positions. Of course, these all have assumed one thing — a 7-year tribulation. However, as was shown earlier, the tribulation consists of but a 3 and 1/2 year period of time. This one point alone, by its very nature, therefore basically eliminates the Mid-Tribulation position from consideration. Thus, it seems only two really remain, leaving us with either a Pre-Tribulation or Post-Tribulation rapture to decide upon. The question thus becomes, "Which one of these two is Scripturally accurate?"

In the vast majority of cases, the Pre-Tribulation rapture is the position embraced by most in the Christian community. The reason, of course, is based upon a statement made by Paul in 1 Thessalonians 5:9, "For God hath not appointed us to wrath, but to obtain salvation by our Lord Jesus Christ." Speaking of the believers in Jesus Christ, Paul says that God, in no uncertain terms, will not allow Christians to experience His wrath, and this is certainly true! Unfortunately, there arises two distinct problems at this point. The first is that this happens to be the most crucial verse used by Pre-Tribbers to place the rapture before the tribulation. The second problem concerns what this "wrath of God" actually is and incidentally, is something of which I believe is of even greater significance. For the Pre-Tribber, this "wrath of God" is none other than the tribulation period itself – that is, they are one and the same. However, what if this isn't true?

What if the tribulation and the "wrath of God" are not the same? To answer this question, we must again ask, "What saith the Scriptures?"

Actually, versus identifying <u>what</u> the "wrath of God" is to pinpoint the timing of the rapture, we need only to identify <u>when</u> this "wrath of God" begins. Incidentally, that God's wrath is some sort of judgment resulting from His anger being provoked should be evident. At the same time, we can also agree that unto the Christian, this "wrath" is not to be appointed. Yet it is equally important to note that to equate God's wrath with this same tribulation, although on the surface would appear to be the case, nevertheless is not Biblical. That is, upon further examination, the Scriptures actually reveal otherwise. We can conclude then that if the Christian is not to be a recipient of this wrath, it certainly would help for us to better determine when it is that God's wrath is actually levied for in so doing, we might thereby better be able to determine the actual timing of this rapture. Thus, it would be worthwhile for us at this point to take a closer look at this judgment specifically referred to as the "wrath of God." Accordingly, it is in the next chapter of this book that we will begin to do this very thing.

Chapter 23

"The Wrath of God"

Believe it or not, a chapter such as this on the "wrath of God" will more clearly explain the Biblical meaning of the "rapture." Most Believers, for one, associate the "wrath of God" with the tribulation and therefore, believing that the Christian is not to experience God's wrath (1 Thess. 5:9), they conclude that they will be raptured before the tribulation ever begins. However, as I discovered and you too soon will, the "wrath of God" is NOT the same thing as the tribulation, but rather is something entirely <u>different</u> and yet, it nevertheless does take place <u>during</u> this tribulation period. If this is to be true, then the premise that the Christian is not to experience God's wrath does not necessarily preclude them from also experiencing the tribulation! This, by the way, is a very key point that God's Word actually reveals upon further study.

Actually, we must first remember that the tribulation period is only 3½ years long. Accordingly, the "rapture" can therefore either take place prior to, subsequent to, or sometime during this same period of time. When I began to further study the "wrath of God," I soon discovered that it was something that specifically took place at the very <u>end</u> of the tribulation. As a matter of fact, the book of Revelation places it as occurring during the "6th seal" judgment. If the Christian is not to experience God's wrath, then they at least can experience the first five "seal" judgments prior to being raptured. These "seal" judgments, of course, occur <u>during</u> the 3½ years of tribulation.

Interestingly enough, almost the same can also be said upon examination of the seven "trumpet" judgments of Revelation. For example, in this particular case, the "wrath of God" doesn't occur until the 7th "trumpet" judgment, or the final one for that matter. Accordingly, the Christian could therefore possibly experience the first six "trumpet" judgments prior to being raptured. These "trumpet" judgments, by the way, are also to occur <u>during</u> this same 3½ years of tribulation.

Incidentally, there exists in Revelation still another set of seven judgments, only in this latter case, they are called the "vial" (or "bowl") judgments of which are really a set of seven types of plagues. However, although these also occur during the tribulation period, they aren't spread out throughout the full 3½ years. Rather, they all occur collectively at one particular point of time which, by the way, is near the end of the tribulation. Can you guess when? You got it – they occur at the same time as the "wrath of God" or, to be more specific, they ARE the "wrath of God!" Of course, the point here is that as a result, the rapture would have to take place <u>prior to</u> the occurrence of these seven "vial" judgments, though this does not necessarily preclude the Believer from experiencing the tribulation period <u>up to</u> the point of this "wrath of God."

Are you confused yet? The explanation portion of this chapter will provide a more thorough and detailed examination, but by this point you should at least understand this — that the rapture and "wrath of God" are not the same thing. In addition, you should also realize that the rapture will not take place at the end of the tribulation, though at the same time it will NOT take place at the beginning either. The fact is, it will take place <u>near the end of the tribulation</u>, or just prior to the "wrath of God" which, incidentally, does take place at the tribulation's end. Thus, this essentially means that the Believer will actually be around during most of this tribulation period. As far as the time of when the rapture will occur, this will be a subject addressed later in this book. Of probably even greater concern and more importance, however, is what you as a Believer might therefore expect to experience during this tribulation period. Of course, this too will be covered in a later chapter. As for now, I would like to better and more thoroughly explain the above arguments from a Scriptural standpoint.

"The Wrath of God"
Scripturally Explained

First of all, it is important to again note that the tribulation is only 3½ years long. Realizing that much of the end-time discussions involve the book of Revelation, we can immediately see the implications of this. Specifically, attempting to understand this book of the Bible has often resulted in numerous problems, especially in trying to chronologically place the differing periods of 3½ years that are referenced within (see Rev. 11:2,3; 12:6,14; 13:5; also Dan. 12:7). Obviously, to take each such period and interpret it as distinct and then to add each of them together, you would far surpass the assumed 7-year time frame that is traditionally taught. Conversely, to remain within the 7-year limitation, an overlapping of events associated with each reference would somehow have to be necessary. Determining then which of these events are to fall where is difficult at best and thus, attempting to interpret Revelation can be a difficult task with varied results. Yet, in the case of only a 3½ year tribulation, these problems dwindle. Essentially, each 3½ year passage would therefore be a reference to the same period of time, thereby being just a different perspective of that same period. It is interesting to note that in the attempt to interpret Revelation, this point alone results in some amazing and yet profound observations.

Additionally, another problem associated with interpreting Revelation is the placing of and understanding of the three major "7-type" judgments. Specifically, these are known as the "7 seals" (Rev. 6-8), "7 trumpets" (Rev. 8-11), and "7 vials (or bowls/plagues)" (Rev. 16). In the past, these have been interpreted somewhat chronologically with the seals being usually placed in the first 3½ year period, followed by the trumpets in the last 3½ year period, while the vials have had numerous interpretive placements. Nevertheless, the attempted placements of these would often result in many inconsistencies, problems, or other related types of confusion. Obviously in the case of just a 3½ year tribulation, again a different picture appears altogether.

Certainly, to attempt to interpret Revelation chronologically is problematic, at best. This is usually the by-product of one having a preconception before they ever begin their attempt – e.g., believing that the book of Revelation is a description of a single revelation of the Lord, hence the singular name "Revelation." Unfortunately, this is not the case either. Rather, Revelation is a book that is composed of many "revelations" — mini-revelations, if you will - meaning that it is a compilation of visions. Incidentally, more Scriptural proof confirming this particular point will be given in a later chapter of this book! But for now, this is best understood by noting here that every time you observe the Apostle John saying, "And I saw...(or I beheld, etc.)," you can most often interpret it to be a specific recording of a new vision, or mini-revelation, that he experienced. This takes place numerous times, but to give you some immediate examples, check out Revelation 4:1; 5:1,11; 6:1; 7:1; 8:2; 9:1, etc, to name a few. The importance of this principle of interpretation becomes clearly evident when it comes to understanding these three "7-type" judgments, especially in their connection to the "wrath of God."

Simply stated, the recording of the three "7-type" judgments — each being a separate vision by John — are very close to being descriptions of the same thing, that is, they are explanations of various facets of what will happen during the 3½ year tribulation. As a matter of fact, that John would do this — speak of the same thing (describing the 3½ year tribulation period) from different perspectives — is really not a unique thing in Scripture. He and the other three writers of the Gospels each quoted Jesus as teaching in this very same manner. For example, Jesus likewise would often describe the Kingdom of Heaven (or Kingdom of God) — "The Kingdom of Heaven is like unto..." (Mt. 22:2; 25:1; etc.), and then He would give some unique metaphor, simile, allegory, or word picture to help describe it. Yet in most instances, the comparison made or the picture given was something unrelated to the other examples, although the ultimate purpose was one and the same — to attempt to "explain" what the Kingdom was like. In the case of Revelation, the same is true. Many "visions" are experienced by John, each providing a different perspective related to the overall "Revelation of Jesus Christ" (Rev. 1:1). Accordingly, in the case of the three "7-type" judgments, you will notice a similar pattern. With a closer look and comparison of the details within each, this becomes even more evident. But what makes this understanding so remarkable regarding this discussion happens to be the calculated placement of the coming "wrath of God" within each of these "7-type" judgments. As a matter of fact, its importance is magnified when you realize that what we are really attempting to do is <u>determine the timing of the rapture</u> based upon the so-called understanding that the Christian is not to experience this "wrath of God."

Upon closer examination, one thing becomes clear. At some specific point within each of these different visions of "7-type" judgments, a statement to the intended recipient of this "wrath of God" is made to indicate just exactly when this wrath would begin. For example, in the case of the 7 seals (Rev. 6; 8:1), the "wrath of God" does not begin until the introduction of the 6th seal! In other words, the first 5 seals are already introduced by this point (in Revelation 6:1-11). Then in Revelation 6:16-17, John details how the intended recipients of God's wrath will cry, "...hide us from the face of him that sitteth on the throne, and from the wrath of the Lamb: <u>For the great day of his wrath is come</u>; and who shall be able to stand?" This cry, of course, is made within the description of details corresponding to the 6th seal. As a matter of fact, you will find that the 7th seal that follows does not actually take place until John speaks of it much later, in Revelation 8:1. But what is of most significance here is two very important factors associated with this wrath. The first is that God does not even appoint His wrath until <u>after</u> the events corresponding to the first five seals have already occurred. Upon further examination, you clearly realize that these first 5 seals that will have already transpired by this point embody the events that occur <u>during</u> the tribulation. The second factor, however, involves the very details associated with this wrath, stated as follows:

> *vs. 12 -* "*And I beheld when he had opened the sixth seal, and, lo, there was a <u>great earthquake</u>; and the <u>sun became black</u> as sackcloth of hair, and the <u>moon became as blood</u>;*"
>
> *vs. 13 -* "*And the <u>stars of heaven fell</u> unto the earth, even <u>as a fig tree casteth her untimely figs</u>, when she is <u>shaken</u> of a mighty wind.*"
>
> *vs. 14 -* "*And the heaven departed as a scroll when it is rolled together; and every mountain and island were moved out of their places.*"
>
> *vs. 15 -* "*And the kings of the earth, and the great men, and the rich men, and the chief captains, and the mighty*

> men, and every bondman, and every free man, <u>hid themselves</u> in the dens and in the rocks of the mountains;"
>
> vs. 16 - "And said to the mountains and rocks, Fall on us, and <u>hide us</u> from the face of him that sitteth on the throne, and from the wrath of the Lamb:"
>
> vs. 17 - "For <u>the great day of his wrath is come</u>; and who shall be able to stand?"

Notice, if you will, what happened to the sun (it darkened), moon (it darkened as blood), and stars (they fell). Take note also of the impact that this has on the heavens (they were shaken). Accordingly, the effect it has on the people of the earth is one of them crying out, or mourning, or even becoming distressed with great fear. Now, could it be that we have seen these same results mentioned elsewhere in Scripture? Ironically, the answer is an affirmative, "Yes."

Take a look again, in His Olivet Discourse, at the very words of Jesus in Matthew 24:

> vs. 29 - "Immediately **AFTER THE TRIBULATION** of those days shall the <u>sun be darkened</u>, and the <u>moon shall not give her light</u>, and the <u>stars shall fall from heaven</u>, and the powers of the <u>heavens shall be shaken</u>:"
>
> vs. 30 - "And then shall appear the sign of the Son of man in heaven: and then shall all the <u>tribes of the earth mourn</u>, and they shall see the Son of man coming in the clouds of heaven with power and great glory."
>
> vs. 31 - "And he shall send his angels with a great sound of a trumpet, and they shall gather together his elect from the four winds, from one end of heaven to the other."

Again, notice here that these events do not even occur until, according to Jesus Himself, **"AFTER THE TRIBULATION!"** Also, lest there be a question of whether the "tribes of the earth mourn(ing)" is reflective of the people of Revelation 6:15-16 hiding and crying out in fear, Luke provides us with this in his Gospel, "...and upon the earth <u>distress</u> of nations, with <u>perplexity</u>; ...<u>Men's hearts failing them for fear</u>, and for looking after those things which are coming on the earth" (Lk. 21:25-26). Of course, if this is not convincing enough, then we need only to review the Old Testament passage from which this idea originated, "And they shall go into the holes of the rocks, and into the caves of the earth, <u>for fear of the Lord</u>, and for the glory of his majesty, when he ariseth to <u>shake terribly the earth</u>. In that day a man shall...go into the clefts of the rocks, and into the tops of the ragged rocks, <u>for fear of the Lord</u>, and for the glory of his majesty, when he ariseth to <u>shake terribly the earth</u> (Is. 2:19-21)." It is fairly obvious, wouldn't you agree, that he is speaking of this very same event?

Of course, John also adds an additional detail in Revelation 6:14, telling us that "every mountain and island were moved out of their places." Incidentally, Luke also mentions this detail in his account, though it is merely by him alluding to it when he tells us that, "the sea and the waves (were) roaring" (Lk. 21:25).

You will notice also that John even describes a "great earthquake" (Rev. 6:12) taking place. Could it be that the phrase, "the powers of heaven shall be shaken," from Luke 21:26 is also to be understood as a <u>description</u> of this "great earthquake?" Or else maybe this phrase describes that which actually <u>causes</u> it? At any rate, we also learn that there are the mountains and rocks to which the people cried, "Fall on us" (Rev. 6:16). Could it be that this appeal is what results in this "great earthquake?" Uncertain the answer is, I admit, but notice at least what God pronounces in Hebrews 12:26, "<u>Yet **once more** I shake not the earth only, but also heaven</u>." I guess the point can be made then is that if God is only going to shake the heaven and the earth **ONE** more time, then it seems that these two events (the tribulation and the shaking of the heavens) will have to occur <u>simultaneously</u>, don't you think? In other words, the tribulation occurs for 3½ years, with the great earthquake being at the end of it — this earthquake being one of the events resulting from the "wrath of God."

Still another, albeit vastly important, event occurring at this time is the "heaven depart(ing) as a scroll when it is rolled together" (Rev. 6:14). Of course in most cases, people connect this occurrence with the rapture. If this is the case, then notice its timing, for it also takes place <u>after</u> the occurrence of the previous 5 seals. Incidentally, this particular event is referenced also in Isaiah 34:4 which states, "And all the host of heaven shall be dissolved, and <u>the heavens shall be rolled together as a scroll</u>: and all their host shall shall fall down, as the leaf falleth off from the vine, <u>and as a falling fig from the fig tree</u>." Notice the fig tree reference here which connects it again to this passage in Revelation 6 (see vs. 13). Essentially, the relationship of these 7 seal judgments to the "wrath of God" can be depicted on a timeline as follows:

```
     (Revelation 6:1-11)              (Rev. 6:12-17)      (Rev. 8:1)
       (first 5 seals)                  (6th seal)        (7th seal)
|---------------------------------|  |--------------------|  |---------|
     (3½ year tribulation period)       ("wrath of God")    ("silence")
                                        (great earthquake)
```

To summarize for a moment, we can definitely see a connection between this passage in Revelation 6:12-17 and the one in Matthew 24:29-31. This being the case, then it is important to point out verse 32 of Matthew 24 because of its reference also to the fig tree, "Now learn a parable of the fig tree..." Again, realizing that the rapture is the "gathering (of Christians) together unto him (Christ)" (2 Thess. 2:1), then would not the "gathering together of his elect" in Matthew 24:31 be speaking of this same event (the rapture) as well? Again, the only reason others have stated that it would not is because of their belief that the Christian is not to experience the "wrath of God," which they believe means the full tribulation period. But here, in this discussion of the 7 seal judgments, we clearly see that His wrath does not even begin until the end of the tribulation period. Of course, I have yet to even discuss both the "7 trumpet" and "7 vial" type judgments.

As far as the 7 trumpets go (Rev. 8:2 - 11:19), again we discover the same case — the "wrath of God" does not even take place until after some of these trumpet judgments have already occurred, only this time it is not until after the completion of the first <u>six</u> trumpets. The 7th trumpet judgment is then introduced in Revelation 11:15-19 as follows:

> *vs. 15* - "*And the seventh angel sounded; and there were great voices in heaven, saying, <u>The kingdoms of this world are become the kingdoms of our Lord, and of his Christ; and he shall reign for ever and ever</u>.*"
> *vs. 16* - "*And the four and twenty elders, which sat before God on their seats, fell upon their faces, and worshipped God.*"

>   vs. 17 - "Saying, We give thanks, O Lord God Almighty, which art, and wast, <u>and art to come</u>; because thou hast taken to thee thy great power, and hast reigned."
>
>   vs. 18 - "And the nations were angry, and <u>thy wrath is come</u>, and the time of the dead, that they should be judged, and that thou shouldest give reward unto thy servants the prophets, and to the saints, and them that fear thy name, small and great; and shouldest destroy them which destroy the earth."
>
>   vs. 19 -"And the temple of God was opened in heaven, and there was seen in his temple the ark of his testament: and there were lightnings, and voices, and thunderings, and an earthquake, and great hail."

Here we see that it is not until verse 18 that the introduction of God's wrath even occurs. Notice also that in this case, it is in conjunction with the Lord's return, because the Millennial Kingdom is by this point already established (vs. 15). Of course, a careful analysis of verse 17 will cause you to identify an apparent problem and conclude otherwise in that it says of our Lord God Almighty that He still NEEDS to come — meaning that He therefore would NOT have returned yet and thus, neither would His kingdom have been established. However this apparent problem, as it typically appears in the King James Version, is actually the result of an unfortunate bias on the part of the translators and instead disappears once one examines what is stated in the original Greek. In other words, the phrase in the King James Version, "and art to come," is non-existent in the original Greek text – AT ALL! — though the translators have for some reason still chosen to include it! In actuality, a proper translation of this verse should have read as follows, "**...We give thee thanks, O Lord God Almighty, <u>which art, and wast</u>; because thou hast taken to thee thy great power, and hast reigned.**" Had this been the case, certainly a different understanding would have resulted. Thus, <u>at this point in the trumpet judgments</u>, the proper understanding would be that <u>Christ has already come</u>, confirmed then by His Kingdom being already established in verse 15 and thus, the reason for the actual omission of the phrase "and art to come!" Why would the translators have made this mistake of adding this phrase to the verse? Most likely, it was based upon their preconceived understanding of the book of Revelation. In other words, they probably felt justified in so doing because Christ Himself was referred to this way much earlier in the book, well before He had ever returned – i.e., way back in Revelation 1:4, "...from him which is, and which was, and <u>which is to come</u>." In other words, I guess they probably felt the need to "add to" (see Revelation 22:18-19 for a stern warning against doing this very thing!) this phrase here in Revelation 11:17 in order to provide some consistency with chapter 1. However, with the proper rendering, it once again changes considerably the interpretation of the entire book of Revelation — for now you instead have Christ having already returned and thereby establishing His Kingdom in as early as the 11th chapter of the book of Revelation, prior even to such chapters as 13 (involving the beast, his image, the mark of the beast, and 666), chapter 16 (regarding the 7 vial judgments), and even chapters 17 and 18 (about Mystery Babylon)!

Another matter indicative of Christ's return having already occurred at this point is the verse prior to this passage, "The second woe is past; and, behold, the third woe <u>cometh quickly</u>" (Rev. 11:14). In other words, if this third woe, which refers to the 7th trumpet (see Rev. 8:13), is in fact speaking of Christ's return, then notice its similarity to other verses which also speak directly of Christ "coming quickly" (see Rev. 2:5, 16; 3:11; 22:7, 12, 20). In what is even more of a convincing proof regarding the timing of His return, notice the verse preceding this one, "And the same hour was there a <u>great earthquake</u>, and the tenth part of the city fell, and in the earthquake were slain of men seven thousand: and the remnant were <u>affrighted</u>, and gave glory to the God of heaven" (vs. 13). Here, immediately prior to His return, we see again the "great earthquake" taking place as well as the "fear" amongst the people. Then in the verse prior to that, we read also of this amazing event, "And they <u>heard a great voice from heaven</u> saying unto them, <u>Come up hither</u>. And they <u>ascended up to heaven in a cloud</u>; and their <u>enemies beheld them</u>" (vs. 12). Sounds pretty much like the rapture to me, don't you think? By the way, notice also that this event follows all of the other events up to this point which have already occurred, which incidentally make up the first 6 trumpets (Rev. 8:2 - 11:11)! Accordingly, the relationship on a timeline between the 7 trumpet judgments and the "wrath of God" can be depicted as follows:

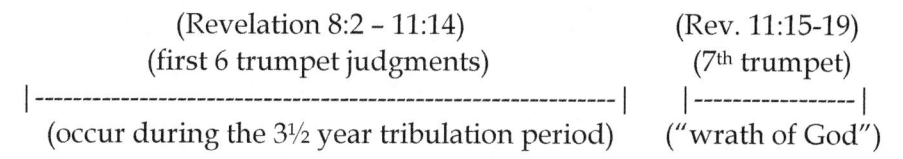

```
         (Revelation 8:2 – 11:14)              (Rev. 11:15-19)
         (first 6 trumpet judgments)             (7th trumpet)
|-----------------------------------------------------| |-----------------|
    (occur during the 3½ year tribulation period)    ("wrath of God")
```

There still "appears" to be (no pun intended) one other event in connection with this passage of Revelation 11:15-19 that seems to also help in the placement of its (this passage's) correct timing, but it involves the verses that follow this passage. Actually, it begins with the verse that opens the next chapter, "And there <u>appeared</u> a great wonder <u>in heaven</u>..." (Rev. 12:1). The word for "wonder" in this verse happens to be translated as "sign" meaning basically that John now sees a sign in heaven. Incidentally, in the original Greek text, we must remember that there are no chapter divisions, or even numbered verses, and thus it appears that the thought from verse 19 of chapter 11 carries right on into verse 1 of chapter 12. Of course, the importance of this factor is seen when we recall the words of Jesus in Matthew 24:30, "And then shall <u>appear the sign</u> of the Son of man in heaven." Could it be that chapter 12 of Revelation, specifically verses 3-5, is also describing this same sign of the Son of man that appears in heaven, "And there <u>appeared another wonder (sign) in heaven</u>...And she brought forth a <u>man child</u> (Son of Man?)..."

Having now discussed the "7-type" judgments of both the seals and trumpets, we turn our attention next to the 7 vials (Rev. 15:1, 7; 16:1-21). Differing a bit from the former two "7-type" judgments, it is important to note that during these 7 vials the coming of the "wrath of God" does not occur at a particular or designated point at all. Rather in this case, it is these 7 vials as a whole that are actually the "wrath of God." In other words, these vials make up a picture of, or even give us a description of, what this "wrath of God" actually is. Notice at first what is stated in Revelation 15:1, "And I saw another sign in heaven, great and marvellous, seven angels having the seven last plagues; <u>for in them is filled up the wrath of God</u>." Then in Revelation 15:7 John describes these plagues as "...seven golden vials <u>full of the wrath of God</u>." In other words, these plagues actually ARE the "wrath of God" and this becomes evident when the seven angels are then told, "Go your ways, and pour out the <u>vials of the wrath of God</u> upon the earth" (Rev. 16:1).

What is interesting at this point regarding these vials is that, since these contain the very "wrath of God," we should notice again their specific timing. For example, John informs us that the first vial would consist of this event, "and there fell a noisome and grievous sore upon the men which had the <u>mark of the beast</u>, and upon them which <u>worshipped his image</u>" (Rev. 16:2). Obviously from this verse we can see that the "wrath of God" comes AFTER the mark of the beast event as well as the image worship (Rev. 13:15-18) which, as was previously discussed, clearly takes place DURING the tribulation period. Thus, the 7 "vial" judgments and its relationship to the "wrath of God" could be depicted on a timeline as follows:

```
      (mark of the beast & image worship)           ("wrath of God")
|----------------------------------------------|   |-----------------|
      (occurs during the 3½ year tribulation period)   (7 vial judgments)
              (Revelation 13; 16:2)                    (Rev. 15:1, 7; 16)
```

Incidentally, during the third vial John says, "And I heard the angel of the waters say, Thou art righteous, O Lord, which art, and wast, <u>and shalt be</u>, because thou hast judged us" (Rev. 16:5). As was earlier stated, in the original Greek text the phrase "and shalt be" is non-existent, which leaves us once again with the understanding that by this point, the Lord has already returned, or at least is in the process of returning. But most important is the next two verses which clearly pinpoint that the timing of God's wrath is to be connected with Christ's return, "Behold, <u>I come as a thief</u>. Blessed is he that watcheth, and keepeth his garments, lest he walk naked, and they see his shame. <u>And he gathered them together into a place called in the Hebrew tongue Armageddon</u>" (Rev. 16:15-16). Certainly, we know that the battle of Armageddon will not take place until Christ has returns to the earth.

Finally, you will notice that during the seventh vial we have numerous events occurring, the likes of which are described as follows, "a great voice out of the temple of heaven" ...(saying,) "It is done" (vs. 17), "voices, thunders, and lightnings" (vs. 18), "a great earthquake" (vs. 18), "islands (fleeing) away, and the mountains (therefore) were not found" (vs. 20), and "great hail (coming) out of heaven" (vs. 21) — all of which parallel descriptions of verses earlier discussed in this chapter that we already established as being associated with the Lord's return.

Of course, our overall concern in this discussion regards the timing of the rapture. Could it be that the preceding factors, especially in light of the timing of the "wrath of God," are indicative of a post-tribulation rapture? It would be worthwhile to discuss at this point the "great sound of a trumpet" (Mt. 24:31). We just saw in Revelation 16:17 that "there came <u>a great voice</u> out of the temple of heaven, from the throne, saying, It is done." We also saw that in Revelation 11:12 John said, "And they heard <u>a great voice</u> from heaven saying unto them, Come up hither. And they ascended up to heaven in a cloud; and their enemies beheld them." In each of these cases there was a great voice from heaven with God speaking. But because of the already discussed timing of, or placement of, the events discussed above, this voice becomes an even more significant factor to consider, especially when we compare it to what John in Revelation 1:10 recorded, "I was in the Spirit on the Lord's day, and heard behind me <u>a great voice, AS OF A TRUMPET</u>." Here we see that this voice is that of the Lord Jesus Christ's (Rev. 1:11). But what really is important here is that <u>John describes God's voice as sounding like a trumpet</u>. This being the case, it sheds some light on the trumpet sound with respect to the rapture and/or Second Coming. For now we know that the great voice in Revelation 11:12 and 16:17 is, from a Scriptural standpoint, the same as the trumpet sound of Matthew 24:31. So also, it sheds some light on some other interesting passages. First, we can look at what Paul says in 1 Thessalonians 4:14-18:

> *vs. 14 - "For if we believe that Jesus died and rose again, even so them also which sleep in Jesus will God bring with him."*
> *vs. 15 - "For this we say unto you by the word of the Lord, that <u>we which are alive</u> and remain unto the coming of the Lord shall not prevent <u>them which are asleep</u>."*
> *vs. 16 - "For <u>the Lord himself shall descend from heaven with a shout, with the voice of the archangel, and with the trump of God</u>: and the dead in Christ shall rise first:"*

> *vs. 17 -"Then we which are alive and remain shall be <u>caught up together</u> with them in the clouds to meet the Lord in the air: and so shall we ever be with the Lord."*
>
> *vs. 18 - "Wherefore <u>comfort</u> one another with these words."*

Now, notice what Paul says in the very next chapter, specifically in verses 9-11 of 1 Thessalonians 5:

> *vs. 9 - "<u>For God hath not appointed us to wrath</u>, but to obtain salvation by our Lord Jesus Christ,"*
>
> *vs. 10 - "Who died for us, that, <u>whether we wake or sleep</u>, we should live together with him."*
>
> *vs. 11 - "Wherefore <u>comfort</u> yourselves together, and edify one another, even as ye also do."*

It seems that Paul in this second passage is really referencing what he just said in the first passage, by mentioning both of these phrases, "whether we wake or sleep" and to "comfort...one another." Of course, notice also his mentioning of the voice (his shout), the trump (of God), the rapture (being "caught up together" with the dead "in the clouds"), and the "wrath of God."

Speaking of the trump, and also of those who are either asleep (the dead in Christ) or alive, we can look at another of Paul's writings in 1 Corinthians 15:51-52:

> *vs. 51 - "Behold, I shew you a mystery; <u>We shall not all sleep</u>, but we shall all be changed,"*
>
> *vs. 52 - "In a moment, in the twinkling of an eye, <u>at the last trump</u>: for <u>the trumpet shall sound</u>, and <u>the dead shall be raised</u> incorruptible, and <u>we shall be changed</u>."*

Clearly it seems that Paul also connects the rapture with the return of Christ, especially since the "wrath of God" — of which we as Christians are not to experience — is something that does not take place until the very end of the tribulation period. An additional question regarding the trump (or the voice of God) is, "Since we know that the rapture is to take place at the last trump, are we able to determine what this last thing that God says (or "trumpets") will be?" Of course, I will admit my uncertainty here, but I would like to draw our attention, once again, to Revelation 16:17, "And the seventh angel poured out his vial into the air; and there came a <u>great voice</u> out of the temple of heaven, from the throne, saying, <u>It is done</u>." That this might be that last trump – or last statement that God makes — is certainly worth considering, especially when you recall the last words of Jesus on the cross before He died, as also recorded by this same Apostle John, "When Jesus therefore had received the vinegar, he said, <u>It is finished</u>: and he bowed his head, and gave up the ghost" (John 19:30). Another possibility, however, is that this "last trump" relates back to the 7th trumpet blown during the 7 trumpet judgments which pronounces the establishment of the Millennial Kingdom at Christ's return, "And the <u>seventh angel sounded</u>; and there were <u>great voices in heaven, saying</u>, The kingdoms of this world are become the kingdoms of our Lord, and of his Christ; and he shall reign for ever and ever" (Rev. 11:15). Of course again, to this I admit my uncertainty, although it certainly is worth considering or "chewing on."

Chapter 24

"The Marriage Supper"

There is one last thing regarding the "rapture" that I would still like to discuss and that is its purpose. That is, what is it for or even why is there a rapture? The answer of course can be found in the title of this chapter. In other words, it really has something to do with the "marriage supper" of the Lamb. Of course, this begs the question of what is the marriage supper? Just like so many other end-time topics, on this I was again groomed on a traditional explanation that I have since realized is really not Biblical. Rather, God's Word has once again revealed an altogether different understanding than I was accustomed to on this subject of the "marriage supper." As a matter of fact, on this subject I was truly shocked, to say the least, at what I discovered God actually had to say. I am confident that you too will be just as shocked upon further examination.

My idea of the "marriage supper" was for so many years one that consisted of incredible pageantry, festive celebration, joyous euphoria, and spiritual bliss, to say the least. Jesus was getting married and this would be the wedding of all weddings! We Believers, making up His bride, would in no way be lacking. Christ would sweep us off our feet and this would be just the beginning of an eternity beyond description. Allowing your mind to wander into dreamland was almost expected when it came to this subject. It seemed that this was meant to occur and was even part of the package deal. This celebration was something to look forward to and you could rest assured, knowing that in no way would God let us down. At least it seemed that my having this ideal was the typical sentiment. But then one day, I guess you could say, I studied this subject in the Bible and actually discovered a totally different picture.

The "marriage supper" is an event that takes place immediately following the rapture. It is referred to in a couple of different ways, such as the "marriage supper," the "marriage supper of the Lamb," the "wedding supper," the "wedding feast," and even the "wedding banquet." Yet it is understood to be a celebration of the uniting of the Groom with the Bride – specifically meaning Jesus Christ with the

Church! This is basically what I was taught, and was what I also found to be the generally accepted understanding, again, until I looked further into God's Word.

Would you like to know what I discovered? Amazingly, I found that John the Revelator revealed a vision that he had that symbolically described this wedding feast. Unfortunately, what I found in his account was no record of any pageantry, neither any celebration, and certainly no festivities. Rather, what I discovered was that this supper was a portrayal of, of all things, the <u>battle of Armageddon</u>! In other words, imagine the Church, united with Christ, returning to earth to battle against the Arab/Moslem empire! With Christ leading the way, the Church would reign in victoriously and, in defeating this "beast," would metaphorically be said to have "eaten" their prey! Although this sounds disgusting, this is essentially the vision John receives and, believe it or not, it is referred to as the **"<u>marriage supper of the Lamb!</u>"** With this explanation, I guess you now know why I was so shocked the first time that I discovered this. Of course, this brings me back to the primary question of why the rapture?

The purpose of the rapture is therefore basically <u>to sound the alarm in order to gather in the troops for this very battle</u>. Jesus will rally His Church together and lead them into the battle of Armageddon in order to destroy the oppressors of Israel, which of course will be the Arab/Moslem empire. That this is a supper is symbolically revealed to us by John in Revelation 19. Of course, it isn't exactly what we normally would have envisioned, but it nevertheless is Scripturally sound and is something of which I will further demonstrate in the second part of this chapter. But just to get you thinking further on this explanation, consider for a moment this one question. Why, if God is going to, at the start of the Millennium and for the rest of eternity, bring <u>heaven down to earth</u>, would He bring <u>us up to heaven</u> for seven years, which is the traditional thinking? In other words, why for seven years? What would be the reason? What I have found is that God's reasoning for the rapture is simply to gather us together, in this case into the clouds, in preparation for the battle, for which we will actually return to the earth to fight. In other words, there is no need of seven years to accomplish this objective. Rather, it requires a significantly less amount of time to do so. Incidentally, in a later chapter of this book I will Scripturally provide for you God's revealing of that very amount. For now however, the need is to further explain this "marriage supper" and to do so, we will examine more closely John's 19th chapter of Revelation.

"The Marriage Supper"
Scripturally Explained

There is one last thing I would like to discuss regarding the rapture and that is its purpose – that is, what is it for? To understand the answer to this question, we need to first realize another title that the Bible gives for our Lord — it is the position of "Captain" (Heb. 2:10). Essentially, we should understand that He is the Captain of those who are saved. But to state it another way, Scripturally speaking He is the Captain of His armies of which Christians are a part. This is important when we recall that in Biblical times, when a nation's army was ready for battle, the signal given to move them out was the blowing of a trumpet by that army's captain signifying that he was ready to move. Essentially, the purpose for the captain's blowing of the trumpet was to gather his troops into battle. In the same way, the purpose of the rapture, which involves the blowing of the "trump of God" (1 Thess. 4:16), is for the Captain — the Lord Jesus Christ — to gather together His armies for the preparation of the battle. In this case, the meeting place for getting in rank with the Captain is within the clouds of the air, "Then we which are alive and remain shall be <u>caught up together with them in the clouds to meet the Lord in the air</u>: and so shall we ever be with the Lord" (1 Thess. 4:17). Incidentally, as is often the case in Scripture, clouds are representative of the Lord's "shekinah" glory and therefore, it is quite possible that our meeting the Lord in the air is another way of saying that we will meet Him in His Glory — "When the Son of man shall <u>come in his glory</u>" (Mt. 25:31). Nevertheless, it is at this particular point that we will forevermore be with Him (1 Thess. 4:17). But again, the purpose that God has for doing it this way is to make preparation for the impending battle, which would be the battle of Armageddon (Rev. 16:16). Notice what John says in Revelation 19:19, "And I saw the beast, and the kings of the earth, and their armies, gathered together to make war against him that sat on the horse (according to Rev. 19:11, this is Christ), <u>and against his army</u> (God's army)." Clearly we see here that this battle includes not only Jesus, the Captain, but also His army. Now notice also what John says about our weapons, or how we will fight this battle, "and <u>in righteousness</u> he doth...make war" (Rev. 19:11). In effect, "the weapons of our warfare are not carnal, but are mighty through God" (2 Cor. 10:4), for we find ourselves using God's righteousness in this war as our weaponry.

Amazingly, another thing we discover from Scripture is that this battle consists of something like birds eating people because John actually states in the verses preceding the 19th verse, "And I saw an angel standing in the sun; and he cried with a loud voice, saying to all the fowls that fly in the midst of heaven, Come and gather yourselves together unto the supper of the great God; That ye may eat the flesh of kings, and the flesh of captains, and the flesh of mighty men, and the flesh of horses, and of them that sit on them, and the flesh of all men, both free and bond, both small and great" (Rev. 19:17-18). Strange it seems, does it not, that this battle would include not only God's army, but also a bunch of fowls that are flying around in heaven? And stranger yet is that God would have these same fowls participate in that so-called "honorable" event known as "the supper of the great God?" Or might it just be that this supper is, once again, symbolic of something else? Fortunately, John gives us the answer to this question in this very same chapter. For instance, notice what he says in verse 7 of Revelation 19, "Let us be glad and rejoice, and give honour to him: for the marriage of the Lamb is come, and his wife hath made herself ready." Then notice verse 9, "And he saith unto me, Write, Blessed are they which are called unto the marriage supper of the Lamb." With this, John makes it very clear that symbolically, "the marriage supper of the Lamb" is also "the supper of the great God" (vs. 17), which is therefore actually the battle of Armageddon. We see now also that "his wife," which we know consists of the saints of God (which is also His army, don't forget!), happens to be characterized as the "fowls that fly in the midst of heaven." This happens to sound amazingly similar to a description of the rapture, as it is just taking place, now doesn't it! Remembering again that the weaponry used during this battle is the righteousness of God, notice now verse 8, which speaks of His wife, "And to her was granted that she should be arrayed in fine linen, clean and white: for the linen is the righteousness of saints." In other words, we Believers (being His wife) are actually clothed here with what we would use to fight this battle — the righteousness of God! Incidentally, John also says that God's army, much like the Captain Himself (vs. 11), will travel by horses, "And the armies which were in heaven <u>followed him upon white horses</u>, clothed in fine linen, white and clean" (Rev. 19:14). Obviously from these details given to us by John, we can therefore conclude that the purpose of the rapture is actually to prepare the Christians for the battle of Armageddon, known also for the Christians as the marriage supper of the Lamb — or even the wedding feast! Incidentally, since this supper involves us as the Lord's Bride, it would serve us well to further examine what God has to say regarding His Bride. Accordingly, we will do so in the next chapter as we evaluate the significance of what is really being referred to by the subject of "The New Jerusalem."

Dennis Crump

Chapter 25

"The New Jerusalem"

In the last chapter, we learned that "marriage supper" more than likely will be something entirely different than what we normally would have expected. Nevertheless, it still will involve the Groom, Jesus Christ, and His Bride, the Church. Speaking of the Bride, there is another passage in Scripture which also mentions Christ's Bride, only in this case it is a city. If you have any church background, by now I am sure that at some point you have at least heard of the "new Jerusalem." This is another end-time subject that conjures up pictures that are for most people, quite the same. After all, as normal human beings, we too are generally trained to understand only what we have been taught. The potential problem we have then is, what if we have been taught wrong? The traditional teaching on this subject is not only what is popularly believed, but is also what I was taught. Yet what actually is this "new Jerusalem?" Like so many of the other topics already discussed, I only needed to search God's Word in order to discover His explanation and, once again, it is not what I had imagined.

I really think as Believers that sometimes we just don't think. I don't mean that in a critical way, but rather more in a challenging sense. In the case of the "new Jerusalem," this would be a classic example. Oh yeah, I for so long didn't "think" either. When it came to the "new Jerusalem," I imagined a brand new city somehow coming out of the clouds and amazingly descending from heaven to earth. It would replace the "old," or current, city of Jerusalem. This new one would however be absolutely stunning! I had heard of the streets of gold. I had heard of the precious stones, and even the pearly gates. This city would have those things. In fact, it would be something to behold! I had even heard of how big it would be – 1500 miles wide, by 1500 miles long, by 1500 miles high. Absolutely breathtaking! And what a grand entrance it would have, as well. The sky would open up and down it would come, straight from heaven, a miraculous event and splendorous sight indeed! Yep! This is what I was taught and of course, I was rather enthusiastic in just imagining it.

But then I studied my Bible and you know what I discovered? I found out that the "new Jerusalem" was also referred to as the Lord's Bride, which almost didn't faze me until I began to think. How could the Lord have two wives? We all teach in Christianity that God's position on marriage is that monogamy alone is all that is allowed. Why then would He have more than one wife?

Once I began to question this, I continued to think some more? If the "new Jerusalem" is 1500 miles cubed, then where would it go when it is placed on earth? The old city of Jerusalem is not very big. I have been there. In fact, the whole nation of Israel is not very big, being less than 100 miles wide and only about 200 miles long — and we are supposed to expect a city to replace the old one that is that big? I decided to do some calculating and discovered that this "new Jerusalem" is almost half the size of the United States! But probably its most incredulous trait is its heighth. The former World Trade Centers, two of the tallest buildings in the whole world, were less than 1500 FEET! How could a city then be 1500 MILES high? It just didn't make any sense! So I studied some more.

Amazingly, the "new Jerusalem" is best understood as being symbolic. That is, it is not literal, but rather it is to be understood as representing something else. What it actually represents then is the Bride of Christ. In other words, the "new Jerusalem" is really symbolic of the Church Body of Christ! Let me give you a few examples to help you begin to understand this. First of all, it is called both the "bride" and the "Lamb's wife." Second, the city is made up of gates and foundations, actually of 12 each. The 12 gates represent the 12 tribes of Israel and the 12 foundations represent the 12 Apostles of Christ. Symbolically, the gates relate to God's people from the Old Covenant while the foundations relate to God's people from the New Covenant. Of course collectively, they make up the whole Body of Christ. Third, when the city is said to descend to earth from out of the clouds, this is really a picture of the Church returning to earth with the Lord at His Second Coming. Remember, we would have been raptured previous to this point, being already up in the clouds. Fourth, the city is also made up of stones, which is simply a metaphor for God's people of whom He calls "living stones." Last, God already said that He would no longer dwell in a building made up of stone (or a real building), but instead would dwell in a living temple of which we Believers collectively make. Incidentally, these proofs are discovered by studying the 21st chapter of Revelation of which, accordingly, is about John's vision that God gave him of this "new Jerusalem." I will now provide a more thorough explanation regarding this symbolic city in the next part of this chapter.

"The New Jerusalem" *Scripturally Explained*

As was mentioned in the previous chapter on the marriage supper, the participants would be the saints of God, collectively referred to as the <u>wife</u> of Christ. As John tells us, "the marriage of the Lamb is come, and his <u>wife</u> hath made herself ready" (Rev. 19:7). The Apostle Paul in another passage makes it clear that the Body of Christ is also called the <u>Bride</u> of Christ (Eph. 5:22-32) and that this is also another one of those mysteries. But another reference by the Apostle John makes this mystery appear even more mysterious. In Revelation 21:2 he says, "And I John saw the holy city, <u>new Jerusalem</u>, coming down from God out of heaven, prepared as a <u>bride</u> adorned for her husband." He then adds, "<u>I will shew thee the bride, the Lamb's wife</u>. And he carried me away in the spirit to a great and high mountain, and <u>shewed me that great city, the holy Jerusalem</u>, descending out of heaven from God" (Rev. 21:9-10). We can certainly admit that this is a mystery, but doesn't it also seem a bit strange? Consider for a moment the idea that Christ is married to a city. That certainly seems strange. Consider also then that from these passages it seems He now has two wives — the Body of Christ and the "new Jerusalem." Something here is definitely mysterious, albeit wrong, unless of course the two wives are really one and the same. Could this be possible? Could the "new Jerusalem" actually be symbolic for the Body of Christ? Again we ask, "What saith the Scriptures?"

This puzzling question becomes all the more troubling when you consider just how John later describes this city, eventually even giving the dimensions of it, "And he <u>measured the city</u> with the reed, twelve thousand furlongs. The length and the breadth and the height of it are equal" (Rev. 21:16). Twelve thousand furlongs, as translated in other versions, is equivalent to approximately 1,500 miles. Think of it for a moment — Christ's bride is essentially a giant Rubick's cube: 1,500 miles wide by 1,500 miles long by 1,500 miles high! But just as this bride's size seems strange and is even more difficult to imagine, consider the implications of these dimensions even if this city was not to be considered His wife. A city – new Jerusalem — is to come down from the sky to the earth. When it lands, it will have the dimensions of 1,500 miles cubed. This is simply astounding, albeit impossible. For example, imagine if you will the United States being split in half, such as with the Mississippi River. The result would leave with you with each half being approximately 1,500 miles long by 1,500 miles wide – the same dimensions as the base of this city. This is basically the same as half of the Continental United States! Are we to now consider just one city being this size? To top that off (no pun intended), now the heighth of this city is to be 1,500 miles as well. This alone should prove its impossibility, especially when you consider that the tallest building in the entire world is less than 1,500 FEET! And we are talking 1,500 **MILES** here. In fact, even the highest mountain in the world extends to only around 30,000 feet – a mere 6 miles high. But are we to now add another 1,494 miles on top of that? I mean, can you imagine yourself being assigned a window room on the top floor of this cubed city of which is 1,500 MILES high? I sure hope those windows are those extra thick ones because I would hate to accidentally fall through one!

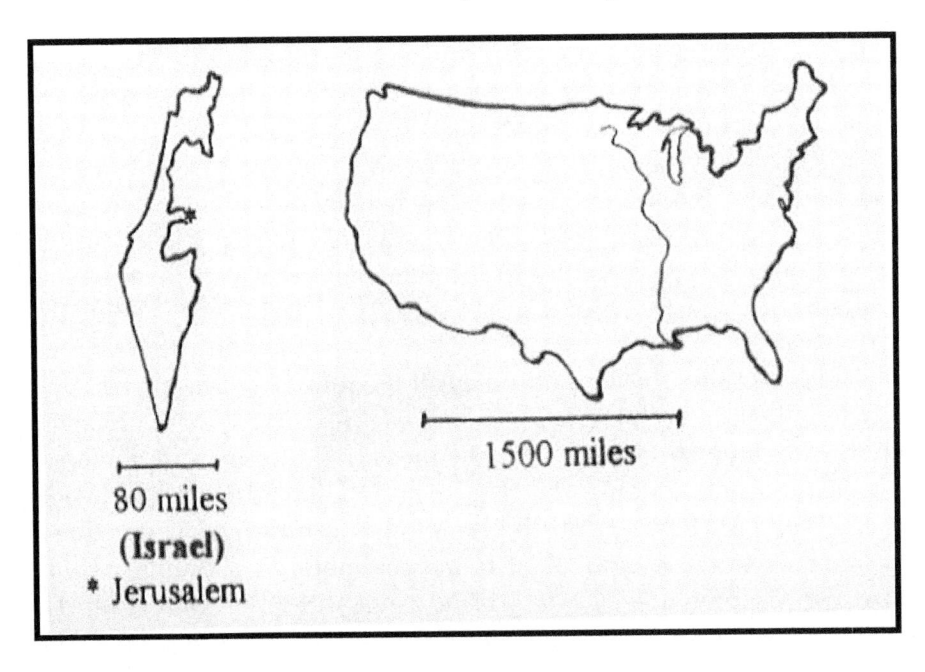

1500 miles

80 miles

(Israel)

* Jerusalem

To fully understand this apparent mystery, one only has to compare Scripture with Scripture. John himself begins to describe the measurements of this unique city and, in so doing, it becomes clear that this city, or the new Jerusalem, is really a picture of the Bride (or Body) of Christ. For example, in verse 12 this city is described as follows, "And had a wall great and high, and had <u>twelve gates</u>, and at the gates twelve angels, and names written thereon, which are the names of the <u>twelve tribes of the children of Israel</u>." Accordingly, from this verse we can now see that <u>the 12 gates are actually based upon the 12 tribes of Israel from which we also get our Old Testament saints</u> (or God's people) — the chosen nation of Israel.

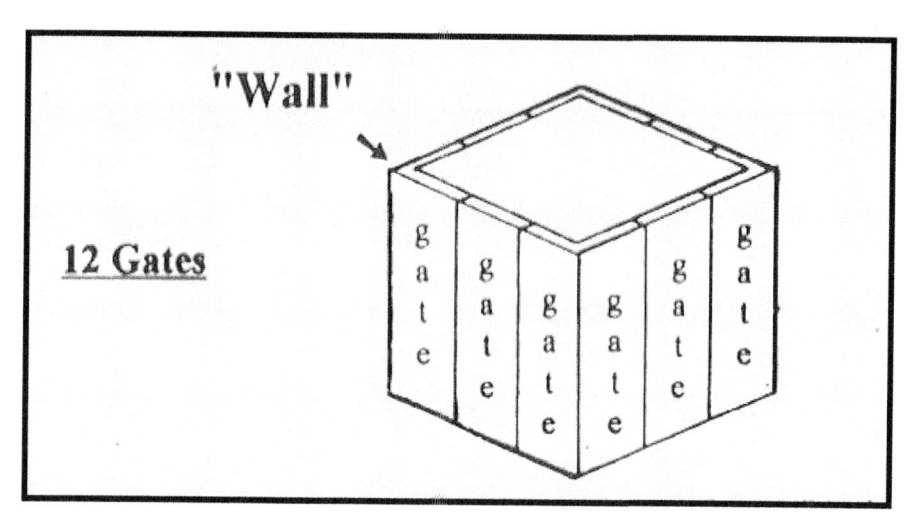

[Figure: A cube labeled "Wall" with an arrow pointing to its top edge, and "12 Gates" labeled on the side, showing gates along the vertical faces of the cube.]

Then in verse 14, the description of the city continues, "And the wall of the city had <u>twelve foundations</u>, and in them the names of the <u>twelve apostles of the Lamb</u>." Remember now that it was Jesus' 12 apostles of whom He used as the foundation upon which to build the New Testament Church. In so doing, this verse takes on new meaning for, in effect, <u>this is a picture of the New Testament saints</u>. For example, Paul wrote in Ephesians of the believers in Christ, "Ye are...fellow citizens with the <u>saints</u>, and of the <u>household</u> of God; And are built upon the <u>foundation of the apostles</u> and prophets, Jesus Christ himself being the chief corner stone; In whom all the <u>building fitly framed together groweth unto an holy temple</u> in the Lord: In whom ye also are <u>builded together for an habitation of God</u> through the Spirit" (Eph. 2:19-22).

12 Foundations

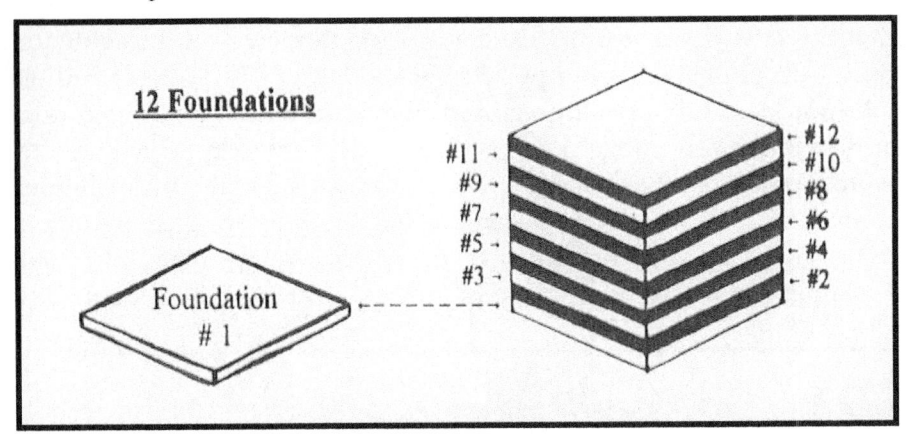

Clearly, we see that Paul identifies all of the saints as that which makes up God's new household, the place from whence He will take residence, symbolically referred to as the building that becomes His new temple. Of course, its foundation is the work of the 12 apostles. John also had a vision of this same habitation in Revelation 4, describing it partly as such, "And round about the throne were four and twenty seats: and upon the seats I saw <u>four and twenty elders</u> sitting" (Rev. 4:4). Interestingly enough, Jesus even told us clearly who would be sitting in at least twelve of these seats when He spoke to His disciples, "And Jesus said unto them, Verily I say unto you, That ye which have followed me, in the regeneration when the Son of man shall sit in the throne of his glory, <u>ye also shall sit upon twelve thrones</u>, judging the twelve tribes of Israel" (Mt. 19:28). With 12 of these 24 seats being occupied by these 12 apostles, certainly we can conclude that in the other 12 will be the representatives of the 12 tribes of Israel, them most likely being the prophets (Eph. 2:20).

Another New Testament verse of great significance is given to us by the Apostle Peter, speaking also of this precious Holy City, "As newborn babes, desire the sincere milk of the word, that ye may grow thereby: If so be ye have tasted that the Lord is gracious. To whom coming, as unto a <u>living stone</u>, disallowed indeed of men, but chosen of God, and precious, Ye also, as <u>lively stones</u>, are <u>built up a spiritual house</u>, an holy priesthood, to offer up spiritual sacrifices, acceptable to God by Jesus Christ. Wherefore also it is contained in the scripture, Behold, I lay in Sion a chief corner stone, elect, precious: and he that believeth on him shall not be confounded" (1 Pt. 2:2-6). Here, Peter clearly indicates that **this household of God is not**

material, but rather spiritual, consisting of stones that are not physical, but rather human (the Believers). Of course, this same spiritual house is none other than the Bride of Christ, now understand as the "new Jerusalem."

One other interesting verse to look at is found in Galatians 4:26 wherein Paul writes, "But <u>Jerusalem which is above</u> is free, which is <u>mother of us all</u>." Amazingly, this "new Jerusalem" is not only referred to as a wife (of Christ), but also is now personified as a mother (of us Believers). Of course, this is best understood upon evaluating the context of this verse for in so doing, we find that this statement is actually connected with Abraham (the Father of all of us in the faith) and all of his descendants (that is, those who are called the "children of faith" – Gal. 3:6-9; 4:22-31). Speaking of Abraham, we find also another amazing verse in Hebrews which says of him that he "looked for <u>a city which hath foundations</u>, whose builder and maker <u>is God</u>" (Heb. 11:10). What are these foundations? Obviously, from evaluating other Scriptures, they are the New Testament Apostles and the Old Testament Prophets. Remembering that it is God alone who saves a person, we once again see that this is the "new Jerusalem," the city that is built and made also by God alone. As a matter of fact, Paul even seems to agree with this understanding (Eph. 2:19-22). Thus, when it comes to Scripturally understanding the "new Jerusalem," we should in no way think of it as being a literal or material thing. Rather, it is but a symbolic picture of all the Saints of God who collectively make up the new Temple, or residence, or even habitation, of the Living God Himself upon our entering into that new era that we know as the Millennial Kingdom. Of course, with this understanding, it brings us to yet another related question being, "What about my mansion?" This, by the way, happens to be the subject of our next chapter.

Dennis Crump

Chapter 26

"But What About My Mansion?"

In the last chapter, it was established that there actually is no literal or physical type of city to expect to come back to earth that is called the "new Jerusalem." This teaching alone can be a shock for some. However, this ought to stir up even more questions that would result from this understanding. For example, there is one question that is a definite – "What about my mansion?" You know, the one we expect to get in heaven! There is a phrase that I like to use that identifies things we tend to learn in church, oftentimes beginning while we are yet children. It is what I call "Sunday School Theology!" In other words, it refers to some of the things that we learn while in the developmental stages of being a Christian. Quite often, and unfortunately, these things tend to be some of the basic things that help to formulate our theology, although they actually lack a true depth that is supported fully in Scripture. The effect of "Sunday School Theology" is that it can be embraced dogmatically even after one has further developed as a Christian. In the extreme cases, you find adults who continue to operate from the same theological mindset that they initially received in the beginning. The sad reality is that God's wisdom far surpasses this theology and in many cases, the result is that these Believers never really discover the deeper things of God. This is not to, however, completely fault "Sunday School Theology." I have kids and you quickly realize that you have to teach them in steps and increments, so as to not confuse the learner. At the same time, the simple things eventually can be more thoroughly or deeply explained as they develop, thereby increasing the understanding of the learner. Unfortunately, there exists today far too many adults, to include even pastors and teachers, who still embrace, quite dogmatically as a matter of fact, many of the elements of "Sunday School Theology."

Now, having said that, how does one escape this outcome? I personally have realized that there are two distinct solutions. One is for you to become surrounded by or exposed to diligent teachers of God's Word. The second is to hungrily seek after God and study His

Word for yourself. Why? Because God rewards those who diligently seek after Him and He also considers as noble those who diligently search the Scriptures. Thus in doing so, you can begin to learn the deeper things of God and, in turn, be able to distinguish that which is truly Biblical from that which is of the "Sunday School Theology" category. At any rate, I think that the challenge to overcome this must be given and for the Church, it is time to really respond.

In the case of our "mansions," it is time to file them away as "Sunday School Theology." Actually, they do relate somewhat to the "new Jerusalem." However, the flaw has been a direct result of our erroneous understanding that this "new Jerusalem" was actually a real or literal city. Having properly determined its true meaning though, it again raises that necessary question of, "What about my mansion?"

The typical understanding has been broadly embraced – while yet being here on earth, we as Christians continue to await an eternity in heaven. At the same time, while Christ is reigning in heaven, He supposedly is at work preparing for each one of us some type of mansion. Upon stepping over to the other side, we would then be able to take residence in our mansion and begin the enjoyable lifestyle of eternal bliss. This type of teaching is a part of our typical diet and begins for us even while yet being children. I still remember, for example, the song I learned as a child in Sunday School, "In My Father's House are Many Mansions!" Unfortunately, this teaching is Biblically not correct!

Guess what? There are no mansions! We as Believers have sadly been the recipients of "Sunday School Theology!" The <u>Bible</u> never says that we are to receive a mansion. You might have a <u>version</u> of the Bible that indicates that you do, but that is where the problem begins. The most popular and original version of the Bible that we as Americans have had is the King James. In this version, it actually indicates that Jesus is preparing for us a mansion. But unfortunately, this is the result of an error in the translation process. The original Greek manuscripts indicate that Christ is preparing for us not mansions, but rather "abodes." An "abode," quite simply, is a loose term to describe an "habitation." It is a more general term as opposed to being specific, but for good reason. Jesus, if you recall, reminded us to "abide" in Him in order to successfully live as a Christian. To abide in Him means to be <u>"in Christ."</u> In other words, to fully grasp this means that after Christ went to the cross, He provided a new way for people to relate to Him by faith. This new way, referred to as the New Covenant, provided for us as Believers to actually be "in Christ," or <u>to abide in Him</u>, through the supernatural and unique work of the Holy Spirit. This then is the "abode" that Christ has been able to prepare for us as a result of Him eventually leaving the earth. By leaving, He was able then to send the Holy Spirit which in turn, enabled us to therefore "abide in Christ!" In other words, this proper Biblical interpretation is in no way even remotely close to the teaching of a mansion being prepared in heaven for each one of us. Thus, it is considerably different from that which is a part of our normal "Sunday School" teaching on this subject.

"What About My Mansion?"
Scripturally Explained

With the understanding of the "new Jerusalem" being a city that is symbolic, we must address a very popular verse learned by so many of us, even as children in Sunday School, in which Jesus said, "In my Father's house are many <u>mansions</u>: if it were not so, I would have told you. <u>I go to prepare a place for you</u>" (Jn. 14:2). In other words the question must be asked, "What about my mansion?" Incidentally, since we are discussing end-time topics, it is worth noting that in connection with this particular verse, Jesus actually alludes to His return in the very next verse when He says, "And if I go and prepare a place for you, <u>I will come again</u>, and receive you unto myself; that where I am, there ye may be also." Funny, but with respect to the mansions, if you notice Jesus' statement of, "if it were **not** so, I would have **told** you," the truth of Scripture is that <u>it really is not so</u>! Of course, this is not to suggest that Jesus is a liar. Rather, the truth is that Jesus never really did say that there were "mansions" in His Father's house. In other words, the actual truth is that there are no mansions. That's right, **NO MANSIONS!** What Jesus actually did say has not been translated properly. This unfortunate misunderstanding is again due to the biased work of our beloved translators.

What is actually recorded in the original Greek is, **"In the house of my Father are many <u>ABODES</u>."** In other words, we need to realize that "abodes" are not the same thing as mansions, especially as we today understand mansions. This being the case, the ramifications of it are truly eye opening. First of all, we again see a direct reference to the house (or <u>household) of God</u> as we already saw in Ephesians 2:19 – a verse which points us once again to the "new Jerusalem." Second, we also see a reference to Christ's Second Coming (in John 14:3), as was indicated above – again, it too connecting us to this "new Jerusalem." And last, with the proper rendering of this verse ("abodes"), we see a reference to the believers in Christ of whom we now know make up this "new Jerusalem." Incidentally, this word for "abodes" is of the same word in the Bible for "abide," which brings us to the 15th chapter of the Gospel of John.

In this chapter, Jesus tells of Himself as being the true vine (Jn. 15:1-17). While explaining this, He also indicates that for Believers to live victoriously and thereby bear fruit, they have to learn to **ABIDE** in Him. For example He says, "He that abideth in me, and I in him, the same bringeth forth much fruit: for without me ye can do nothing" (Jn. 15:5). Interestingly enough, He uses this very same word at least 8 other times in just this one passage (Jn. 15:4, 5, 6, 7, 10). Essentially, the point here is that in John 14:2, though the word "abode" is used of a place metaphorically (mistranslated as "mansion"), it really is to be understood as "a place of being in" or "the state of remaining in" Christ. Thus in the case of the Believer, this is an eternal abode that forever puts us in Christ. Unfortunately, with the use of the word "mansion," especially in light of what our normal understanding of what a mansion is, the intended message of what Jesus was really trying to communicate has instead become very misleading. Although a "mansion" may be popular for our "Sunday School Theology," it nevertheless only distorts the message of what Christ was truly trying to communicate to us – that He would provide a way for people to spiritually "abide" in Him and therefore be able to live as a part of the household of God. At the same time, it also demonstrates in yet another way just how the "new Jerusalem" is not to be understood as a real or literal city. Rather, it is symbolic. This, incidentally, brings us to still another end-time subject related to this "new Jerusalem" – that being "The 144,000" witnesses of Revelation.

Chapter 27

"The 144,000"

You probably noticed already that the last few chapters have been basically devoted to the subject of the "bride" of Christ, meaning the Church. It was pointed out how the "new Jerusalem" is a symbolic portrayal of God's people from both the Old and New Covenants. It was also demonstrated that there aren't to be any future mansions prepared for us. Additionally, we covered the uniqueness of the "marriage supper" that we are to some day partake in. Of course, each of these explanations provided are far from the normal or traditional point of view. But I can't apologize for that. God's Word speaks for itself. Of course, there is still another subject that can be discussed that is also not traditional in its Biblical explanation. So also does this subject relate to the Body of Christ. As you can gather from the above title, I am speaking of the topic of the 144,000 sealed witnesses of Revelation.

The subject of the 144,000 sealed witnesses was revealed to the Apostle John in a couple of different visions. The primary question for us regards just who they actually are? They are viewed as being already in heaven and thus, one religious persuasion has actually organized itself based largely on this very belief. The Jehovah's Witnesses consider these as the cream of the crop as far as God's people are concerned and therefore resign themselves to the belief that these 144,000 have already been identified (or sealed). Thus, they believe that they (the 144,000) alone already are assured of their future blessed standing with God whereas everyone else has to still work to earn somewhat of an intermediate type of standing with Him. This is due to the belief that these 144,000 are said to have already been sealed!

The traditional bent regarding the 144,000, however, is somewhat varied. Some understand it as being a literal amount while others treat it as symbolic. Unfortunately, it seems neither viewpoint does the Bible justice when it comes to diligently examining this subject. For all intents and purposes, the 144,000 are identified as being 12 groups of 12,000 each. They are characterized as being witnesses while also originating from the 12 tribes of Israel. They are already sealed by God and additionally, even have His name written on their foreheads. But how to fully comprehend their actual role in the end-times continues to be in question? And yet there is a clue to help open up the understanding on this subject that few seem to realize, even though it too is found in John's book of Revelation.

Believe it or not, the 144,000 is a symbolic picture of, once again, the Body of Christ. The understanding of this is derived from the same 21st chapter of Revelation that John used to describe the "new Jerusalem." As John described this city, he indicated many unique characteristics that seemed to highlight how it was constructed, only these were again to be understood as symbols as opposed to being taken literally. The tendency to interpret the "new Jerusalem" as a literal city would normally presuppose that. However, God's Word has indicated otherwise. That the "new Jerusalem" is now understood as being symbolic therefore requires the same general treatment for its characteristics. Accordingly, this includes the interpreting of the city's wall, its measurements, and also its foundations. In so doing, God's Word actually portrays the building up of this city, or the Body of Christ, on the part of 12 foundations, each symbolizing the work of the 12 Apostles of the Lord Jesus Christ. It also reveals how the wall of this city is formed uniquely from 12 precious stones, each symbolizing one of the 12 tribes of Israel. Taken together, these symbols are provided to reflect both the Old and New Covenant Believers of whom collectively make up the overall Body of Christ. Of course, a more thorough examination of this explanation is provided in the next section of this chapter. But again, the thing to realize in general is that God's Word reveals more than we realize and in particular, this is especially true in the case of the end-time city known as the "new Jerusalem." This, incidentally, becomes even more evident with a proper understanding of these 144,000 sealed witnesses.

"The 144,000"
Scripturally Explained

At this point, bearing in mind the symbolic interpretation of the "new Jerusalem" along with its lack of mansions, you might still wonder, "But what about all the precious stones and the streets of gold, etc. that we have heard about?" — such as what is listed in Revelation 21:17-21. To be sure, these also are simply metaphorical or symbolic representations that help to identify this city as actually being the Body of Christ. For example in verse 19, John says of the 12 <u>"foundations of the wall of the city</u> that they are garnished with all manner of <u>precious stones</u>." The 12 precious stones are then listed which, ironically, relate back to both the <u>old</u> city of Jerusalem as identified in the Old Testament as well as the particulars regarding the priesthood's role of leading worship. Specifically the priest, in representing those participating in worship, was ordered by God to wear an ephod. This ephod, which was an important and unique part of his garment, had four individual rows of three stones each on it, thereby totaling 12 individual stones. Each one of these stones, incidentally, represented one of the 12 tribes of Israel. Of course they each were different (see Ex. 28:15-21), just as the 12 stones of the "new Jerusalem" also were as we find in Revelation 21:19-20. The bottom line though is that these 12 stones symbolically reflected the 12 tribes of Israel and thus, they are representative of God's own people as according to the Old Covenant.

It is important to note that it is in this city's wall where these 12 stones are actually found. Incidentally, it is in this very same wall that we also find 12 foundations. Remembering then that these same 12 foundations are symbolic of the New Testament's 12 Apostles, we can therefore conclude that they, on the other hand, are representative of God's people according to the New Covenant. Essentially, we can see then that this wall is actually a very telling sign for from it, we symbolically see a portrayal of both the Old and New Testament Saints of God. Interestingly enough, John gives us another amazing verse at this point. In Revelation 21:17, he says of an angel (of whom he is conversing with about this particular city), "And he measured the wall thereof, an <u>hundred and fourty and four</u>

cubits, according to the measure of a man." Remembering again that this "new Jerusalem" is actually a symbol for the Body of Christ, we now find that it has a very unique wall and that this wall not only has a measurement that is symbolic, but that it also happens to total 144 cubits. So also does John tell us in the verse prior to that, in verse 16, that "the city lieth foursquare, and the length is as large as the breadth: and he measured the city with the reed, twelve thousand furlongs." Here, we likewise see that the city's collective length and breadth are measured and, in fact, total out at 12,000 furlongs. To help us better understand them, these two important measurements are depicted below according to the way that John actually described them:

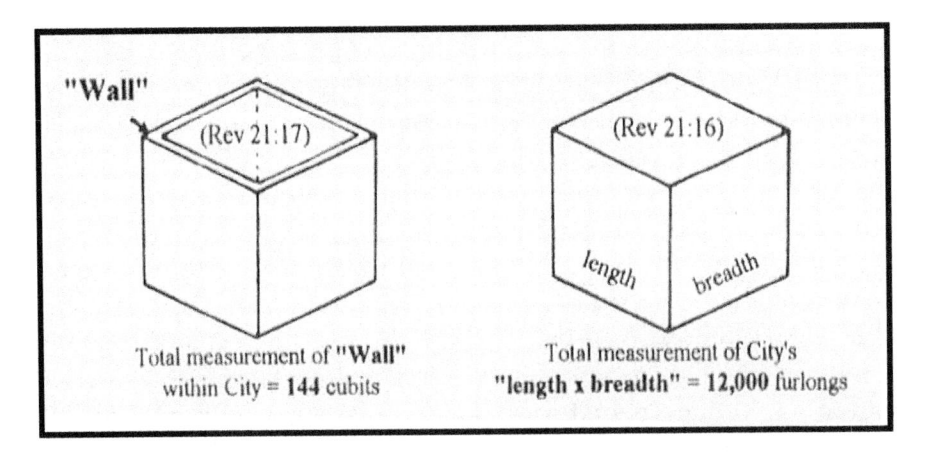

"Wall"
(Rev 21:17)

Total measurement of "Wall" within City = 144 cubits

(Rev 21:16)
length   breadth

Total measurement of City's "length x breadth" = 12,000 furlongs

Notice, however, that up to this point the heighth has been left out in describing this city's measurements. Still, we at least have the basic understanding regarding this city that the "length and the breadth and the height of it are equal" (vs. 16). With the heighth not really being specified, we instead have the measurement of 12,000 furlongs that was given to compute this height, though we understand it to be merely that of the city's foundation. However, another of this city's important characteristic given that can help us in this regard is found in verse 14, in which we are told that "the wall of the city had twelve foundations." It is from this very detail that we can now determine the heighth (given as 12 foundations) and, as a result, therefore add it into the equation, thereby computing the city's total measurement as 144,000 furlongs (12 foundations of 12,000 furlongs each computes to 144,000 total furlongs). Again, the following pictures help to illustrate this calculation:

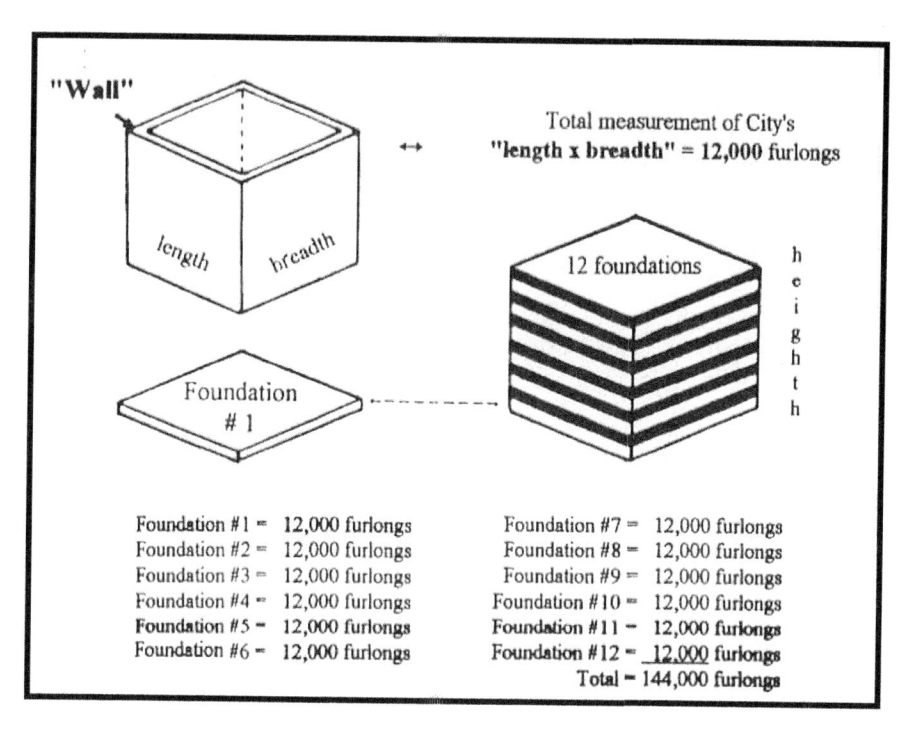

```
"Wall"
                                    Total measurement of City's
                                    "length x breadth" = 12,000 furlongs

length   breadth              12 foundations     h
                                                 e
                                                 i
                                                 g
                                                 h
Foundation                                       t
   # 1                                           h


Foundation #1 =  12,000 furlongs    Foundation #7  =  12,000 furlongs
Foundation #2 =  12,000 furlongs    Foundation #8  =  12,000 furlongs
Foundation #3 =  12,000 furlongs    Foundation #9  =  12,000 furlongs
Foundation #4 =  12,000 furlongs    Foundation #10 =  12,000 furlongs
Foundation #5 =  12,000 furlongs    Foundation #11 =  12,000 furlongs
Foundation #6 =  12,000 furlongs    Foundation #12 =  12,000 furlongs
                                            Total = 144,000 furlongs
```

Now, remembering also that the wall's measurement (of 144 cubits) is said to be "according to the measure of man" (vs. 17 — the definite article "a" is not in the Greek text, thereby rendering it this way), we can therefore conclude that the unit of measurement used here (as "cubits") is actually symbolic for people ("men"). This, of course, leads us to yet another end-time subject, that being the 144,000 sealed witnesses of Revelation 7:4 and 14:1. In each of these cases, what really is being referred to is another symbolic portrayal of the "new Jerusalem" (or again, the Bride of Christ). For example, in the case of Revelation 14:1 we read, "And I looked, and, lo, a Lamb stood on the mount Sion, and with him an hundred fourty and four thousand, having his Father's name written in their foreheads." Remembering again the earlier discussion of the "mark of the beast," it was noted that a "mark" represented spiritual allegiance. That it went on the forehead was a reference to the Old Testament practice of the priests putting Scriptures on their foreheads in order to signify their allegiance to Jehovah God. In effect then, they too would have their "Father's name written in their foreheads," demonstrating that they belonged to God. Likewise, in a similar manner this applies to God's people of today. In other words, the mark of God's Spirit has now been written on our hearts and is therefore, spiritually, seen as being in our minds (we have the "mind of Christ" according to 1 Cor. 2:16) and on our foreheads. Thus, this reference to the 144,000 sealed witnesses again symbolically refers to God's people. Of course, this does not at all mean that there are only 144,000 such people. Rather, this is simply a symbolic picture of the whole of it. In this particular reference, we see also that John is giving us a picture of Jesus Christ having just returned, standing on Mount Zion, together with His Bride (symbolically portrayed as the 144,000 sealed witnesses). Of course, this still does not explain for us that other reference given of these 144,000 sealed witnesses, or Revelation 7:4. For an explanation of this reference, we will continue on into the next chapter and examine the Biblical meaning of "The Fullness of Times."

Chapter 28

"The Fullness of Times"

There is a particular passage in Revelation that while describing some of the details to occur during the tribulation period, John also indicates that prior to their occurrence, the sealing of the 144,000 must take place. This again brings us back to the subject of the 144,000 sealed witnesses. In that we have just established that the sealing of the 144,000 is actually a symbolic portrayal of the whole Body of Christ, it allows for us to discover even more insights into God's Word. In effect, what we can learn is that the precondition for the occurrence of these end-time events, of which John is referring to, is what is called "the fullness of times." As a matter of fact, the Apostle Paul in another passage of Scripture tells us that prior to Israel's experiencing God's deliverance, "the fullness of times" must first be fulfilled, or completed. This of course begs the question of what exactly is meant by "the fullness of times?"

Most of us already believe that God is omniscient — that is, He is all-knowing. Accordingly, we can therefore assume that God already knows not only all who will become Believers in His Son, but also just exactly who they are. In other words, He knows already, by name, each person that is to become one of His children. Of course, this also implies that the entire process necessary for all that are to become His children has yet to fully occur. In others words, the full period needed is not yet complete. Applying some logic here, we can imagine then that at some point in the future, there will actually be a last or final person that will respond to Him, thereby completing the full "list" of Believers, if you will. That person would then complete the Body of Christ, if you know what I mean. Applying this particular logic then, it allows for us to now imagine this – what if you could determine just exactly when it will be that the last person to come into the fold will take place? Could you then quite possibly have a better timetable to work with as far as calculating some of these end-time events? The answer of course is yes, in theory, but not necessarily in actuality. Unless of course, God in His Word tells us otherwise. Again, using this same logic, I would like to begin a process of examining some additional passages of Scripture that at least for me, I find very intriguing, yet I believe you will too.

In this case, it seems God establishes in Scripture that He has already determined the times and the seasons. In particular, He even knows just when the Body of Christ will have been completed. As a matter of fact, He even has it further broken down into two categories – Believers that are Jews and Believers that are non-Jews. These non-Jews, incidentally, are called in Scripture "Gentiles." Interestingly enough, God has prescribed a period of time already for the allowance of the Gentiles to become a part of His people. Accordingly, this age of the Gentiles will eventually come to a close. As a matter of fact, at some particular point in the future, the last Gentile will enter into the Body of Christ. Of course, it will be at this exact point in time that this era will then be considered complete. It seems, incidentally, that both the Apostles John and Paul were very much aware of this and accordingly, each made some form of reference to it in their writings. Of course in John's case, it comes up in this very same passage regarding this symbolic reference to the 144,000 sealed witnesses. In that he tells us that this is a condition (the sealing of the 144,000) necessary to be completed prior to some stated end-time events, we can therefore determine that these same events then are not to occur at least until after the completion of this period of when the Gentiles in full are a part of the Body of Christ. Of course, because of its symbolism, we already know that this is not limited to just a mere 144,000 people! That being said, what is amazing then is what John tells us for in this same passage, He essentially informs us that it is that divine consequence known as the "wrath of God" that is what is NOT to occur until after the Gentiles have fully come in. In other words, if you recall from our discussion of the "wrath of God," this is an event of judgment of which is to occur at the end of the tribulation period and yet, it is also to immediately precede the return of Christ. Of course, it likewise immediately follows that event known as the rapture. Thus, this essentially is one more clue provided by God to help indicate that Christians will in fact be around during the bulk of the tribulation period. But don't fret! Instead, remember again that the tribulation is predominantly an Israeli-Arab affair to be experienced primarily in the region of the Middle East.

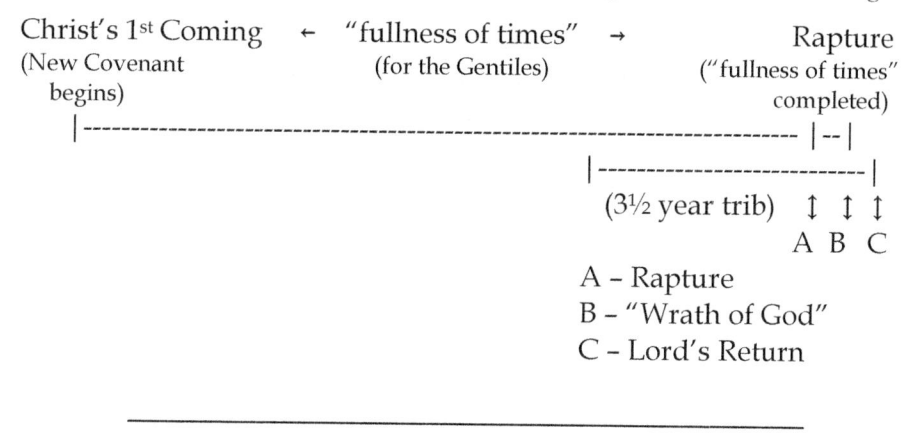

Christ's 1st Coming ← "fullness of times" → Rapture
(New Covenant (for the Gentiles) ("fullness of times"
begins) completed)
--	--

(3½ year trib) ↑ ↑ ↑
                                                A B C

A – Rapture
B – "Wrath of God"
C – Lord's Return

"The Fullness of Times"
Scripturally Explained

In reference to the other mentioning of the 144,000 sealed witnesses, we read of the Apostle John saying in Revelation 7:2-4:

> vs. 2 – "And I saw another angel ascending from the east, having the seal of the living God: and he cried with a loud voice to the four angels, to whom it was given to hurt the earth and the sea,"
>
> vs. 3 - "Saying, Hurt not the earth, neither the sea, nor the trees, **till <u>we have sealed the servants of our God in their foreheads</u>**."
>
> vs. 4 - "And I heard the number of them which were sealed: and <u>there were sealed an hundred and forty and four thousand</u> of all the tribes of the children of Israel."

It is necessary to note here that a key word in this passage is the word "till" found in verse 3. Although we see that the angels are prepared to hurt the earth, sea, and trees, we also are told that they must first wait for the fulfillment of a condition given them — that is, until all the servants of God have become sealed. From reading this passage, we can conclude at this point that the process of sealing all the witnesses has yet to be completed. At the same time however, although John specifies that these 144,000 come specifically from the 12 tribes of Israel, we now also understand that this is a symbolic representation for the entire Body of Christ. Of course, God provides us many other Scriptures to help back this same conclusion up.

For example, from Ephesians 1:13 we find that Paul indicates the important truth **that all Believers are sealed already by God the Holy Spirit**, "In whom ye also trusted, after that ye heard the word of truth, the gospel of your salvation: in whom also <u>after that ye believed, ye were sealed with that holy Spirit of promise</u>." As a matter of fact, we then can turn our attention to what Paul tells us in Romans 11:25-26, "That blindness in part has happened to Israel, <u>until the fulness of the Gentiles be come in</u>. And so <u>all Israel</u> shall be saved: as it is written, There shall come out of Sion the Deliverer, and shall turn away ungodliness from Jacob." This passage, although referring to Israel, actually gives us also an important detail regarding the Gentiles. In other words, conditional to Christ's return is first the completion of the "sealing" of Gentile Believers. God actually tells us this important detail for a reason. He is outlining His schedule regarding His divine plans and yet, He says here also that then, and only then, will all of Israel be considered saved. Of course, Israel in this case happens to actually be what is referred to as "spiritual" Israel. This, by the way, is a very important point for what many people do not realize is that even the Gentile Believer of today, from a Scriptural standpoint, is considered as being a Jew — of the tribe of Israel as a matter of fact, "And <u>if ye be Christ's</u>, then are ye <u>Abraham's seed</u>, and heirs according to the promise" (Gal. 3:29). In other words, because we are Believers, we are therefore also considered "spiritual Jews!" This of course is true because of the way God looks at things, "For he is not a Jew, which is one outwardly; ...<u>But he is a Jew, which is one inwardly</u>; and circumcision is that of the heart, <u>in the spirit</u>" (Rm. 2:28-29). Thus, we can see then that the Second Coming of Christ is actually conditioned upon the completion of "the fullness of times" of the Gentiles. This, of course, relates to the purpose of the New Covenant and, incidentally, it brings us to yet another verse of which few understand.

In Galatians 4:4, Paul gives us a verse in which again, few people have been able to fully explain its meaning, "But when the <u>fulness of the time</u> was come, God sent forth his Son, made of a woman, made under the law." From this verse, few have given an adequate explanation for what God meant by His Son coming in the "fullness of time." Incidentally, Paul continues in the next verse with this stated purpose, "<u>to redeem them that were under the law</u>, that we might receive the adoption of sons." Obviously, this verse helps to somewhat qualify the meaning of the phrase, "the fullness of time." However, Paul also adds in the preceding verse, "Even so we, <u>when we were children, were in bondage</u> under the elements of the world" (vs. 3). In other words, what this passage as a whole is attempting to say is that the Law, meant to help redeem people, was actually inadequate and therefore, in the "fullness of time," Christ came instead. This of course is speaking of His First Coming. Accordingly, we should understand then that it is related to the Old Covenant and therefore, specifically, it represents "literal" Israel. Of course in the same way, just as Christ's Second Coming is to take place when the "fulness of the Gentiles be come in" (Rm. 11:25), this then is based upon the New Covenant and accordingly, it is a representation of "spiritual" Israel. Certainly, we now know that Christ's First Coming took place in the fullness of time of when Old Testament Israel had finally and fully (in a general sense) come into His Body (the completion of the Old Covenant). Of course, it would serve us well at this point to include here something of which, fortunately, the Bible also teaches. As a matter of fact, it is not only encouraging, but also happens to bring about the very completion of this tribulation period. Of course, what I am referring to is that God has decreed that there yet remains a remnant from Israel of whom will eventually cry out to God, finally acknowledge that Yeshua is their Messiah, thereby experience salavation, and thus also become included as part of the seed of Abraham (Zech. 14).

Chapter 29

"Which Generation?"

You probably are aware already that there is a Biblical passage in which Jesus is talking to His disciples telling them of the signs to look for that help indicate that the end is near. These "signs of the times" include the mentioning of earthquakes, wars, famines, pestilences, and the like, and are said to precede the Lord's return. Incidentally, within this very same passage Jesus makes a statement addressing also just who it is that will be the witnesses of these same end-time signs. What Jesus says is found in Matthew 24:34 wherein He indicates that, "This generation shall not pass, till all these things be fulfilled." Because He specifies that a certain generation will experience these signs, one only needs to question just whom it is that He is referring to determine an approximate period of time in which to expect His return. In other words, the question of "Which generation?"

Believe it or not, the answer to this question doesn't need to be speculated about. Nor does it need to be thought of as being unknown. Actually, God reveals the very answer in His Word, though it seems that few again have ever connected the answer with this as the supposed question. In so doing, however, we will find the depths of God's Word opening up to us in even greater measure.

There is a unique "generation," incidentally, that is introduced to us within the pages of the New Testament. Amazing as it may be, we happen to discover that it is WE that are this unique generation! That is, we as Believers in Christ are the generation of whom Jesus was alluding to. Within the New Testament, the name given to uniquely identify this generation is that of the "chosen generation." Actually, the Apostle Peter identified us as such. Essentially, the Body of Believers under the New Covenant has been deemed a "chosen" people much like the Nation of Israel under the Old Covenant was also called the "chosen ones." But this generation is NOT one that is but 40 years in length, or 70, or even 120 for that matter, much like the length of some of the other types of generations might be. Instead, this generation spans approximately 2,000 years and, as a matter of fact, will also be that particular one that bears witness to the very signs of the times of which we said Jesus listed. By the way, this particular insight now only serves to reveal in more fullness the very intent of God's Word. For example, it now makes sense what Jesus was actually saying. That is, when He said these things to His disciples nearly 2,000 years ago, knowing that they were to become a part of this "chosen generation," it actually made perfect sense. These signs which to them He listed, He also knew would occur (or experience their fulfillment of) at some point during the existence of (actually near the completion of) this same generation of New Covenant Believers of whom were also referred to as the "chosen" ones.

"Which Generation?"
Scripturally Explained

In order to examine this question we must first return back to Matthew 24. In this chapter, again as was stated earlier, Jesus gives us His infamous Olivet Discourse just prior to His going to the cross. So also in this passage, Jesus foretells numerous events that will precede His Second Coming, to include the signs of the times, the tribulation, the rapture, and His return (vs. 3-33). Then in verse 34, Jesus says something very key to our understanding of these end-time events — "Verily I say unto you, <u>This generation shall not pass</u>, till all these things be fulfilled." Of course, the question to ask here is <u>which generation</u> was He referring to that "shall not pass," for He then indicates in verse 35 that "Heaven and earth <u>shall pass</u> away, but my <u>words shall not pass</u> away." Certainly, much debate has taken place regarding the proper interpretation for the question of "which generation" that Jesus was referring to. Upon further study, it becomes clear that there is not just one usage in Scripture of this word "generation" either, but rather many and thus the debate. For example, at times in Scripture a generation meant 70 years. Still other times, it meant 40 years. Yet even these two are not comprehensive in the word's use. Nevertheless, the most popular interpretations for the "generation" in this particular passage involve these same two usages. On the one hand, it was believed by many that Christ meant that those who witnessed Israel's reemergence as a people upon the climax of the First World War (the use of a 70 year generation) would also witness His return. On the other hand, others believed that those who actually witnessed Israel's rebirth as a legitimate or independent nation in 1948 (in this case, both the 40 and 70 year generations have been used in the interpretation) would witness His return. Yet even today, the infamous Six Day War of 1967 is considered by some for this interpretation (by using a 40 year generation). In any case, the bottom line is that the debate continues with little assurance either way of which interpretation adequately fits the equation. Nevertheless, bearing in mind all this debate regarding this subject, there yet remains another possibility which, although found in

Scripture, it seems no one even considers. Of course, it is this very possibility of which I would like to examine.

In First Peter 2:9, Peter tells us of the formation of another specific and yet unique "generation." The number of years assigned to this generation is really unknown at this time, yet it currently is still in existence and in fact, has been so for almost 2,000 years. Interestingly enough, this particular generation is none other than the same one referred to in the Bible to describe the whole of the New Testament believers in Christ — "But ye are a <u>chosen generation</u>, a royal priesthood, <u>an holy nation</u>, a peculiar people: that ye should shew forth the praises of him who hath called you out of darkness into his marvellous light: <u>Which in time past were not a people, but are now the people of God</u>." Specifically, this generation (referred to here as the "<u>chosen</u> generation") began to develop with the arrival of God's Son, Jesus Christ, at His First Coming and upon His death on the cross. Incidentally, it is still developing today and will continue to do so until ultimately, the Second Coming of Jesus Christ takes place. Of course, this generation is none other than that of the Body of Christ which has formed <u>as a result of the New Covenant</u> and therefore consists of all resultant believers in Christ, both Jew and Gentile alike. As a matter of fact, in God's eyes, He even refers to them as "an holy nation." This is especially significant because of the preceding parable which Jesus gives us in this same chapter of Matthew 24, "Now learn a parable of the <u>fig tree</u>; When his branch is yet tender, and putteth forth leaves, ye know that summer is nigh: So likewise ye, when ye shall see all these things, know that it is near, even at the doors" (Mt. 24:32-33). Of course as you probaby already know, the fig tree in Scripture is symbolic of the <u>actual</u> nation of Israel. Yet we must remember that Israel, in both Scripture and therefore in the eyes of God, is characterized also as being a <u>spiritual</u> nation, in this case consisting of the New Covenant Believers. In fact, in this very passage in First Peter they are actually referred to as "an <u>holy nation</u>," wherein God now calls them His people as well — a term reserved under the <u>Old Covenant</u> for the then "actual" nation of Israel, but instead here under the <u>New Covenant</u> as the now "spiritual" nation of Israel! Certainly then, it is this unique "chosen generation" referred to here of which now Scripturally fits the conditions given us by the Lord Jesus in Matthew 24:34. Interestingly enough, it is this very same generation of which, before it actually "passes away," we know will also witness the occurrence of all these end-time signs. God's Word seems to make this clearly evident. Hence, God's Word is truly amazing for once again, we discover that it not only speaks for itself, but it even does the interpreting for us.

The following timeline is provided to help portray this understanding of the "chosen generation," thus revealing how this same "generation" of whom Jesus was speaking to will also bear witness of the "signs of the times," the tribulation, and His return:

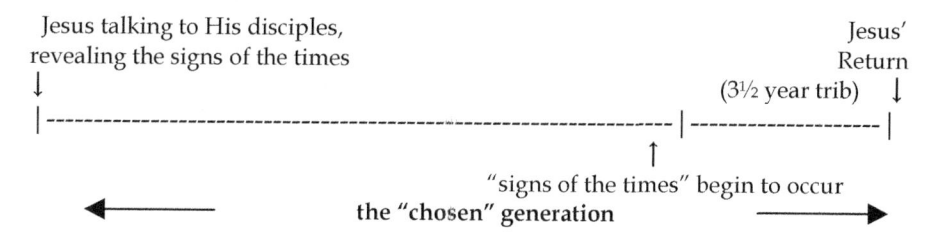

```
Jesus talking to His disciples,                                    Jesus'
revealing the signs of the times                                   Return
↓                                             (3½ year trib)   ↓
|----------------------------------------------|-------------------|
                                          ↑
                              "signs of the times" begin to occur
     ←————————          the "chosen" generation          ————————→
```

Dennis Crump

Chapter 30

"Heaven and Earth Pass Away"

In the previous chapter, it was explained that the "generation" that would witness the "signs of the times" was the "chosen generation." This subject arose from within the Olivet Discourse that Jesus gave us as recorded in the 24th chapter of Matthew. From this same chapter there arises yet another subject meriting discussion – that of the "heaven and earth passing away." If you recall, Jesus actually tells us that "heaven and earth shall pass away" in Matthew 24:35. But what does He really mean by this statement? To most people, it seems fairly obvious. That is, upon the return of Jesus Christ, God would create a new heaven and earth to replace our existing one. At least this is what I was taught for so many years. But is this really what we should expect? If we examine the Scriptures more thoroughly, the answer is amazingly different than this supposed conclusion.

Consider at first this question. If God, after completing this original creation by the end of those first six days on earth, told us that it was finished, why then would He create anything more, especially after already indicating that He was done creating things? Obviously, if we assume the earth is going to be destroyed, it would make sense that God would have to create another one. However, could it be possible that we have assumed this wrongly, that is, that the actual planet called "Earth" is not going to be destroyed? Upon further examination of Scripture, you will discover that the answer is a definite yes!

Actually, the earth is not going to be completely destroyed, and neither is heaven. Instead, there is going to be what would be considered as a major "change" that takes place, in this case in both heaven and upon the earth. This particular "change," if you will, will actually be the third time that a change of this type takes place. The type of change that I am referring to is, however, one that you probably would not normally consider. It is actually a change in the way that the spiritual realm is governed as well as the natural realm. In this particular case, the spiritual realm is referred to as "heaven" with the natural realm being "earth." Thus, the "passing away" of the "heaven and earth" is a statement used to describe this particular process of change. Of course, this is probably not something you would normally be taught, although it is Biblically sound.

If you have had any Biblical background, you will recall that from the time that God first created the heaven and earth up until the time of the great flood and Noah's Ark, a certain type or form of government controlled both the spiritual realm and the natural realm. For instance, the entire earth was basically tropical in climate and there had yet to be any form of rain. However with the post-flood era, in the natural realm came the climactic changes of the four seasons, to include the introduction of both rain and snow. In the spiritual realm and therefore in God's relationship to man, you had Him relating to Adam and Eve in the Garden of Eden, you also had the strangely unique experience of the Nephilim (giants/angels) cohabiting with humans, and you even had the amazingly recorded lifespans of people being well over hundreds of years in age, just to name a few examples. In other words, the Biblical record of this type of government or administration (or this period of time) was what was called the "first heaven and earth."

Following the flood, a second type of "heaven and earth" began. This form of government included, again as was just stated above, the seasons and changes in climate. Additionally however, there was the introduction of covenant theology to help govern the spiritual realm. In other words, God began to relate to man on the basis of first, the old covenant, followed by the new covenant. Basically, you could say that there existed now various new and/or different "principles" to help govern both the spiritual and natural realms. Essentially then, this is what the Bible would imply as being the "second heaven and earth."

As you can see, because there was <u>no newly created</u> "heaven and earth," human life therefore transitioned naturally from the first one right on into the second one. Of course when it comes to the subject of the end-times, God's Word still tells us of a future or "new heaven and earth" — one that will soon follow these other two. Nevertheless, this new one is not to be understood as actually being a <u>newly created</u> "heaven and earth," but rather as a new <u>form of government</u> in both the spiritual and natural realms. In other words, at the time of the Lord Jesus Christ's return to earth, He will set up this new type of government, thereby bringing to pass at that particular point the so-called <u>passing away</u> of the old one (or the second "heaven and earth"). The bottom line is that this will therefore constitute that fulfillment of Jesus' words wherein He states, "<u>Heaven and earth shall pass away</u>" (Mt. 24:35). Hence, this is the Bible's interpretation for this end-time subject. Once again, in order to better help you understand this explanation from a Biblical basis, I will go into further detail in the next portion of this chapter.

"Heaven and Earth Pass Away"
Scripturally Explained

In yet another end-time event worthy of discussion from that very same passage in the last chapter regarding the "(chosen) generation," Jesus informs us that at some point in the future "heaven and earth shall pass away" (Mt 24:35). Of course, the question to be asked is what is the Scriptural meaning of this? Interestingly enough, this event is given even more attention in other passages of Scripture. For example, the Apostle John writes in Revelation, "And I saw a new heaven and a new earth: for the first heaven and the first earth were passed away" (Rev. 21:1). He mentions this also in Revelation 20:11. So too, the Apostle Peter addresses this event in his second letter (in 2 Peter 3:1-13). Even the Apostle Paul makes mention of this event in 2 Corinthians 12, although in his case it is less obvious to the reader, of which I will discuss in the next chapter of this book. But first, let us consider what Peter said about this subject because, unfortunately, it seems that another misrepresentation of what the Bible truly has to say has taken place due to our traditional understanding of it.

In Peter's account, he wraps up the handling of this particular event by saying, "Nevertheless we, according to his promise, look for new heavens and a new earth, wherein dwelleth righteousness" (2 Pt. 3:13). This he mentions immediately following an allusion to Christ's Second Coming in which he says, "the heavens being on fire shall be dissolved, and the elements shall melt with fervent heat" (2 Pt. 3:12). He states this very same thing, however, in another way in verse 10, "But the day of the Lord will come as a thief in the night; in which the heavens shall pass away with a great noise, and the elements shall melt with fervent heat, the earth also and the works therein shall be burned up." It seems that from these verses, most have concluded that God is going to replace (or recreate) the planet Earth, as well as His Heaven, with new ones. In other words, He will actually destroy the current ones, doing so by the process of using a great fire with extreme heat. As a matter of fact, many prophecy students have even gone so far as to speculate here on the cause of this fire and heat, offering an all-out nuclear holocaust as their suggested way for its fulfillment. Unfortunately, not only is the Bible silent on this fire's actual cause, but actually this entire interpretation lacks Scriptural merit. Let's consider again what the Bible really says regarding this event of the "heaven and earth passing away."

To be sure, Peter himself does an adequate job of handling this subject, though it has escaped the attention of so many. What has been the problem with most peoples' interpretations, unfortunately, is not their understanding regarding the <u>removal</u> of the "heaven and the earth," but rather their idea of WHAT it is that God actually meant by the "heaven and the earth." To better explain this, first realize that Peter, beginning in verses 3 and 4 of chapter 3, while alluding to the scoffers of that day concerning the talk of Christ's second coming, nevertheless gives a reminder to the reader that "all things continue as they were from the beginning of the creation" (2 Pt. 3:4). Then, beginning in the very next verse, Peter starts to describe what would be considered in Scripture as the very <u>first governing period</u>, or "heaven and earth" which, for the purpose of being able to better understand this event, I will refer to here as a dispensation. In other words, this first "heaven and earth" dispensation can therefore best be understood as the first administrative type of system or rule, designated by God, which He used to order the activity and operation of both the heavens and the earth. Bearing this in mind, now notice what He says next, "For this they willingly are ignorant of, that by the word of God the <u>heavens</u> were of old, and the <u>earth</u> standing out of the water and in the water: Whereby the world that then was, being overflowed with water, perished" (vs. 5-6). In other words, this first dispensation of the "heavens and the earth," according to Peter, lasted from the beginning of creation up until and culminating with the great flood of Noah's day (Gen. 6-9). Then at that point, the <u>second</u> "heaven and earth" dispensation began and, incidentally, has continued on even until now. Amazingly, notice what Peter then says as he continues in the very next verse, "<u>But the heavens and the earth, which are now</u>, by the same word are kept in store, reserved unto fire against the day of judgment and perdition of ungodly men" (vs. 7). Specifically, you should notice that up to this point, Peter has only spoken of a "heaven and earth" type of dispensation <u>twice</u> — the former one being from the very beginning up until the flood and the current one being from the flood until now, even lasting up until the return of

Jesus Christ. Then upon Christ's return, Peter tells us in verse 13 to look for what would then be a new "heaven and earth" dispensation which, in this case, would be the THIRD such one. This, of course, takes place during the Millennial rule of Christ as the "King of Kings and Lord of Lords" in which, by the way, the order of rule will then be "righteousness" (again see 2 Pt. 3:13). Accordingly, a chronological picture of these three such "heaven and earth" periods looks something like this:

"Heaven & Earth" Dispensations:

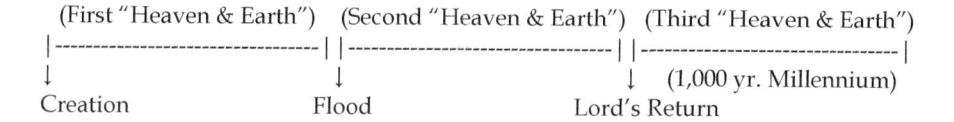

```
(First "Heaven & Earth")   (Second "Heaven & Earth")   (Third "Heaven & Earth")
|-------------------------| |-------------------------| |-------------------------|
↓                           ↓                           ↓  (1,000 yr. Millennium)
Creation                    Flood                       Lord's Return
```

It is worth noting here a few additional points regarding this subject. We are told also that the first "heaven and earth" type of dispensation was destroyed because of the great wickedness of man that at that time existed (Gen. 6:5-7). The means for destruction then was water, as in the great flood of Noah's day. Ironically in Matthew 24:35, immediately following Jesus' statement of the "heaven and earth passing away," He then added, "But as the days of Noah were, so shall also the coming of the Son of man be. For as in the days that were before the flood they were eating and drinking, marrying and giving in marriage, until the day that Noah entered into the ark, and knew not until the flood came, and took them all away; so shall also the coming of the Son of man be" (vs. 37-39). In other words, in the case of the second "heaven and earth" dispensation, so too will the cause for its destruction be, as stated by Peter, because of a great deal of ungodliness on the part of the people (2 Pt. 3:7). As a matter of fact, prior to Paul's description in another passage of the great depravity that God indicates will occur, he actually stated this as being the case, "For the wrath of God is revealed from heaven against all ungodliness and unrighteousness of men" (Rm. 1:18). Paul then followed with a description of our present condition of great depravity among mankind (vs. 19-32). The means of destruction however, as earlier indicated by Peter, would this time be by fire as opposed to being by water as in Noah's day (2 Pt. 3:7).

Incidentally, with respect to this "fire," another point to consider is just how the Bible uses this particular word for in many cases, it is actually symbolic of judgment. For example, Paul writes, "Every man's work shall be made manifest: for the day shall declare it, because it shall be revealed by fire; <u>and the fire shall try</u> every man's work of what sort it is" (1 Cor. 3:13). Here we see that Paul uses the analogy of a trial, by court of law, in which fire is used symbolically as the means for bringing about judgment. As far as the second "heaven and earth" is concerned, whether the fire that destroys it is actually real, symbolic, or even both is admittedly uncertain. What is certain, however, is that our planet (and heaven for that matter) will not literally or fully be destroyed, or else how would Jesus afterwards be able to set up His Millennial Kingdom on it (see Rev. 20:4), especially when you consider that He has already finished His work of creating things (Gen. 2:1-4, Ex. 20:11)? Remember also that in the case of the <u>first</u> "heaven and earth," neither did the flood back then actually destroy the whole entire planet, but rather just the face of it. Yet the result of this "limited" destruction was still a significant change in the systematic or administrative order of rule on earth – resulting actually in our current <u>second</u> "heaven and earth." Remaining consistent then, we can therefore expect a similar "limited" type of destruction when it comes to the ending of this current "heaven and earth" – that is, some form of change on the face of the earth will be manifested more so by the changes in both the spiritual and natural realms.

As a matter of fact, another point to consider from Peter's passage is the Bible's interpretation for the word "elements" since he says that they too will be melted with fervent heat (2 Pt. 3: 10, 12). Unfortunately, this word having been translated as "elements" has resulted in what is actually a misinterpretation of this particular passage for, in actuality, the original Greek word that is used is more properly rendered as "principles." In other words, versus thinking of the earth's various "elements" (such as the metallic ones, etc.) as being destroyed, we should understand these rather as being "those basic principles that govern the world's system" (ELEMENTS, Vine's, p. 22-23) as being destroyed. The Greek word used here is "stoicheion" which, by the way, is used elsewhere in the New Testament just five other times. For example, Paul used it in a verse to indicate that before salvation, we actually "were in bondage under the <u>elements</u> (principles) of the world" (Gal. 4:3). He also used this word twice in the book of Colossians, only in these instances it is translated as "rudiments" rather than "elements" — "Beware lest any man spoil you through philosophy and vain deceit, after the tradition of men, after the <u>rudiments</u> (Greek word "stoicheion," meaning principles) of the world, and not after Christ" (Col. 2:8) and "Wherefore if ye be dead with Christ from the <u>rudiments</u> (principles) of the world, why, as though living in the world, are ye subject to ordinances...?" (Col. 2:20). In each case, you will clearly notice that the word translated here in no way is speaking of the earth's metallic elements, but rather as the <u>principles</u> that govern the way the world operates, known more or less as the principles or laws of worldliness. Of course, this makes all that Peter was saying regarding the "heaven and earth" all the more plausible. In other words, what we should understand is that God is going to destroy (or "try") the world (or its "principles") with judgment (or "fire") and thereby replace it with a new system of rule (or a "new heaven and earth") wherein, or in this case, dwelleth righteousness — this of course being fulfilled by the establishment of the coming Millennial Kingdom that will take place here on earth.

Dennis Crump

Chapter 31

"The Third Heaven (or Paradise!)"

In that the last chapter demonstrated that the "new heaven and earth" would actually be the third such type of "heaven and earth" governing system set up by God, the next question for us regards, in particular, the subject of the "third heaven!" How do we explain the "third heaven" that the Apostle Paul talked about in 2 Corinthians 12? It is in this chapter that Paul tells us of man who experienced being caught up into this "third heaven." Paul also in this chapter describes his own personal struggle with the temptation of being proud, as in wanting to boast. It is in this context that the teachers of tradition then provide an interpretation for this passage that unfortunately denies an amazing truth of which God has already conveyed to us. The popular belief is that Paul is the sole person referred to in this passage. That is, he was the one caught up into the "third heaven." This experience, evidently being so blissful and glorious for him, accordingly became the cause of a constant battle within him – that is, the personal struggle with wanting to boast of this surreal experience. In other words, I was taught that Paul was describing himself in this passage, that his previously recorded initial and amazing encounter with the Lord Jesus Christ was probably this "third heaven" experience (more than likely a spiritually transcendent type of experience in which he encountered Christ as no one ever before had), and thus he probably even witnessed things in the highest levels of heaven. Strangely however, he supposedly was also forbidden from then even sharing about them. Because these things were so glorious, he in turn encountered a constant struggle within himself of pride due to what he now knew. Thus, Paul was the apparent recipient of this "third heaven" type of experience, or at least this is what I was taught. However upon further examination, it seems God's Word amazingly and, once again, tells us a different story altogether.

Somewhere along the way, tradition seemed to figure that a "third heaven" was something that was two levels higher than the first one. In other words, the idea crept in that heaven was arranged with different levels, if you will, each ascending higher than the last. It was assumed then that each level represented a higher and/or deeper level in experiencing heaven (deeper spiritual experiences). This presupposition then became the window from which this subject would always be evaluated and in turn, it never seemed to be questioned, almost as if there was a veil over our eyes to prevent us from doing so. However, as is so often the case with God's Word, the depths of it seem to never fully be discovered and, in time, God even begins to incrementally open up our eyes in order that we might see more fully various aspects of His message to us. In this matter, this seems to once again be the case. The "third heaven" is not to be understood in terms of three separate levels, but rather as three separate periods of time. As in the last chapter, the third heaven is that third period of time depicting the unique type of rule that eventually will be governing the atmosphere of both the heaven and earth. In other words, Paul is actually referring to the same "new heaven and earth" that was discussed in the previous chapter.

Because this "third heaven" of 2 Corinthians 12 is therefore a reference to the Millennial Kingdom of Christ, then it also demands further explanation regarding the very man who witnessed it. Was it really the Apostle Paul? In most cases, a casual reading of this chapter just leaves one confused, especially in trying to determine who Paul was referring to. But when it is considered to be Paul himself as the one of whom he is referring to, it seems even all the more confusing. The very style of writing that he used, admittedly, comes off as awkward and sounds confusing. Yet again, there is that presupposition when reading it that it must be Paul, even though that cannot be adequately proven. However, it is necessary to know at this point that there definitely exists another character in Scripture who also experienced this "third heaven." As a matter of fact, he actually experienced it by both visions and revelations. On top of that, he even experienced it while being "in the spirit," meaning that it cannot be determined whether he was in the body or out of it. Another important detail is that he even had his experience at least 14 years prior to Paul's recording of it. This being the case, it surely ought to put into question whether Paul was actually speaking of himself, again as is supposed. And oh, by the way, this other character happened to even be forbidden from uttering anything about it! So then, who is it that I am referring to? Think "Revelation" as a hint. That's right, it is the Apostle John! John is the person who was actually caught up into the "third heaven" when he, while in the spirit, had visions of the Millennial rule of Christ. He had these some 14 years earlier than the writing of Paul's Second letter to the Corinthians and incidentally, he was even prohibited from uttering to anyone the details of some of this experience. Of course, this "third heaven" was also referred to as a "paradise" in Scripture and thus, he even experienced that! Understandably, this is not exactly your typical explanation for this subject and yet, it remarkably is Scriptural of which I would like to share with you just exactly how as we continue in the next section of this chapter.

"The Third Heaven (or Paradise!)"
Scripturally Explained

In what is yet another topic with end-time implications, we need to examine the "third heaven." In other words, we must ask the question, "Who was it that was caught up into the third heaven?" For this we must return again to the Apostle Paul's writings, only this time in Second Corinthians chapter 12. Here, Paul first tells us of a man who had "visions and revelations of the Lord" (vs. 1). He also indicates that from the actual time of his penning this Epistle, to him their occurrence was some "fourteen years ago" (vs. 2). He then goes on to tell of some of the circumstances surrounding this experience (vs. 2-4) while even sharing of the great temptation to boast that for this man followed (vs. 5-10). For most scholars, the interpretation of this passage is that the Apostle Paul was referring to himself. They base this conclusion primarily on the time element (at least 14 years earlier) and, of course, the previously understood circumstances surrounding Paul's initial encounter with the Lord while on the Damascus Road (Acts 9, 22). Unfortunately this interpretation, although possible circumstantially, still leaves the passage confusing at best, especially when you consider from a literary perspective how Paul chooses to describe this encounter. Yet aside from having Paul as being this man, few other seemingly adequate explanations have really been made. Of course, when it comes to identifying whom Paul was truly speaking of, since we can be assured that the Bible is capable of speaking for itself, we can again ask, "What really saith the Scriptures?"

Notice first of all verses 1 through 6 of this passage in Second Corinthians 12 which are stated as follows:

>*vs. 1 - "It is not expedient for me doubtless to glory. I will come to visions and revelations of the Lord."*
>
>*vs. 2 - "I knew a man in Christ above fourteen years ago, (whether in the body, I cannot tell; or whether out of the body, I cannot tell: God knoweth;) such an one caught up to the third heaven."*
>
>*vs. 3 - "And I knew such a man, (whether in the body, or out of the body, I cannot tell: God knoweth;)"*

> vs. 4 - "*How that he was caught up into paradise, and heard unspeakable words, which it is not lawful for a man to utter.*"
>
> vs. 5 - "*Of such an one will I glory: yet of myself I will not glory,* but in mine infirmities."
>
> vs. 6 - "For though I would desire to glory, I shall not be a fool; for I will say the truth: but now I forbear, lest any man should think of me above that which he seeth me to be, or that he heareth of me."

Interestingly enough, the person Paul is talking about here is really not himself, but rather the Apostle John, and this becomes increasingly more obvious when comparing this passage with John's book of Revelation. Speaking of the man who had "visions and revelations of the Lord," notice what John actually says in his opening record of Revelation, "The <u>Revelation of Jesus Christ</u>, which God gave unto him, to shew unto his servants things which must shortly come to pass; and he sent and signified it by his angel unto his servant John" (Rev. 1:1). Here we see that John has a "revelation of the Lord" and, although the word is singular, it is indicative of the overall revelation which, as earlier pointed out, consists not of just one revelation, but rather of a series of mini-revelations or as Paul also calls them, "visions." Paul then states that John had these revelations at least fourteen years earlier. What is important to note at this point is that although the Bible is inerrant and infallible, historians are not. In other words, although many historians seem to think that John wrote his book around 90-95 A.D. (2 Corinthians is believed to be written around 57 A.D.), this is really not conclusive. In fact, there exists numerous evidence otherwise to indicate that this book may have been written earlier, even before Paul's writings. Nevertheless, even if John had written his book in the 90's, it would not necessarily have meant that he would have had to have his experience right at that same time. Certainly, he could have had his revelations years earlier, only choosing to instead document them at this point in time. There is, however, yet another clue (in the Bible as a matter of fact) to help us better determine the date of John's writing of Revelation. The Apostle Paul himself tells us that, as far as the Bible is concerned, he was the last writer of Scripture. In other words, God actually commissioned Paul to be the one who would ultimately complete the writing of His Word. Notice this commentary, for example, given us by Paul, "Whereof I am made a minister, according to the dispensation of God which is given to me for you, <u>to fulfil the word of God</u>" (Col. 1:25). Believe it or not, this word "fulfil" in the original Greek text actually means "to complete," thus indicating to us that John would have had to have written the book of Revelation sometime before the completion of Paul's writings, else Paul would not be the one "to <u>complete</u> the word of God." Incidentally, the historians also believed that Paul's writings were completed sometime by the year 70 A.D..

At any rate, as Paul continues his explanation of this account in 2 Corinthians, he mentions also of how he was unsure whether this individual was actually in the body or out of it when he experienced these revelations. Of course in Revelation, neither does John indicate the same regarding himself. Rather, John only says of himself regarding these visions that either "I was in the spirit" (Rev. 1:10; 4:1), or "I saw" (Rev. 6:1; 7:1), or even "I beheld" (Rev. 5:6,11; 6:5,12; 7:9), etc. — in most cases, each of these statements indicating either the explanation of or else the beginning of a brand new vision. At any rate, it is Paul who then shares how this man was "caught up to the <u>third heaven</u>." Unfortunately, many erroneous teachings have emanated from this statement, to include the teaching of three (or even more) levels supposedly being up in heaven — the third being the most glorious and ecstatic level of which they teach Paul so enjoyed experiencing. Nevertheless, having earlier discussed that the meaning of the "new heaven and earth" was to be interpreted as the third dispensation of God's order of rule in heaven and on earth, we see now that this here is speaking rather of the Apostle John (versus Paul). In Revelation, John accordingly states, "And <u>I saw a new heaven and a new earth</u>: for the <u>first</u> heaven and the <u>first</u> earth were passed away" (Rev. 21:1). Of course for John, this <u>new</u> heaven would actually be the "third heaven." In other words the <u>first</u>, having already passed away as a result of the flood, therefore meant that at the time of John's writings, he would have only been living in the <u>second</u> "heaven and earth" time period. Obviously then, this would mean that the "new heaven and earth" which he witnessed, as recorded in the book of Revelation, would therefore logically be the <u>third</u> "heaven and earth" — which of course was really a vision of the Lord's future Millennial Kingdom. Incidentally, not only does

Paul tell us that this man (John) experienced the "<u>third</u> heaven," but he also states that "he was caught up into <u>paradise</u>" (2 Cor. 12:4). Again, this also points to John the Revelator as we read how, by way of an angel, this too was revealed to him, "He that hath an ear, let him hear what the Spirit saith unto the churches; To him that overcometh will I give to eat of the tree of life, <u>which is in the midst of the paradise of God</u>" (Rev. 2:7). Incidentally, as Paul ends his account of this man who experienced these revelations, he says of him that he "heard <u>unspeakable words</u>, which it is <u>not lawful for a man to utter</u>" (2 Cor. 12:4). Again, does this statement point also to John? Amazingly, the answer is yes. Notice what John tells us in Revelation 10:3-4, "...and when he had cried, <u>seven thunders uttered their voices</u>. And when the seven thunders had uttered their voices, I was about to write: and <u>I heard a voice from heaven saying unto me, Seal up those things which the seven thunders uttered, and write them not</u>." Here we again see that, because he was told not to share what he had heard, it was therefore unlawful for John to utter or write about these unspeakable words. Amazingly, John's account in Revelation parallels Paul's account in Second Corinthians and, once again, it becomes clear to us that the Bible speaks for itself, telling us just exactly who it was, as described by Paul, that had received these visions and revelations – that is, the Apostle John!

> *"Third Heaven"* = *"Paradise!"*
> or
> ***Third "heaven and earth" (dispensation)*** = ***Millennial Kingdom***

Incidentally, there is still one last factor regarding this passage by Paul worth mentioning. In the very next verse, when Paul writes, "Of such an one will I glory: yet of myself I will not glory" (2 Cor. 12:5), it is assumed by most that the "one" Paul is referring to is the person who supposedly had these revelations of the Lord. However, with verses 2 through 4 being what is referred to as a parenthetical clause, then the "one" of whom Paul is actually referring to is not the individual who had these visions, but rather the Lord Himself of whom these visions were of. This, too, makes this passage that much more clearer and thus, points once again to John as being the correctly interpreted recipient of these revelations.

Chapter 32

"Holy Days:
The Seven Feasts of Israel"

When it comes to the subject of the end-times, one of the more critical positions that determines which camp you put yourself into involves the issue of date-setting. Either you do believe in the possibility of forecasting dates with the various events, or else you don't. At least that seems to be the reality, whether intended or not. For those who don't believe in date-setting, there is one primary reason – Jesus said so! Jesus is accordingly quoted with His statement given us in Matthew 24:36, "But of that day and hour knoweth no man, no, not the angels in heaven, but my Father only." This one statement has become the bedrock for Believers who fall into the camp that denies the idea of date-setting. As a matter of fact, it becomes the rule of thumb for not only subjects such as the Lord's return and/or the rapture, but also for just about any event in general. In my opinion, this is very unfortunate and even grievous because it usually prevents people from even ATTEMPTING to further search the Scriptures regarding possible dates of occurrence of either these or any of the other subjects. The result, I have discovered, is that they then never get to uncover some of the more amazing insights God has to offer and even, when others offer them such insights to consider, they immediately reject and close their minds off to them. Again, this is unfortunate because it actually denies a pattern in Scripture that is very much the opposite, and that is that GOD IS A DATE-SETTER!

With this being the case, certainly the question now becomes why would Jesus say what He did then? I certainly understand the grave concerns that are raised concerning this subject and for this reason, another chapter will be specifically devoted to this issue. However at this point, the thing to consider is that maybe our understanding of what Jesus actually said has, unfortunately, not really been adequately interpreted. If so, then the original premise of no date-setting could lead to all kinds of error in our attempts to interpret the many subjects of the end-times. In this particular chapter, I would like to call attention to one of those patterns in Scripture in which God reveals that He is, in fact, a legitimate date-setter. Of course from the title given, you can determine that it involves the specific topic of the feasts of Israel.

In the Old Testament, God gives particular attention to the idea that the feasts of Israel, of which there are seven of them, have specific meaning in the very observance of each one of them. Then in the New Testament, He informs us that they also are actually prophetic in nature. Each of these Holy Days, as a matter of fact, specifically find a prophetic fulfillment in the very life of the Messiah, Jesus Christ! In researching this truth, one soon discovers that these feasts provide for us somewhat of a timetable in the fulfillment of prophecy and therefore also begin to invite us into this issue of date-setting. In particular, the life of Jesus reveals a fulfillment in two very separate and distinct settings – referred to more or less by what is known as His first coming and His second coming. For example, during His first coming to earth, various events in Jesus' life became a fulfillment for the first four of these feasts – specifically, the feasts of Passover, Unleavened Bread, First Fruits, and Weeks (or Pentecost). As a result, one can now go back and even connect actual dates with each one of these events, thereby revealing that God is actually very concerned not only with specific dates, but that He even can be understood as being a so-called date-setter!

But what about the last three feasts? Can the same be said of God regarding these? Again, in searching out the Scriptures, the answer is without a doubt a yes! Except that in this particular case, only time will ultimately tell for us if this is true. However, the pattern has already been set and therefore in following it, a tremendous amount of insight becomes apparent, to include the narrowing down of, if not actual <u>dates</u>, at least what would be considered periods or <u>seasons</u>. For example, there yet exists three feasts to have a fulfillment occur in the life of Christ. These three are referred to as the feasts of Trumpets (or Rosh Hashanah), Atonement (or Yom Kippur), and Booths (or Tabernacles). From the pattern already set, it can be inferred that their fulfillment will occur in some connection with not His first coming, but rather in this case with His second coming, and therefore can provide for us some insight with respect to identifying the potential seasons to look for as to when they might actually occur. Yet doing this is not to be considered as something wrong, such as in what some people would consider as going against what Jesus earlier said. Rather, this is actually what God intends for us to do. He already hinted so when He told us that the very purpose of these feasts are to help provide for us clues regarding various events to come in both the life of Christ as well as His Body, being the Church (see Col. 2:16-17). Thus, upon searching the Scriptures, it seems that the last three feasts also, in an orderly fashion, reveal a prophetic timetable involving His return. Specifically, there are three future events that correspond to these three feasts and, collectively, help to ultimately usher in His return. The first is the feast of Trumpets (or Rosh Hashanah) which corresponds to the rapture of the Church. The second is the feast called the Day of Atonement (or Yom Kippur) which corresponds to the atoning of the nation of Israel wherein they finally repent and thereby acknowledge Yeshua (Jesus) as being their Messiah. Finally, the feast of Booths (or Tabernacles) is the actual Second Coming of Christ in which He returns to the earth and thereby forever "tabernacles" among us. This of course is the start of the Millennium.

In that these last three feasts are still observed today, as God commands, among many of the Jews, one can therefore look to them to potentially narrow the season in which these events might possibly occur. Incidentally, not every feast is merely one day long, thus in these cases it would be difficult to set an actual date. Instead, you could only identify the particular period (such as the seven day period for Tabernacles). Strictly attempting to identify just the day and hour would be next to impossible. At any rate, it again should be more clear now that God is, in fact, a date-setter and that He even encourages us to be the same. For example, during His first coming there were two individuals in particular and a group of men in general who also could have been considered date-setters of whom were each honored accordingly. Both Simeon and Anna awaited the Messiah's first coming, sitting in the Temple (Lk. 2:25-38) while the magi we are told, were looking to the stars to determine His arrival (Mt. 2:1-2). Evidently, they must have been doing some form of date-setting. Likewise it seems then that for us, God in no way would be anything but honored if, in fact, we also diligently search for the same in order that we too might be more than ready for His arrival at His second coming (1 Thess. 5:6).

"Holy Days: The Seven Feasts of Israel"
Scripturally Explained

In the book of Colossians, there is another key passage with end-time ramifications that the Apostle Paul gives us. He says this, "Let no man therefore judge you in meat, or in drink, or in respect of an holyday, or of the new moon, or of the sabbath days: Which are a shadow of things to come; but the body is of Christ" (Col. 2:16-17). In this passage, although the context regards something entirely different, Paul still clues us in on a very integral end-time principle. Essentially, the Jewish Holy days, meaning the seven feasts of Israel, are to be understood as being prophetic in nature. In fact, by the time Paul wrote this, the prophetic purpose of the first four of these seven feasts had already been fulfilled. Amazingly, they were fulfilled in the life of Jesus Christ and, even more amazing, their fulfillment each took place during His first coming to the earth. The significance of this, of course, is that if the first four were prophetically fulfilled in connection with His first coming, then it makes sense to ask if the last three could therefore be fulfilled in conjunction with His second coming? The answer, I hope, seems now fairly obvious to you.

The Biblical origin of Israel's feasts is the Old Testament book of Leviticus, specifically chapter 23. The first four feasts are listed as Passover (vs. 5), Unleavened Bread (vs. 6-8), First Fruits (vs. 9-14), and the Feast of Weeks (or Pentecost, vs. 15-21). As was just stated, in the case of His first coming, Jesus Christ already fulfilled the prophetic purpose for each of these four feasts as follows:

1. **Passover** = His Crucifixion (1 Cor. 5:7 & Jn. 19:14-16)
2. **Unleavened Bread** = His Burial (Lk. 22:1-2,7 & 1 Cor. 5:7-8)
3. **First Fruits** = His Resurrection (1 Cor. 15:20-23 & Mk. 16:9)
4. **Feast of Weeks** = Pentecost (Acts 2:1,4)

Incidentally, these first four not only were fulfilled during Christ's first coming, but they also were connected specifically with the 3½ year period of Christ's ministry on earth (which again is also that first 3½ year period of Daniel's seventieth week – Dan. 9:24-27), although their fulfillment covered just over 50 days at the very end of this period of time (His earthly life). In contrast, the prophetic fulfillment of the last three feasts amazingly takes place in connection with the last 3½ year period of Daniel's seventieth week (meaning the tribulation). The period of time separating the fulfillment of the first four from the last three, however, is an interval of years known to us as the Church age, or also "the last days" (Heb. 1:2). This period of time is also characterized as an age of grace (Jn. 4:35; Mt. 13:38-39) wherein the New Covenant is operative, thereby allowing the Gospel to go out to the Gentiles. Incidentally, ushering in this "end of the age" will therefore be those last three feasts, Scripturally known also as the "feasts of the ingathering" (Ex. 23:16).

Accordingly, the first of these last three feasts is known as Trumpets (Lev. 23:23-24) and is fulfilled by the rapture of the Church. The second of these is the Day of Atonement (vs. 26-28) and is fulfilled at the point in the future when Israel finally repents and acknowledges Jesus as their Messiah. Of course, the last feast then is Tabernacles (vs. 33-34) and is fulfilled by the ushering in of the Millennial Kingdom, whereby Jesus returns to the earth to dwell (or "tabernacle") among us. Scripturally, these are validated in part as follows:

5. **Trumpets** (Rosh Hashanah) = Rapture of the Church
   (Mt. 24:29-31; 1 Thess. 4:16-17; 1 Cor. 15:51-52)
6. **Atonement** (Yom Kippur) = Repentance by the nation of Israel (Zech. 12:10; 13:9; Zeph. 3:20; Mt. 23:39) (incidentally "atonement" also means "reconciliation" – 1 Cor. 7:11; Dan. 9:24; Ezk. 45:17)
7. **Tabernacles** (also "Booths") = Set up of Millennial Kingdom with Jesus dwelling among us
   (Acts 15:16; Zech. 14:8; Jn. 7:37-38; Rev. 20:4; 21:3)

It is important at this point to note that according to Leviticus 23, there is a definite pattern given us with the order of these 7 feasts. For example, the first 4 feasts take place in just over a 50 day period at the start of the Jewish New Year which, incidentally, begins with Passover and always occurs in the Fall. There is then a period of about 6 months which takes place prior to the occurrence of the last 3 feasts. Finally, it is within a short period of just 15 days that these last 3 feasts occur, being of course in the Spring. In consistent fashion, the same pattern is similarly followed when it comes to the Scriptural fulfillment of these last 3 feasts — that is, in the prophetic sense. For example, with respect to the prophetic fulfillment of the first 4 feasts in Christ's life, as previously mentioned, they all again occurred within a period of just over 50 days. Of course, a prophetic gap of time then follows with that interval known as the church age. Finally, in consistently following the Scriptural pattern already given us in Leviticus 23, we can therefore conclude that the last 3 feasts will prophetically be fulfilled in Christ's life also, upon His return, in a matter of just 15 days. In other words, the rapture will take place on Trumpets, followed 10 days later by Israel's repentance, with this followed 5 days later by the establishment of His Kingdom. Of course, as Jesus Himself informed us, again all three of these would therefore occur "immediately <u>after the tribulation</u> of those days" (Mt. 24:29-31).

The 7 Feasts of Israel

(as prophectically fulfilled in the life of Jesus Christ and the Church)

```
1. Passover = Crucifixion
↕          2. Unleavened Bread = Burial
     ↕          3. First Fruits = Resurrection
          ↕          4. Feast of Weeks (Pentecost) = Birth of Church (H.S. came)
                ↕
                         (Church Age)
|---------------|---------------|---------------|------------------------------------|---------------|---------------|
                                                                        ↕
                                                   5. Trumpets = Rapture          ↕
                                                          6. Atonement = Israel Repents          ↕
                                                                  7. Tabernacles = Millennium Begins
```

Certainly, the question at this point to ask is, can we therefore now predict or determine just exactly when the tribulation period will start? Well, the Scriptures do indicate that, in a general sense, we can know not WHEN it begins, but rather WHAT IT IS that begins this tribulation period - and that being the encircling of Arab armies around Passover of the city of Jerusalem (see again Lk. 21:20). Accordingly then, having now already determined that the rapture's occurrence, being on the Feast of Trumpets, is subsequent to the start of the tribulation period by almost 3½ years, we can therefore mathematically backtrack by this same amount of time (3½ years) to determine that the tribulation will actually begin on some future Jewish Passover Feast. In other words, although uncertain as to the exact year it will begin, we can at least conclude and therefore anticipate that the tribulation will start on some future Passover Feast.

3½ Year Tribulation

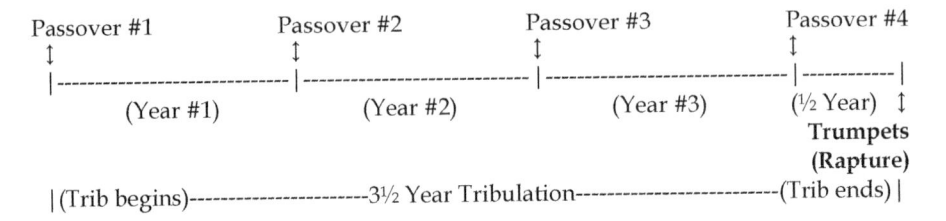

```
Passover #1           Passover #2           Passover #3           Passover #4
    ↕                     ↕                     ↕                     ↕
|------------------------|---------------------|---------------------|-----------|
      (Year #1)               (Year #2)              (Year #3)        (½ Year)  ↕
                                                                      Trumpets
                                                                      (Rapture)

|(Trib begins)---------------------3½ Year Tribulation---------------------(Trib ends)|
```

The importance then of the 7 Feasts of Israel are that they are to be considered by us as a prophetic timetable, if you will, helping the Christian to become more aware of God's pending plan. This awareness will therefore allow him to be "not in darkness," but rather "of the light" (1 Thess. 5:4,5) concerning the anticipated timing of Christ's return. Incidentally, although it is not one of the annual feasts, there is yet one other Holy Day mentioned in both these passages of Colossians 2 and Leviticus 23 that deserves some discussion — and that being the weekly Holy Day called the Sabbath. This is a very interesting factor because, according to the Scriptures, the 1,000 year Millennium is also called the 1,000 year Sabbath rest, primarily because of the peace that will prevail on earth during that period. For example, remembering that the Law of God required of the people to rest on the seventh day (or Sabbath day) after their previous 6 days of labor, so too, the Millennium will be a time of spiritual rest for God's people from all their spiritual labors (Heb. 4; Rev. 14:13). Interestingly enough, a more in-depth study of this Holy Day brings us to yet another interesting end-time conclusion of which we will likewise discover in the following chapter entitled, "The 7 Day Principle."

Chapter 33

"The 7 Day Principle"

In attempting to dissect the overall puzzle that exists as part of the end-time picture, there remains still another Biblical principle that is key in our understanding of it, even though it again is one which is largely overlooked by so many. It is the principle of which, in the eyes of God, one day is equivalent to a thousand years just as a thousand years is equivalent to one day. This principle is mentioned twice in Scripture, initially in the Old Testament (Ps. 90:4) and again in the New Testament (2 Pt. 3:8). Although the way that it is stated is seemingly confusing, even implying that God is poor with His mathematics, it nevertheless is a very unique and vital principle in Scripture, especially when it comes to the study of the end-times. Essentially, the meaning of it is that there are unique correlations or patterns that exist when you evaluate Biblical history from both a microscopic and macroscopic (or panoramic) viewpoint. In other words, God has provided for us a tool to help us in evaluating the end-times that will reveal a pattern that He initially set up, even as far back as during the first week of creation.

In the very beginning of the Bible we learn that God created the world in six days and then rested on the seventh. In the same way, there is a 7,000 year timetable to evaluate the end-time picture from which has some amazing similarities to this initial 7-day week of creation. For example, on the fourth day of creation God gave us the sun. Likewise in the 4,000th year of creation, He gave us also, as the anointed Messiah, His Son — being the "Sun of righteousness" according to Malachi 4:2. As another example, we already know that on the seventh day of creation God rested, declaring it as a Sabbath day of rest. Likewise, the 1,000 year period known as the Millennium is also a period of rest, additionally referred to in Scripture as the "Sabbath rest." As you can see, this principle is both amazing and helpful in evaluating God's divine timetable and yet, it is one which often is overlooked and in fact, even avoided — unfortunately due once again to the supposed belief that God is not wanting us to be date setting. However, one only needs to begin with the very first man (Adam) and follow the various genealogical details given us in Scripture to find that God has not, in fact, IS NOT withholding from us certain clues to help us in the seeking out of His divine plans, especially in this area of the end-times.

Actually, an amazing discovery takes place as you begin to follow the genealogical timetables in Scripture, beginning first with Adam. Essentially, you discover that from the very beginning with Adam, up until the day that Jesus (by John the Baptist in the Jordan River) was anointed with the Holy Spirit as the Messiah, there existed a total of exactly 4,000 years (supporting detail for this is provided in the explanation section of this chapter). Then from that day on up until the present, there has existed almost 2,000 additional years. Of course, we know already that there yet remains the 1,000 year period of the Millennium, thus giving us a grand total of just under 7,000 years. The only other component not factored in is that of a "little season" of years to occur following the Millennium in which the devil is let loose on the earth in an attempt to deceive the nations for one final time. The length of this "little season" is currently unknown, but nevertheless it will complete this 7,000 year divine timetable from which it appears God is working from. Ultimately of course, only time will tell just how accurate this assessment really is. At any rate, this timetable definitely needs to be considered if we are to both honestly and diligently search out the Scriptures for His answers regarding the many and various end-time subjects.

"The 7 Day Principle"
Scripturally Explained

Going way back to the beginning of the Bible, we find that God used a total of 6 days to complete His creation (Gen. 1). Then on the seventh day we find that God rested from all of His labors in this work of creation (Gen. 2:1-3). Eventually, as revealed in the requirements of God's Law, this pattern would also be one for His people to follow (Ex. 20:9-11). Interestingly enough, this very pattern would become especially significant from a prophetic standpoint as well. Keeping in mind what the Apostle Paul advised us regarding the Sabbath (that it was to also be understood as a "shadow of things to come" – Col. 2:16-17), we next learn from the Apostle Peter regarding the perspective God takes on time that "<u>one day is with the Lord as a thousand years, and a thousand years as one day</u>" (2 Pt. 3:8). It is from this very principle, initially established in the Old Testament in Psalms 90:4, that we can identify a pattern set for the creation account of life as paralleling a pattern set for the prophetic account for the world. In other words, for each one day of creation that initially occurred, there likewise exists for the world an additional 1,000 years. Or to put it another way, by the time that Jesus Christ actually returns, the age of the world will be around a mere 6,000 years old.

To be sure, although the vast majority of the world's people would have you to believe, because of its bias towards the theory of evolution, that the world is millions of years old, the Bible on the other hand gives us a different picture altogether. As a matter of fact, within the very pages of Scripture are the recording of a number of different genealogical accounts and other relevant historical references given to matters such as the number of years a person lived, or that they lived before having certain children, or even the length of certain kings' reigns. For example, we are told in Scripture that Adam <u>lived</u> 930 years before he died (Gen. 5:5). Amazingly, by utilizing these references given, one can actually determine that from the very first man (Adam) up until the time Jesus Christ was baptized in the Jordan River, the earth's age was precisely 4,000 years old. Colin Deal of Rutherford College, North Carolina, who has authored a handful of books on prophecy and has his own End-Time Ministry, did this very research and gave me permission to include it in this book. Utilizing the following table and Biblical references, he concluded that from the initial creation of Adam up until the point of Jesus' anointing as the Messiah in the Jordan River, there was exactly 4,000 years that transpired:

God's 4,000 Year Timetable

A. From Adam to the Abrahamic Covenant:

Patriarchs	Genesis reference	Lineal Years
Adam	5:3	130
Seth	5:6	105
Enos	5:9	90
Cainan	5:12	70
Mahalaleel	5:15	65
Jared	5:18	162
Enoch	5:21	65
Methuselah	5:25	187
Lamech	5:28	182
Noah	(*a)	502
Shem	11:10	100
Arphaxad	11:12	35
Salah	11:14	30
Eber	11:16	34
Peleg	11:18	30
Reu	11:20	32
Serug	11:22	30
Nahor	11:24	29
Terah	(*b)	130
Abraham	17:1,2 (*c)	99
	Sub-total	2107

*B. From the Abrahamic Covenant to the time of the Exodus (*c):*
Gen. 17:1,2; Ex. 12:40,41; Gal. 3:17   **430**

C. From the time of the Exodus to the Building of the Temple:
1 Kgs. 6:1   **480**

D. From the time of the Building of the Temple to the beginning of the Babylonian Captivity:

Kings of Judah	Reference	Years of Reign
Solomon	1 Kgs. 11:42 (*d)	36
Rehoboam	1 Kgs. 14:21	17
Abijam	1 Kgs. 15:2	3
Asa	1 Kgs. 15:10	41
Jehoshaphat	1 Kgs. 22:42	25
Jehoram	2 Kgs. 8:17	8
Ahaziah	2 Kgs. 8:26	1
Athaliah	2 Kgs. 11:1-4, 20-21	7
Jehoash	2 Kgs. 12:1	40
Amaziah	2 Kgs. 14:2	29
Azariah	2 Kgs. 15:2	52
Jotham	2 Kgs. 15:33	16
Ahaz	2 Kgs. 16:2	16
Hezekiah	2 Kgs. 18:2	29
Manasseh	2 Kgs. 21:1	55
Amon	2 Kgs. 21:19	2
Josiah	2 Kgs. 22:1 (*e)	31
Jehoiakim	2 Kgs. 23:26 (*e)	11
Zedekiah	2 Kgs. 24:18	<u>11</u>
	Sub-total	**430**

E. Babylonian Captivity: Jer. 25:11; 29:10; Dan. 9:2   **70**

F. End of Babylonian Captivity to the Anointing of the Messiah:
Dan. 9:25 (*f)   **483**

Grand Total   **4,000**

* Notes:

* *a* - Noah's 3 sons were not born the same year. In Genesis 7:6, we are told that Noah was 600 years old when the flood came. We are told in Genesis 11:10 that Shem was 98 years old (100 minus 2) when the flood came. Thus, Noah would have been 502 years old (600 minus 98) when Shem was born.

* **b** - From Genesis 11:26 we know that Terah had 3 sons. We also know from Genesis 12:4 that Abram (his name was later changed to Abraham) was 75 years old when he departed Haran immediately following his father's death (Acts 7:4). Incidentally, Genesis 11:32 tells us that Terah was 205 years old when he died. Thus, Terah would have been 130 years old (205 minus 75) when Abram was born.

* **c** - God changed Abram's name to Abraham and made a covenant with him at the age of 99 years old (Gen. 17:1-7). From the time that this covenant was confirmed with Abraham to the end of the exodus was 430 years (Gal. 3:16-17), "even to the selfsame day" (Ex. 12:40-41).

* **d** - We are told in 1 Kings 11:42 that Solomon reigned 40 years. However, according to 1 Kings 6:1, construction of the Temple did not begin until the 4th year of his reign. Thus, only the last 36 years of his reign is considered in this calculation (40 minus 4). Incidentally, the first 4 years of his reign were considered to be a part of the last 4 years of the 480 year exodus (1 Kings 6:1).

* **e** - After Josiah's death, we are told that his son, Jehoahaz, reigned for 3 months (2 Chron. 36:2). Also, after Jehoiakim's death, his son, Jehoiachin, reigned for 3 months and 10 days (2 Chron. 36:9). However, neither of these 2 sons occupied the throne at the time of the civil Jewish New Year. Thus, according to the Hebrew counting of regal years, both sons' reigns are reckoned as zero years. Had either been on the throne at the time of the New Year, they would have been credited with a 1 year reign, as was the case for Ahaziah.

* **f** - According to 2 Chronicles 36:21-23, Cyrus ascended the throne of Persia at the end of the 70-year Babylonian captivity. He promptly issued a decree in his first year permitting the Jews to return to Palestine. According to Daniel 9:25, Jesus was anointed as "Messiah the Prince" 483 years (69 weeks of years x 7 years per week) later when He was baptized in the river Jordan (Lk. 3:21-23).

Just as God created the first Adam as a mature man, He also anointed Jesus as the Messiah, the last Adam, at maturity (approximately 30 years of age – see Num. 4:47; Lk. 3:21-23). Thus, from the time of Adam's creation up until the Messiah the Prince was precisely 4,000 years!

Amazingly, the above 4,000 year table gives Scriptural proof that precisely 4,000 years elapsed from the creation of Adam at maturity to the very baptism of Jesus at maturity (Lk. 3:21-23). Incidentally, the ancient Jewish rabbis taught that Adam was created at the Autumn season (or Rosh Hashanah). Of course, we know that Jesus' ministry was 3½ years long, ending at His death on Passover (Mt. 26:2). If we go back 3½ years from this Passover, we discover that Jesus also was baptized in the Autumn season (believed by the rabbis to also occur on Rosh Hashanah), or 4,000 years to the very season (possibly even being to the very day if the rabbis' teaching is correct). In other words, the bottom line is that this evidence alone strongly suggests that God is working on a calculated and predetermined timetable – and that being a 7,000 year timetable according to the initial principle given as the subject matter of this chapter.

Additionally, still using this same principle of time from the point of view of God, we see that the earth would have only been considered 4 days old at this point, since a day is considered to be like a thousand years. This is really interesting when you consider that according to the Scriptures, Jesus happened to also be referred to as "the Sun of righteousness" (Mal. 4:2). If you recall on the fourth day of the actual creation account, the primary thing that God made was, in fact, the greater light called the sun (Gen. 1:14-19). Or to put it another way, while the impact of creation's fourth day was that on this particular day light was provided for the whole world (Gen. 1:16), we see also on the 4,000th year of creation (being the 4th day in God's eyes) that Jesus (also being "the light of the world" according to John 1:4-9; 8:12), via baptism in the Jordan River, began His ministry on earth upon His being anointed as the Messiah by the Holy Spirit.

Of course, the implication of this 4,000 year timetable is that if it does, in fact, take us up to the point of Jesus' ministry commencing, then how many years do we have left on this 7,000 year timetable? More than likely, we can conclude that Jesus began His ministry in the Autumn of 29 A.D.. He was then crucified 3½ years later in the

Spring of 33 A.D.. However, if you were to add another 2,000 years from the time of His anointing (or 29 A.D.), that would take us up to the year 2029 A.D.. In that it is currently 2001 at the time of my writing this book, does this mean that we still have 28 more years prior to the Lord's return? Probably not.

There yet remains another period of time to be fulfilled on the 7,000 year timetable that also needs to be considered. Only in this case, it is a period that comes on the other side of the 1,000 year Millennium. In Revelation 20:1-3, John tells us, "And I saw an angel come down from heaven, having the key of the bottomless pit and a great chain in his hand. And he laid hold on the dragon, that old serpent, which is the Devil, and Satan, and bound him a thousand years, and cast him into the bottomless pit, and shut him up, and set a seal upon him, that he should deceive the nations no more, till the thousand years should be fulfilled: <u>and after that he must be loosed a little season</u>." He adds in verses 7 and 8, "And when the thousand years are expired, <u>Satan shall be loosed out of his prison</u>, and he shall go out to deceive the nations which are in the four quarters of the earth, Gog and Magog, to gather them together to battle: the number of whom is as the sand of the sea." Obviously, we are to understand from this that the devil is going to be allowed by God to test the people for an additional short season following the completion of the 1,000 year millennial period. How long will this short season be? I have been unable to determine this exactly thus far, though there might be some clues in Scripture yet to be realized to do so. At any rate, on an overall scale of a 1,000 years, as in this Millennial period, a short season then could more than likely be measured in terms of years. With this in mind, the length of this short season would therefore make up the difference on this 7,000 year timetable. In other words, the 7,000 year divine timetable looks something like this:

7,000 Year Divine Timetable

```
                                                              Devil let loose
Creation                        Jesus' anointing (baptism)   Jesus' return    ↑
|-------------------------------------------------------|-------------------------|---------|--|
                                                29 A.D.              2005? to 2029?
                  4,000 years                   (almost 2,000 yrs)   1,000 yrs   ↓
                                                                                "short
                                                                                season"
```

Obviously from the above timetable, the return of Christ is deemed to fall somewhere between 2005 and 2029 A.D.. But is this really correct? As is the case with all Biblical prophecy, no one really knows for sure until after the fact. However, the above clues seem to suggest this as a very plausible interpretation to consider. The short season is really the only above time period yet to be determined. All others we know as either being historical or else literal (the 4,000 years from Adam to Jesus' anointing, the 1,000 year Millennium, and the almost 2,000 years from Jesus' baptism up to our current date). This gives us a very real window of time to view these end-time events from, occurring somewhere between now and around 2029 A.D.. However, the other realities and clues already discussed in this book suggest the Lord's return as being probably much sooner than 2029 A.D.. The reason that 2005 is suggested as the earliest possible time for the Lord's return is because of the following factors. First, there is <u>at the very least</u> the 3½ years that is still needed for the tribulation period (again computing this using the current year of this book's writing, or 2001). Second, the tribulation would also have to start in the Spring season (Passover). Again at the point of this writing, this takes us to no sooner than the Fall of 2005 as the earliest time for the Lord's return. As an <u>example</u>, the below depiction illustrates what I am saying (<u>again, I repeat, this is only an example, depicting the earliest possibility</u>):

Passover (Spring)	Passover (Spring)	Passover (Spring)	Passover (Spring)	Tabernacles ↑ (Fall)
2002 Trib begins?	2003 +1 year	2004 +2 years	2005 +3 yrs	2005 3½ yrs of tribulation

Again since this is only an example, the elements of this timeline would certainly be applicable, but nevertheless be adjusted for whatever year the tribulation would actually begin. Now as far as the rapture goes, we likewise can ask when would it occur on this timeline? If you recall, it would fall on the Feast of Trumpets (or Rosh Hashanah), to occur approximately 15 days prior to the Feast of

Tabernacles (see previous chapter). Thus, it would occur on this timeline just before the end of the 3½ years of tribulation.

Personally, I find the above depiction to have more Scriptural merit than any of the other so-called positional arguments on this subject. However, it would serve to note that there is an awareness of a possible discrepancy with the actual year we are in on our calendar. Supposedly, there exists debate contending that our calendars are off by anywhere up to as much as 6 years. Even if this were to be true, this overall timeline set up still applies.

Now keeping in mind the principle of a day being like a thousand years and vice versa, it brings to mind still another passage of Scripture given us in the book of Hosea regarding the nation of Israel, "Come, and let us return unto the Lord: for he hath torn, and he will heal us; he hath smitten, and he will bind us up. <u>After two days will he revive us: in the third day he will raise us up, and we shall live in his sight</u>" (Hos. 6:1-2). Here, regarding the necessary time passage of "two days," we see an obvious reference to the 2,000 year period known as the Church age in which, during the time of Israel's blindness to the truth, the Gospel instead goes out unto the Gentiles (Rm. 11:25). Of course, this wait of "two days" (2,000 years) will last only until the end of the tribulation, at which point Israel will repent and acknowledge Jesus as their Messiah (again see preceding discussion on the Feast of Atonement in the last chapter). Then immediately thereafter, Jesus will set up His Kingdom in what we now know as the 1,000 year Millennium (see also this same chapter in the particular discussion on the Feast of Tabernacles).

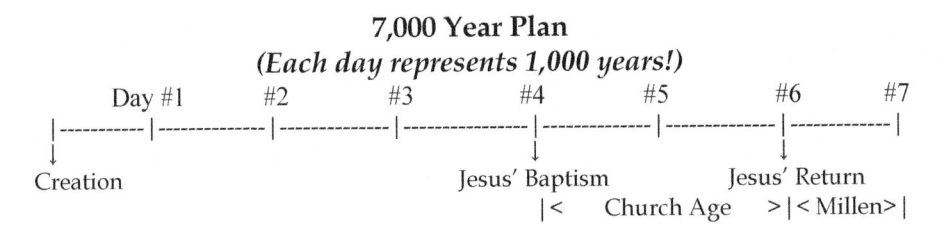

7,000 Year Plan
(Each day represents 1,000 years!)

```
   Day #1      #2         #3          #4          #5          #6         #7
  |----------|------------|------------|-------------|------------|-----------|------------|
   ↓                                   ↓                         ↓
  Creation                      Jesus' Baptism              Jesus' Return
                                        |<     Church Age    >|< Millen >|
```

Obviously from this discussion, we can be sure that Christ's return is very near. In fact, the "signs of the times" (Mt. 24) seem to confirm this, especially when you consider the already many prophetic fulfillments of these signs. Since the next major event – the tribulation – has yet to begin, we can be sure that there remains, at the very least, an additional 3½ years prior to our witnessing Christ's return. Of course, once the tribulation does in fact begin, we will only have to consult our calendars to basically determine when each subsequent prophetic event is to occur. That this is possible is due, in part, to both the fact that the Christian will be around during the tribulation and because the Bible says we also will not be in the dark concerning these events (1 Thess. 5:4-5). Of course as so many already believe, this still does not necessarily mean that we will be able to know the <u>exact</u> day and hour of Christ's return. However, even this particular topic is worthy of a bit of Scriptural discussion as well, of which the next chapter in this book will be devoted to.

Chapter 34

"No Man Knoweth the Day and the Hour!"

The words are from Jesus and the verse is found in Matthew 24:36. It says quite simply, "But of that day and hour knoweth no man, no, not the angels of heaven, but my Father only." But is it really that simple, that absolutely no one is to know the day and hour of His return? Most people would seem to think so. However, not all of Scripture is to always be understood in such basic or simplistic terms. The fact is, we here in America understand Scripture from the Biblical translations that are in English. Unfortunately for us, that is not the language the Bible was first written. Rather, the Bible was originally written in three other languages – the Old Testament predominantly in Hebrew with a trace of Aramaic and the New Testament entirely in Greek. For us to get the original intent of the writers, our best scenario would be for us to be scholars of all three of those languages. Yet this is seldom the case. Thus, we are at the mercy of the translations given us. Though these might be considered adequate, or even excellent in their works, they nevertheless are not infallible, and this is where the problems quite often come. Many times a translation will end up being inadequate for a variety of reasons. Sometimes it is due simply to an attempt to simplify the understanding for the intended recipients. This, however, might result in something being missed, even though it might not be obvious to the average reader. Another problem might result when a number of different words are used in the translation process for a single word in the original text that occurs in what may be more than one location in the Bible. This again might not immediately be realized as lending itself to error, but what is lost is the possible consistency that God might have intended had the same word been chosen to translate it with. In other words, a pattern which might become apparent in the text of the original language due to the one word being utilized would unfortunately disappear in the translated version. Of course, these types of errors potentially taking place are to be understood, even to be expected, as part of the process, despite the honorable efforts of our beloved translators. Were it not for them, where would that leave us? Nevertheless, it is still a noble thing to reevaluate their works as long as the motivation of doing so is not really a critical one, but rather just a desire to better understand God's message to us.

Another possible discrepancy that can result from the translation process is one which actually occurs here with these very words of Jesus in Matthew 24:36. There is an unfortunate reality that occurs when one goes from the original Greek language over to our present English language, and it is one that takes place quite often. The Greek language is a language which in many cases is much more precise, especially in the words that it uses. Quite often, there might be more than one word in the Greek used to communicate various degrees of precision for which in the English we might have only word. The result therefore can be that in the English translation there might be a general thought that is communicated, even though in the original Greek a more precise meaning was intended. Thus, this precision is lost and what is possibly left instead is some particular meaning that is lost, buried, twisted, or even removed, though understandably unintentional. Yet this can be very dangerous and even damaging, for God already warns us that we should not add to or take away from God's Word (Rev. 22:19). In the case of Jesus supposedly saying that no man would know both the day and hour, upon further research this happens to be the very thing that has occurred. In this particular case, we discover that in the Greek language there happens to be eight different words used to indicate various levels of precision for which we have just one English word to translate it with. Thus, as you can see there definitely exists the possibility for error. In this case, what Jesus actually said is unfortunately translated in our English texts to mean that absolutely in no way could one EVER know the day and the hour of His return. As a matter of fact, He amazingly states that this limitation also includes the angels and, by implication, even Himself. However, in a study of the Greek text you will find that He did not actually communicate this same thought after all. Instead, what Jesus communicated was something a bit less absolute. What He said was that no one, <u>at least not without a genuine level of thorough and diligent searching</u>, would ever know the day and hour. In other words, the implication that Jesus left is that SOME MIGHT ACTUALLY <u>AT SOME POINT</u> KNOW! Why?

Because they would do their homework! Plus, if you add into this equation the divine element with the human element, then there is the possibility that they would more than likely receive some new and fresh Biblical understanding on this subject of the end-times as well (knowing that it is God who opens up our spiritual eyes and reveals things – 1 Cor. 2:9-16) as the Holy Spirit unveils new insights during this particular process of diligently seeking to know His ways. But again, this is possible only because Jesus said so, and it becomes more apparent to us in the Greek text as opposed to our various English texts.

Specifically, the reason for this discrepancy is that in the Greek language, there is basically eight different levels of "**know**ing" something. In other words, there are eight different Greek words used in which each communicates a different degree of knowing something. Unfortunately, the problem for us is that in the translation process, most of these words are translated using just a single English word – the word "know." Thus, we would more than likely lose some of the intended meaning when more than one of these Greek words was used in the original manuscripts while a single word is used in the English translations — and incidentally, that is exactly what happened.

To us, the English version of Matthew 24:36 reads as an absolute prohibition, that is, that no man would ever be able to know the day and hour of the Lord's return. It just so happens that in the Greek, there actually is a word that when used would communicate just that. However, that is not the word Jesus used when He made this declaration. Rather, He used a word for "knowing" that is understood instead as communicating one level lower in the degree of not being able to know something. As a result, what Jesus meant was that, although it would be extremely difficult (or pretty much impossible) for one to "know" the day and hour without exerting any effort, one could still possibly know upon a great degree of diligent investigation. This, by the way, is extremely important to us! As a result of Jesus telling us this, it immediately should cast doubt on the teaching of the so-called "Imminence Doctrine" wherein it is taught that Jesus could return (or also that the rapture could occur) at any time — the problem being that we are told that we ought not to be trying at all to determine any dates for these various end-time events. Rather, what it should instead do is to drive us to do further

Biblical study and research, thereby aiming to discern the very times and seasons that we are in. This is the Biblical aim, pattern, and precedent that has been established for us. Again, we only have to do some review to realize us.

First, if you review the first coming of Jesus, you will recall that there were, in fact, some people who KNEW of His coming. Why? Obviously, because they anticipated it. Why? Probably because they did their homework and therefore were ready, even awaiting His arrival. I am speaking, of course, of the two who were hanging out in the Temple anticipating His appearance – Simeon and Anna (see Luke 2:25-38). Second, if you evaluate the transition from the first "heaven and earth" to the second "heaven and earth," you once again see that there were people who knew what was coming. I am speaking of course of the transition from before the great flood in Noah's day to afterwards. In this case, not only did Noah and his family know of this change that was forthcoming, but so did a great deal of others whom he forewarned, though these others failed to heed his warning (see Gen. 6 – 9). However, the pattern and precedent at least was set, and that is that God does in fact set dates and that He also reveals them in His time! Unfortunately, we only do ourselves an injustice by believing the lie that the devil has deceived us with — that God does not want us to even attempt to know the dates of various events. Rather, the actual truth is that God wants to bless us and reward us for diligently seeking to know Him and His ways. Yet not only that, but He has already declared that we are NOT to be in the dark concerning these things, but rather are to be children of the light – that is, He intends for us to know (see 1 Thess. 5:4-6). This, by the way, brings me to one additional but vital truth that only serves to confirm this particular truth all the more. In the book of Daniel, we are told in 12:4, "But thou, O Daniel, shut up the words, and seal the book, **even to the time of the end**: many shall run to and fro, **and knowledge shall be increased**." In other words, what God is telling us here is that we should expect near the end of this age, or just prior to His return, and influx of KNOWLEDGE to occur. Incidentally, this knowledge is not a reference to the advances of technology, science, or intellectual abilities, but rather is a reference to an increase in the understanding of BIBLICAL KNOWLEDGE – that is, <u>the knowledge of God and His ways, which would in great part also refer to an increased understanding of His</u>

<u>plans regarding all of these end-time events and subjects</u>! Thus, this would only serve to strengthen the argument that God intends to reveal more and more of His plans, to include even greater insight regarding the day and hour of His return, even as the day draws all the more closer. By the way, this is the reason for the writing of this book, of which I personally hope has been for you an eye-opening blessing of what it seems God's Word is truly communicating to us.

"No Man Knoweth the Day and the Hour!"
Scripturally Explained

Jesus supposedly made it very clear in Matthew 24:36, "But of that day and hour knoweth no man, no, not the angels of heaven, but my Father only." Admittedly, this verse has been the source for and cause of many debates. Unfortunately, it has also resulted in numerous unnecessary and yet divisive arguments. On the one hand, from it has come the unscriptural and yet very popular "Imminence Doctrine," that is, that Christ could return at any time – period! Actually, the usual application by those adhering to this doctrine is that it is the rapture which could take place at anytime. Yet, in that Christ was not even referring to the rapture in this particular statement that He makes, we can see that this idea of "imminence" is unscriptural, and therefore untrue. Still, even if this doctrine of imminency were correct, then based upon all the teachings derived from or associated with it (a Pre-trib rapture, a 7 year tribulation, etc.), upon the occurrence of the rapture, one could still count ahead 7 years to determine when in fact Christ would return (of course, they would then be unbelievers, having not been raptured). As a matter of fact, they would also be able to calculate and therefore date many of the other prophetic events as well. Apart from this doctrine, however, and yet taking into consideration all of the other prophetic Scriptures, principles, and patterns given us, it would therefore be very difficult to not have some sense of certainty regarding the dating of these yet to be fulfilled prophetic events, especially in light of the prophetic nature of the Jewish Feasts. Nevertheless, when it comes to evaluating what Jesus really meant by His statement, the truth of the matter is actually found in examining just exactly what Christ did say in this verse for, from it, the logical implications become very clear.

When Jesus made His statement, He made it in connection with numerous other events He was discussing. Of course, all of His discussion in this Olivet Discourse was generated by a question given Him by His disciples in verse 3 of Matthew 24, "Tell us, when shall these things be? and what shall be the sign of thy coming, and of the end of the world?" Incidentally, you should notice here that there are three parts to this question. Breaking this verse down, we can determine that part one ("when shall these things be?") is in reference to Jesus' question to them in the preceding verse, "See ye not all these things?" (vs. 2). This particular question that Jesus asked, of course, pertained to His preceding comments concerning the "buildings of the temple" (vs. 1) and specifically, the stones thereof, "There shall not be left here one stone upon another, that shall not be thrown down" (vs. 2). Of course, we know historically that the destruction of the Temple actually took place in 70 A.D. at the hands of the Roman Empire and certainly, as it turned out, no one was able to predict the exact day and hour of its destruction! Nevertheless though, the second part of this question by the disciples is not really a question of "when," but rather of "what," and specifically pertains to a sign, "What shall be the sign of thy coming?" Of course, the answer to this question is given by Jesus in verse 30, "And then shall appear the sign of the Son of man in heaven...and they shall see the Son of man coming." Thus, we see here that this was not really a "day and hour" question at all. As a matter of fact, the third part of the disciples' question also appears as a "what" ("what shall be the sign...of the end of the world?"). An examination of the Greek text here, however, could possibly make it imply a question of "when" as well, for the rendering in the Greek has it essentially regarding "the completion of the age." In other words, by implication the word "completion" has a time element associated with it — that is, it is not complete until and only when it becomes completed, meaning that a certain amount of time would have had to have passed first! Nevertheless, you should notice that the question of its "completion" is not about the end of the "world," but rather concerning the end of the "age." This, of course, is a reference more specifically to the "age of the Gentiles," its end of which we know immediately precedes the Millennium. Obviously, we cannot conclude very easily from the disciples' question(s) just exactly what Jesus was referring to with His statement in Matthew 24:36. Nevertheless, this statement by Jesus does happen to follow some other statements He made in which He again referred to the "these things" phrase (see vs. 33 and 34). In addition, He referred to the age of the Gentiles again when He said in verse 34, "This generation shall not pass, till all these things be fulfilled" (Remember, "this generation" is a reference to the "chosen generation" under the New Covenant period — see earlier chapter on

"Which Generation?"). Nevertheless, in the verse (vs. 35) that immediately preceded His statement regarding "the day and the hour," Jesus talked of heaven and earth passing away even though His words would not pass away, while in the verse that followed it (vs. 37), He alluded instead to His coming. Certainly, this seems confusing, unclear, and somewhat vague as to just exactly what Jesus was referring to by His statement. Accordingly, it seems that we too should probably be uncertain regarding the exact day and hour it was that He was referring to. Of course, the point of all of this is that for one to therefore use the Feasts of Israel, as was demonstrated in an earlier chapter, to help pinpoint a more general **"period of time"** versus an exact **"day and hour"** in which certain prophetic events might be fulfilled, should NOT really be a cause for great alarm. Rather, they would actually be very helpful!

You will notice also that I purposely and selectively used the phrase "period of time" in the preceding sentence. This particular phrase, certainly of a more general nature than the specific periods of time referred to by Jesus in His statement regarding the "day and hour," is purposely and selectively used because of the nature of most of the Feasts of Israel. For example, in the case of the last three feasts, which have yet to have their prophetic fulfillment occur in the life of Christ or His Body (the Church), neither of these are for merely an "hour" long. Instead, quite the opposite is the case and in particular, one of these three is even <u>more</u> than a full "<u>day</u>" long — that being the final one, or Tabernacles, which actually lasts a full 7 days. Of course, knowing that this Feast (which is prophetic of Christ's return and the establishment of His Millennial Kingdom) consists of a 7 day length, we would be hard-pressed to pinpoint the <u>exact day and hour</u> of the beginning of its prophetic fulfillment. Still, in the case of both the 5th feast (Trumpets — pertaining to the rapture) and the 6th feast (Atonement — referring to the repentance of Israel and its acknowledgement of Yeshua as their Messiah), although each is limited to but a single day, nevertheless we know that neither of these two is prophetic of either the end of the world (which ends when the new heaven and earth are established, during Tabernacles, with the beginning of the Millennium Kingdom) or the return of Christ (also during Tabernacles).

Of course, the conclusion here regarding Jesus' statement of no one knowing the day and hour is the obvious — that all Jesus really said is that you would not know the <u>day and hour</u>. In other words, what He did not say is that you would not know possibly the week, month, season, or year, etc.. As a matter of fact, one may conceivably be able to narrow it down to as little as just a two day period. Realize, of course, that even if you did know the specific day — and even hour (for example, let's say it was to be at 3:00 PM) — how could it really be binding, unless of course this time was divinely given and was also exclusive for, as an example, only those in Israel's time zone? In other words, realize that today we have extending across the globe a grand total of 24 different time zones, each with a different HOUR! Thus to illustrate as a hypothetical example, if someone was to say that from Scripture they could point out that the day and hour was to be at 3:00 PM on the 5th day of the 4th month, then that could therefore be true for only those in one particular time zone, else Christ would have to return 24 times — once each for each of the 24 different time zones — in order to fulfill the Scriptural requirement for those individuals living within each of these different time zones. In addition, because of these 24 different time zones, you will find that there is just but one tick on the clock — that is, one second in the day — in which all 24 of these time zones are experiencing the exact same <u>DAY</u>! With just the very next second, at least one time zone enters into a new day altogether. Thus considering all of these factors, when it comes to prophecy, we can conclude that to narrow an event down to just the day and hour is very complicated and even confusing at best, albeit it is unscriptural. Thus, on the one hand, even if a Feast of prophetic significance is deemed to be the fulfillment of a key end-time event, we can in no way truly pinpoint the exact day and hour of its anticipated fulfillment. On the other hand however, we can narrow it down to within, quite possibly, a two-day period, or even a particular week, month, or year. This is an amazing truth when you really think about it, especially when you take into consideration the content already provided you within this particular book. Of course, I will add one other important point at this time and that is that, at the very least, <u>attempting to set dates is NOT to be understood as the purpose of the writing of this book</u>.

Nevertheless, the truth is that Jesus did NOT say that we could not in any way know the day and hour. That is, He did NOT say that our not knowing was to be understood as an absolute! Rather, what

He actually said was that <u>it would be extremely difficult to know</u>, especially apart from a great deal of effort. The problem is that we would not immediately understand this from our English versions of the Bible. This is because the English versions do not always use words that are the equivalent of some of the Greek words used in the original manuscripts. In Matthew 24:36, this happens to be one of those cases. In particular, the word "know" in the English translation is used for one of the many Greek ideas for "knowing" something, even though it, unfortunately, is somewhat lacking in what it fully ought to communicate. In other words, we lose something in the English rendering of the original Greek word that is used. The reason for this is because in the original Greek language, there are as many as eight different levels of (or degrees of) "knowing" something for which we, in the English versions, translate with just a single word – "know." As a result, we in many cases end up lacking in our English versions some key aspects from what the Greek text fully intended to communicate. For example in the Greek, the eighth level of the verb "to know" is the word "ginosko," which means "to get to know, recognize, perceive, understand, or understand completely." In other words, if Jesus had said that no man would "ginosko" the day and hour, then that would have been a rendering that meant that no one in any way, at all, would ever be able to know it – period! It would have been absolute and it would have been understood as such. However, Jesus did not use that word. Had He done so, it would have ended this controversy once and for all – that is, end of subject! But He didn't. Instead He used the Greek word "oida." This word is not a definitive, absolute, unconditional knowing, but rather is a prerequisite, abstract, and conditional (upon circumstances) knowing. In other words, for Jesus to say that no man would "oida" the day and hour meant that no one would know <u>without a great deal of effort</u>! Or to put it another way, if one were to apply a great deal of effort, such as in a genuine and diligent searching of God's Truth for a more fuller understanding of His message, then they just might discern, or figure out, or even come to realize and understand His prescribed dates. In this case, Jesus was communicating to His disciples that as of that point in time (approximately 33 A.D.), neither they, nor the angels, nor even Himself (Remember that though Jesus was God in the flesh, He was living exclusive of His Divine Omniscience, or all-knowing ability. Instead, He was living fully as a man in complete dependence upon the Holy Spirit for knowledge. Thus, even He wouldn't have known intuitively!) would have had any idea of the day or hour of His return.

For us today however, it seems that the possibility to better discern, or at some point even know, the day and hour does in fact exist. With a careful investigation of the given events and a more thorough examination of God's Word, it seems God has left these questions open to possibly being answered. After all, other Scriptures seem to imply this as being the case. Remember, as has been stated already, the Apostle Paul said of the Christian that they are not to be in the dark regarding the Lord's return (1 Thess. 5:4-6). At the same time, we learn from the book of Daniel that as the Lord's return grows nearer and nearer, God in preparation of His people will be increasing our understanding of His Word all the more (Dan. 12:4). The result of this, it seems, would be a greater understanding of the prophetic details surrounding His return, even to include the dates, so as to have us ready as the Body of Christ. This would therefore even prepare us with more of a mindset of taking comfort in all of this knowledge, which is just what Paul exhorted us to do (1 Thess. 4:18; 5:11). In addition, it would more than likely have us all the more focused in reaching out to the lost in anticipation of His return, thereby helping to usher in the last great harvest that is to occur in the final hour! This certainly would not be a bad consequence, but instead would actually even contribute to a greater unity in the faith just prior to His return. Once again, it seems God's wisdom far surpasses that of ourselves, and His plans likewise far surpass what we could ever imagine. Thus, we should all the more be diligently looking to know ("oida") the day and hour of our Lord's soon return.

- Part 5 -

"The End-Time Conclusion"

Dennis Crump

Chapter 35

"The Two Witnesses"

A question that is frequently asked in end-time discussions concerns the subject of the two witnesses. Who are these two witnesses? This is certainly a popular question and is one of great interest, yet one of little debate. The reason they are so popular is due to the role that they have as part of the last days. This subject is discussed in Revelation 11 and is one which certainly appears to be quite amazing. After all, it says that they prophesy during the entire 3½ year tribulation period. But even more so, it says that they demonstrate godly power, able to somehow even shut the heavens and thereby stop the rains on earth. On top of that, they are able to turn the earth's waters into blood. These certainly are some amazing credentials. Nevertheless, it says that they also are able to smite the earth with all sorts of plagues, even as often as they would desire. As a matter of fact, we are told that they even have proceeding out of their mouths fire, and that they are able to therefore devour their enemies with it. This is most definitely a unique portrayal of what seems to be two of the most incredible people. But probably the most amazing characteristic of all is what is described of them at the end of this 3½ year period. We are told that at the completion of their testimony, the most spectacular events as of yet then occur. The Bible says that while they first die at the hands of their enemy, which is the beast, they are then left to lie in the streets of Jerusalem for 3½ days only to miraculously, in view of their enemies, arise from the dead. This is then followed by their amazing ascension into the clouds of heaven. This of course results in a great deal of fear falling upon their enemies of whom we are told will, as a result of this, give glory to God. Still, the city is subsequently hit with a major earthquake which results in the ending of many of these enemies' lives. In its very essence, this is a basic outline of events regarding these two witnesses as given us by the Apostle John in his Revelation. According to this description as given above, these events certainly are spectacular, miraculous, and quite surreal. As a result, this also should help to explain the cause of so much of the fascination, intrigue, and interest that people seem to express when it comes to a discussion of this unusual subject.

So once again, who are these two witnesses? Believe it or not, as was already stated above, there is really very little debate over this unique subject. Why? Probably because there are few options to legitimately consider regarding their actual identity. Probably the most popular answer is that they will be Moses and Elijah. Why? Mostly it is due to Jesus' experience on the "Mount of Transfiguration" in which He transfigured before His disciples and appeared in His glory, while at the same time being flanked by these same two individuals (see Matthew 17:1-9). This is believed to be further supported by the understanding that each was a representation of the Old Covenant — with Moses bearing witness to the Law and Elijah beaing witness to the Prophets — thereby each being deemed a witness already. Probably the second most popular answer, although receiving considerably less support, is that they will be Elijah and Enoch. In their case, this is due to the belief that neither ever died, that they both were instead translated up into heaven and thus, they would be the two who would later come back to be these two witnesses (incidentally, each then would finally experience death). In addition, this is believed to be further supported by the knowledge that Elijah already was the one who was previously able to shut the heavens from their raining on the earth (see James 5:17-18). At any rate, there is little popularity along with little support for most any other possibility given regarding whom these two witnesses might be. At the same time, it is also realized by many people that these two might instead be two entirely new characters arising from our present society, neither of which would therefore be historical and/or a former Biblical character. Again these possibilites, although certainly not exclusive, nevertheless represent a sampling of the most popular views circulating as to whom these two witnesses might actually be.

But who are these two witnesses? Can we identify them from Scripture? I believe we can. As a matter of fact, I believe that God has already revealed them in Scripture, a long time ago to be exact. But this is not necessarily obvious, and for good reason. The problem we have in trying to identify these two witnesses is that we, quite often, are so assuming when it comes to studying God's Word. That is, seldom do we think outside of the box, if you will. Let me give you an example of what I mean. There is an old brain-teaser that goes something like this. A famous surgeon was about to operate on a child who had been in an accident. The doctor, upon examining the child exclaimed, "I can't operate on this boy. He's my son!" However, the surgeon was not the boy's father. Now, how would you explain this? Of course, the problem most people have in trying to figure this brain-teaser out is caused by their preconceived assumptions. That is, they don't think outside of the box. Or in this particular case, they automatically assume that all doctors have to be male. Only no where in this brain-teaser does it ever indicate that this doctor has to be a male. When you remove this assumption, the answer becomes quite obvious and easy in figuring out. The doctor is not the boy's father, but rather his mother! Likewise when studying the Scriptures, it seems we often do this very same thing. That is, we interpret the text from the initial perspective of our preconceived ideas and/or assumptions, therefore blinding us to what in many cases would otherwise make the interpretation all the more easier to actually figure out. In the case of these two witnesses, this is the very problem that I made until someone fortunately brought to my attention what I didn't realize — that I was trying to interpret the passage through my assumptions, thereby blocking me from truly understanding their actual identity. What was the assumption that I was making? Just like most everyone else, I was assuming that these two witnesses were to be understood as two individuals, or two distinct people! Unfortunately, this is an assumption that I was reading into the text, albeit it was probably no different than most anyone else. However, it still blinded me from properly discerning God's intended meaning for this particular passage.

As opposed to automatically thinking that these two witnesses are to be understood as two individuals, there is another approach to properly determining their identity. If you recall from the English classes that you had while in school, you probably will remember learning about a literary skill known as personification. Personification was that method in writing in which one could give to any particular thing or entity various qualities that would normally be associated with people. In the case of these two witnesses, this is the very way in which John chooses to describe them, that is, they are personified with various human characteristics and/or qualities. Incidentally, him doing this makes considerable sense. After all, remember that what John actually received from God was what we call a <u>vision</u>. Thus, and what is so often the case with a vision and/or dream, the object or subject matter that is depicted in the vision/dream is done so by the way of symbolism and/or personification. As a matter of fact, a pattern of God doing this very thing already existed throughout not only the book of Revelation, but the whole Bible for that matter. For example, there is the image that Nebuchadnezzar dreamed about in the book of Daniel which we know was partly depicted through the means of personification (see Dan. 2-3). Likewise in Revelation, there is the Mystery Babylon which is the mother of all harlots. Is she really a lady? Certainly not. Rather, she is actually the city of Jerusalem, only personified as a lady (see Rev. 17-18). Then there is the beast. Is it really an animal? Nope. Or how about a person, or even as some people might think, the antichrist? Not at all. Rather, the beast is that Arab/Moslem empire, again merely personified as such (see Rev. 13). In addition, there is the woman (= Israel – see Rev. 12), the dragon (= Satan – see Rev. 12), the Bride of Christ (= New Jerusalem – see Rev. 21), etc.. In other words, God has already revealed to John many different visions of which, to properly understand them, we must first realize that they could involve personification. In so doing, our capacity to understand His message given to us increases greatly. Thus, in the case of these two witnesses, the secret to our understanding them is in realizing that they, too, are being personified. In so doing, God's Word will open up to us that much more.

However, just realizing that John was using personification in describing these two witnesses only begins to get us into the ballpark of its proper understanding. There is still one other assumption that continues to limit us. It is our assumption of what a "witness" actually means. Due to our culturization of Christianity as we know it, we once again limit our ability to understand, at least somewhat, what God intends to communicate to us. In the case of the word "witness," again we bring our preconceptions of what it means into the interpretation. To most of us, the word "witness" refers to something that we DO. However, or as is quite often the case in Scripture, it actually means something different — that is, it means something that we ARE! In other words, as opposed to our going out into the world and doing this thing that we call "witnessing" — as in the hope that we are doing "witnessing" by telling others about Jesus

Christ — it is instead meant to be something to the world of which we are — as in the hope that we <u>are,</u> with our lives, "bearing witness" of Jesus Christ, thus demonstrating that He is truly alive and therefore God! To state it another way, the responsibility for the action in the first case is on us, while in the second case it is instead on the Lord. Thus, this becomes the final key for our understanding of this passage regarding the two witnesses. What we are to realize is that the responsibility for the action is to be expected as being on God — that is, He is the one that will bear witness to the world of Himself, doing so through these two entities of whom again are personified as two individuals (or witnesses). In turn, what we will discover is that these two entities are actually to be understood as being two much broader entities which, accordingly, are a part of God's broader or overall plan of how He reveals Himself to this world. In other words, these two witnesses are His two uniquely chosen entities through whom He will use to reveal Himself to this world - the Old Covenant Believers and the New Covenant Believers! Or to state it another way, they are God's people from the Old Testament and God's people from the New Testament. Or also, Natural Israel and Spiritual Israel. Or Natural Jews and Spiritual Jews. Even Old Testament Saints and New Testament Saints. Or of most importance for this particular discussion, <u>the natural olive branch (or tree) and the wild olive branch (or tree)</u>! Are you beginning to get the point? These are the two means through whom God has chosen to reveal Himself to the world and in this particular passage, John accordingly details from his vision some of the unique details regarding them during this final 3½ year period known as the tribulation. In the following explanation portion of this chapter, we want to take a closer look at these two witnesses, at the proof God gives us regarding their identities, and at some of their other unusual details.

"The Two Witnesses"
Scripturally Explained

The subject of the "two witnesses" comes from chapter 11 in the book of Revelation. To properly understand this passage, one first needs to realize that the description given actually comes from a vision, experienced by the Apostle John, and is therefore filled with symbols. Thus, it is not to be taken as literal in its entirety, but rather is to be understood by identifying the elements within the vision that the various symbols represent. These symbols are identified by comparing them with other Scriptures, thereby having God's Word itself become the teacher of this passage. Ultimately, the best interpretation results when it best fits within the fullness of what God's Word in its entirety seems to be saying, thus fitting the condition of "rightly dividing the word of truth" (2 Tim. 2:15).

One of the major symbols that is first given in this vision is that of the temple. John writes:

> vs. 1 – "And there was given me a reed like unto a rod: and the angel stood, saying, Rise, and measure the <u>temple</u> of God, and the altar, and them that worship therein."
>
> vs. 2 – "But the court which is without the temple leave out, and measure it not; for it is given unto the Gentiles: and the holy city shall they tread under foot forty and two months."

If you recall from the chapter on "The New Jerusalem," the temple is a symbol for the Body (or Bride) of Christ. In other words, the temple in this passage is not a reference to a literal building, as in the Temple that existed during the Old Testament era. This is because under the New Covenant, God told us He would no longer dwell in a temple made of stone, but rather in a living temple, built together using <u>living</u> stones, which means people who are Believers (1 Cor. 3:16; 2 Cor. 6:16; 1 Pt. 2:5). People who might be looking for a temple to be rebuilt in Jerusalem during the tribulation period are sadly being misled. God has no desire for the temple to be rebuilt. Rather, His temple under the New Covenant is instead one that is invisible, being fashioned together with the addition of each new

Believer. Thus, what John sees first in this vision in an angel instructing him to "measure" this <u>new</u> temple, being the Body of Christ. Incidentally, this word "measure" corresponds to the same word used to describe what Believers essentially receive from God — that is, they receive a portion (or "measure") of faith at the point of when they come into the Body of Christ (see Rom. 12:3). Upon identifying this new temple, John then identifies in verse 2 that which is not considered a part of this temple, being the outer court. This outer court happens to symbolize the actual or literal city of Jerusalem, in this verse being clearly identified as the "holy city." Thus, what John is realizing is that there are two contrasting pictures here – in effect, there is the literal Jerusalem contrasted with the new Jerusalem. He then learns that for this literal Jerusalem (again, being the actual city), it is unfortunately going to experience some form of destruction for a period of 42 months, or 3½ years. Again, this is known as the tribulation period. By the way, as was pointed out earlier in this book, Revelation is to be understood as a compilation of many different visions as opposed to just a single large vision and as a result, each of these visions is to be interpreted NOT as automatically occurring chronologically in the book of Revelation. Rather, many of the visions are actually independent visions of, quite often, either the same thing or else the same period of time, only instead depicting a different perspective of it, or even focusing on a different element within the vision. Thus, this particular vision happens to be a new and independent look at this same 3½ year period, only focusing instead on some new or other elements within this period. At any rate, with John now identifying the old Jerusalem, he in turn learns of it that it is to experience a great deal of tyranny at the hands of a people referred to as the "Gentiles." Although this word "Gentiles" in Scripture quite often refers to anyone who is a non-Jew, thereby implying that it is the rest of the world, it also is often a reference for the immediate neighbors of Israel, of which we have already identified as being the Arabs. Thus, in attempting to rightly divide God's Word, this conclusion as such seems to have more merit, which brings us to verse 3:

> vs. 3 – "And I will give power unto my two witnesses, and they shall prophesy a thousand two hundred and threescore days, clothed in sackcloth."

This verse, quite simply, first introduces the two witnesses, then indicates their collective role of which is to last 1,260 days which, once again, computes to this same tribulation period of 3½ years (42 months of 30 days each). Then in verse 4, there is the inclusion of two very unique symbols which help to identify who these two witnesses are:

> vs. 4 – *"These are the <u>two olive trees</u>, and the two <u>candlesticks</u> standing before the God of the earth."*

Amazingly, as you will see, it is this reference right here which helps to identify for us just who it is that these two witnesses are. Remembering what was said earlier in the first section of this chapter, we have to realize that these witnesses are not to be understood as actual people, but rather as two entities which are being personified as people. This realization will thereby give us a greater understanding of what God's Word is actually saying here. This is due primarily because of what it says regarding these symbols. For example, we have an obvious explanation for the first symbol, the "candlesticks," given us in the first chapter of Revelation wherein John tells us that they represent "churches" (Rev. 1:20). Although he tells us in that passage that there are "seven churches" – one for each candlestick of which there were seven – and though he also discusses each one of these particular churches in chapters 2 and 3 of Revelation, nevertheless neither of these seven churches are to be connected with these two witnesses. However, there is still another "church" which God talks about elsewhere in Scripture. I am speaking, of course, about the Body of Christ, referred to also as His Church Body (Eph. 5:22-33). This happens to be one of the two witnesses and thus, is essentially a reference to the New Covenant Believers. Now, is this Church to actually be a witness for God? Absolutely. God even said so in Acts 1:8, "But you shall receive power, after that the Holy Ghost is come upon you: <u>and you shall be witnesses unto me</u> both in Jerusalem, and in all Judea, and in Samaria, and unto the uttermost part of the earth." Thus, the New Covenant Believers, because of the power that they receive through the Holy Spirit (which, by the way, is a major reason why the New Covenant is much stronger than and an improvement upon the Old

Covenant), make up an entity that is then personified as one of these two witnesses, of whom will in turn bear witness of God to the rest of the world. And this makes perfect sense! But what about the other witness? If the one is the New Covenant Believers, which by the way makes up half of the New Jerusalem, then could the other therefore be the Old Covenant Believers? Once again, the answer is an absolute yes. And this is confirmed by the other symbol in this verse — that being the "two olive trees."

In Romans 11, the Apostle Paul describes for us just how the overall Church Body of Christ is uniquely and amazingly united together with both Jews and Gentiles alike (in this particular reference, the Gentiles are to be understood as being the non-Jews). Essentially, he metaphorically describes the Old Covenant Believers (or Jews) as being a natural olive branch (or tree) that grows out from the root of this good tree, which is Jesus Christ. He then tells of how the New Covenant Believers (or Gentiles), depicted instead as a wild olive branch (or tree), are engrafted also into this good tree. Together, he says, these two branches (or trees) make up the full Body of Christ of which he then informs us is, once again, one of those great mysteries of God (see Romans 11:13-25)! Thus, we are able to identify from Scripture just exactly who these two witnesses are – once again, they are the two groups of Believers from both the Old and New Covenant periods. Together, they make up the New Jerusalem which again was initially identified as the "Temple" back in Revelation 11:1 and which, accordingly, is the main subject of this vision of the two witnesses that John describes for us. Next, we come to verse 5:

> vs. 5 – "And if any man will hurt them, fire proceedeth out of their mouth, and devoureth their enemies: and if any man will hurt them, he must in this manner be killed."

At this point, we begin to learn of the great abilities that these two witnesses will have. However, the best way to examine these characteristics is to first, having now established that these two witnesses are to be understood collectively as the Believers of Christ, remind ourselves of one of the great responsibilities that Christ gave them, and that is that they are to help in the role of judging the world (Lk. 22:30; 1 Cor. 6:1-5). Likewise, it would help to remind ourselves of how this judgment will be administered. God indicates in His

Word that judgment is essentially administered through the use of TRUTH! That is, God's Word is what is used in evaluating people. Though judgment is normally deemed as being negative, it is not always the case. For example, if I am doing something right, but at the same time there is someone who might be questioning me, my desire accordingly is to be judged (or be proven) as being in the right. This is the opposite of being judged as in the wrong, which is what we normally assume the meaning of judgment to be. But the tool used in this process of judgment is, of course, God's Word — or TRUTH! Thus, for the Believers, God will be delegating to them the responsibility of adjudicating people according to this TRUTH — that is, evaluating people as to whether they will be in the right or the wrong. Of course, understanding this is necessary to get the full meaning of John's vision of these two witnesses. Why? Because of what proceeds out of their mouth – FIRE! What does fire symbolize in Scripture? Again, it represents "judgment" (1 Cor. 3:13). Thus, the idea of fire proceeding out of their mouths is reflective of their speaking words of judgment against their enemies. Incidentally, this idea is consistent with verse 3 of Revelation 11, wherein the two witnesses are said to have power to prophesy during this period. Where do they get their power? As we learned from Acts 1:8 above, it comes from the Holy Spirit. And what does it mean to prophesy? Although many people believe that "to prophesy" means to speak about the future, this meaning really is not complete. Rather, a more accurate meaning of "to prophesy" is that it means to speak God's Truth in His name and in His power (meaning in the Holy Spirit). Thus, it connects back to their speaking TRUTH, and thereby administering judgment, which is what they'll have an increased role in doing during this period of tribulation! That one could be killed in so doing has already been proven earlier in Scripture. Just go back to the story of Ananias and Sapphira in Acts 5 to see this happening. In that account we learned that when they answered Peter upon being confronted, they therefore were judged wrongly as lying, and the result was that, as a form of judgment, they fell dead! Could this type of judgment be expected to be on the rise? It certainly seems so from this vision. As a matter of fact, a great deal of other unique manifestations are to be expected as well, which brings us to verse 6 of Revelation 11:

> vs. 6 – "These have <u>power to shut heaven, that it rain not</u> in the days of their prophecy: and have <u>power over the waters to turn them to blood</u>, and to smite the earth with all <u>plagues</u>, as often as they will."

Again, the precedent for these amazing endeavors has also been already established. For instance, we know that Elijah was able to shut the heavens from raining (see James 5:17-18), and we know that Moses was able to turn the Nile River into blood, even administering other plagues as well (see Ex. 7-12). That this possibility would be the same for these two witnesses during this tribulation period seems to be what is also learned from this vision. However, we also learn that all is not well for these two witnesses, which brings us to verse 7:

> vs. 7 – "And when they shall have finished their testimony, the <u>beast</u> that ascendeth out of the bottomless pit shall make war against them, and shall overcome them, and kill them."

From this verse we can see that they also encounter great difficulty. As a matter of fact, these two witnesses experience death. But when and from who? Since we are told in verse 3 that their testimony is to last 1,260 days, it would seem that their deaths would occur at the end of the tribulation. However, since they also will arise afterwards (vs. 9), then this death and ascension are also to be considered as part of their testimony as well. Thus, their deaths would actually have to occur <u>prior to the end of the tribulation period</u>! When? More than likely, it would occur 3½ days prior to the Feast of Trumpets (or Rosh Hashanah), specifically prior to the one that would occur near the end of this 3½ year tribulation period (see chart in chapter on "Holy Days: The Seven Feasts of Israel"). Who would kill them? Those from the Arab/Moslem empire. If you recall from the chapter on "The Beast: The Arab Empire," the beast is a symbol portraying the end-time enemy of Israel, understood to be that of the Arabs/Moslems. Additionally, their origin – "ascending out of the bottomless pit" – is to be understood as a symbol for the region of land immediately outside of the country or land of Israel. This, of course, is identified as that territory ruled by the Arabs/Moslems, which was earlier pointed out in the chapter on

"The Origin of the Beast: The Bottomless Pit (or Abyss)!". Thus, we come to verse 8 of Revelation 11:

> vs. 8 – *"And their dead bodies shall lie in the street of the great city, which spiritually is called Sodom and Egypt, <u>where also our Lord was crucified.</u>"*

From this verse we see that upon their deaths, they are left to lie in the city of Jerusalem. We know that this city is Jerusalem particularly because of the historical fact of it being where Jesus was crucified. Sodom (see Jer. 23:14) and Egypt (Ezk. 23:3,8,19,27) happen to be additional Biblical symbols also depicting Jerusalem. An important and critical note to make at this point from this verse is one that is more or less implied. That is, the city of Jerusalem referred to in this particular verse is, in this case, to be understood as being the literal or actual one. Thus, by implication, it therefore narrows the scope of involvement meant for these two witnesses. In other words, it is at this point that we get a more specific explanation regarding the extent of involvement for these two witnesses, and that is that this vision only refers to the Believers represented by the two witnesses that are in the city of Jerusalem. In other words, because we know that the two witnesses symbolize the Believers that are either Jewish or non-Jewish (again, see Romans 11), then we can learn from John's vision that a tremendous outpouring of God's Spirit is to definitely befall these specific Believers residing in the actual city of Jerusalem. Why would this be the case? Again, because it is the divine plan that God has chosen for these last days to most effectively bear witness of Himself to the non-believing Jews as well as to their enemies, the Arabs/Moslems. But at this point, this plan is not complete, which brings us to verse 9:

> vs. 9 – *"And they of the people and kindreds and tongues and nations shall see their dead bodies <u>three days and a half,</u> and shall not suffer their dead bodies to be put in graves."*

With the control at this point that this beast empire will have over the city of Jerusalem, they in turn will be able to do what is a ruthless and humiliating act, thereby mocking the very lives (or memory) of these Believers which, by the way, will more than likely amount to a significant number of people (or at least more than two!). Upon their killing them, we learn that they will also dishonor them, in this case not allowing them to be buried. Instead, they will be bannered before the world (at this point, the media will probably help to achieve this type of disclosure) for all to see, in what appears to be a celebration of an apparent victory. However, I would like to point out that although the world will probably be fully aware of this event occurring, the real impact will be limited more so to within just the Arab/Moslem empire. In verse 10 we read:

> vs. 10 – "And <u>they that dwell upon the earth</u> shall rejoice over them, and make merry, and shall send gifts one to another; because these two prophets tormented <u>them that dwelt on the earth</u>."

In this verse, what appears to be reflective of the entire world is really not the case. The word "earth" is translated from the Greek word "ge" of which, although it is translated to imply the full earth, it is more properly meant to refer to the "land." This rendering can therefore change the meaning of this passage altogether for now, as opposed to referring the entire world, it instead is referring to just those in the surrounding <u>LAND</u>, which is what this word "ge" really represents – that is, it is a Biblical reference for the land that is over there in the Middle East (i.e., the Land of Canaan, Land of Israel, Promised Land, etc.). Thus, we now see a more probable fulfillment in what this verse is actually saying, that it is the many Arabs/Moslems who will be celebrating, even by giving various gifts to one another – obviously again, a more likely scenario! Of course, the most miraculous outcome that takes place comes in the next verse, verse 11:

> vs. 11 – "And after three days and a half the Spirit of life from God entered into them, and <u>they stood upon their feet</u>; and <u>great fear fell upon them which saw them</u>."

God's greatest miracle used to bear witness to both the Arabs/Moslems and the non-believing Jews that He is God and that the two witnesses' message is true (and that Yeshua is the Messiah), now occurs 3½ days following their deaths. To their enemies' utter amazement, these Believers come back to life! The result, not surprisingly, is that a tremendous "fear" of God befalls them (Don't forget that Proverbs 1:7 says, "The <u>fear of the Lord</u> is the beginning of wisdom," and Proverbs 16:6 says, "by the <u>fear of the Lord</u> men depart from evil."). Of course, is this type of miracle unique? Yes, although it is not original. If you will recall, upon Jesus' resurrection, a number of others also arose from the dead (see Mt. 27:52-53). As was stated earlier, the witnesses' deaths would occur 3½ days prior to the Feast of Trumpets and, accordingly, their resurrections would therefore take place on this Feast of Trumpets. Why? Because of the amazing event of which we are told that occurs in verse 12:

> vs. 12 – "And <u>they heard a great voice from heaven</u> saying unto them, <u>Come up hither</u>. And <u>they ascended up to heaven in a cloud</u>; and <u>their enemies beheld them</u>."

Obviously, this is the rapture, folks! A few other Scriptures will only serve to confirm this. As far as the "great voice," check out the connection between God's voice and the sound of a trumpet (1 Thess. 4:16-17; Matt. 24:29-31; Rev. 1:10). Regarding this ascension to heaven in a cloud while their enemies observe them, this is similar to Jesus' ascension less His enemies, "And when he had spoken these things, while they (disciples and followers) beheld, he was taken up; and a cloud received him out of their sight" (Acts 1:9). Then in verse 13 of Revelation 11 we read:

> vs. 13 – "And the same hour was there a <u>great earthquake</u>, and the <u>tenth</u> part of the city fell, and in the earthquake were slain of men seven thousand: and <u>the remnant were affrighted, and gave glory to the God of heaven</u>."

As far as this great earthquake, again this only confirms the timing of this event, that it is the close of this 3½ year tribulation period. This earthquake occurs in connection with the second coming of the Lord Jesus Christ (Mt. 24:29; Rev. 6:12; 11:19; 16:18), on the Feast of Tabernacles, basically 15 days after the rapture (or Feast of Trumpets). Incidentally, the reference to the tenth of the city falling is not a literal one. In other words, this "tenth" is not to be considered as a partial reference to the city of Jerusalem, but rather as a full reference to it, meaning that it is a symbol for all of Jerusalem, which Biblically makes more sense. That is if you think about it, if there is to be this tremendously great earthquake, why would only a tenth of the city be affected? Rather, this symbol of a tenth is Biblically a representation for Jerusalem, which is revealed to us in Isaiah 6:12-13, "And the Lord have removed men far away, and there be a great forsaking <u>in the midst of the land (Israel)</u>. But <u>yet in it (Israel) shall be a tenth (Jerusalem)</u>, and it shall return, and shall be eaten: as a teil tree, and as an oak, whose substance is in them, when they cast their leaves: so the holy seed shall be the substance thereof." As far as the remnant in John's vision is concerned, it seems that this is a reference to the remnant of Jews who finally acknowledge that Yeshua is their Messiah, which again occurs on the Day of Atonement (once again, see chapter on "Holy Days: The Seven Feasts of Israel"). Finally, we conclude John's vision of the two witnesses with verse 14:

> vs. 14 – "The second woe is past; and, behold, the third woe cometh quickly."

At this point, John begins to describe the details of the third woe which, incidentally, is a zoom-in shot of the very last event of the tribulation, or the second coming of Christ, which again occurs on the Feast of Tabernacles. Thus, the following is provided as a timeline to help depict the events of this vision that John had of these two witnesses:

Wake Up Church: The End is Nigh!

The Two Witnesses:
(Jewish and Gentile Believers in Israel)

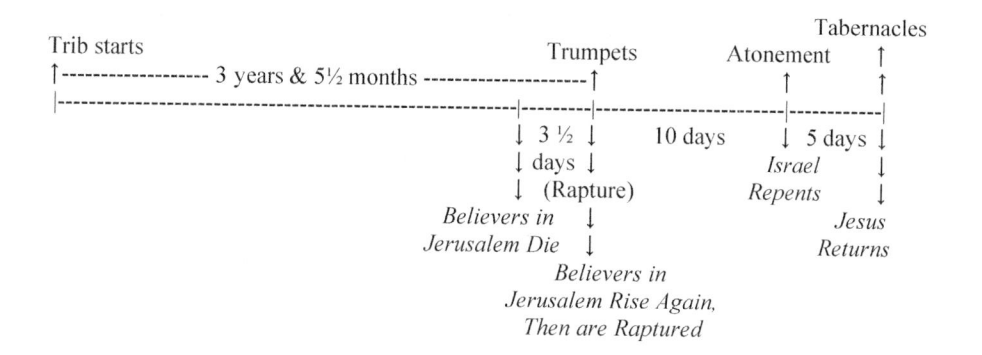

```
                                                      Tabernacles
Trib starts                       Trumpets    Atonement      ↑
↑------------------ 3 years & 5½ months ----------------↑         ↑        ↑
|-----------------------------------------------------|--------|---------------|----------|
                                  ↓  3 ½  ↓   10 days   ↓ 5 days ↓
                                  ↓ days  ↓            Israel     ↓
                                  ↓ (Rapture)          Repents    ↓
                          Believers in   ↓                       Jesus
                          Jerusalem Die  ↓                       Returns
                                  Believers in
                              Jerusalem Rise Again,
                              Then are Raptured
```

285

Chapter 36

"What to Expect for Believers"

By now, it should be fairly evident that the tribulation period is only 3½ years long. It should also be apparent that this tribulation conflict is due primarily to the continuous struggle that exists between the Jews and the Arabs/Moslems. Accordingly, this conflict will primarily be a Middle-Eastern affair. In other words, it is difficult to say just how involved in this conflict the rest of the world will be. On top of that, it should already be evident that for the Believers, they are not immune from this tribulation period. They, too, will be around during this 3½ year tribulation and except for the last couple weeks of it, they should definitely expect to be here. This being the case, the obvious question is what will be their role during this period? Or for that matter, what can they expect?

Taking into account the previous chapter on the two witnesses, this question has to be looked at in two different ways. On the one hand, for the Believers that remain in Jerusalem (and Israel), amazing things can certainly be expected even though the end will result in their deaths. Of course, even this is not their final outcome for as we also learned in the previous chapter, they will later be lifted up, followed also by their being raptured. But what about the rest of the Believers? That is, what about the Christians living throughout the rest of the world?

A key factor to remember in trying to understand God's intended plan from Scripture is that God doesn't address every issue. In other words, not everything is revealed within the Bible. To put it another way, there are many issues and events to occur that God's Word is silent about – meaning that we don't, or even won't, know everything that will happen. When it comes to God's Word, the reality is that He has chosen to address only certain things. In most cases, He only speaks regarding issues and events that pertain to and/or revolve around the nation of Israel. Thus, when it comes to the Believers outside of Israel during the tribulation, we only know just a few things. For example, we at least are aware of what Jesus told us in John 16:33, "These things I have spoken unto you, that in me ye might have peace. <u>In the world ye shall have tribulation</u>: but be of good cheer; I have overcome the world." Thus, it seems that difficulties will definitely exist for the Christian. In addition, it seems that there will also be an increase in lying, deception, rationalizing, and stubbornness. We are told by Paul in 1 Timothy 4:1-2, "Now the Spirit speaketh expressly, that <u>in the latter times some shall depart from the faith, giving heed to seducing spirits, and doctrines of devils; speaking lies in hypocrisy; having their conscience seared with a hot iron</u>." As a matter of fact, it seems he is telling us here that there will also be an ever increasing rise in the dabbling with and participation in the darkside of spiritual matters, such as with a growing interest in witchcraft, satanism, the occult, the new age, etc.. Thus, one can only imagine that there will likewise be a growing sense of spiritual warfare occurring in these last days. Accordingly, it would seem that there would be an increase in both the degrees of and levels of persecution experienced by those within the Church. But even though the assumption can be made that these times will be tough and very serious for the Believers, quite the opposite may in fact be the reality.

By its logical development, the Christian can actually prepare, during these end-times, for quite an outpouring of God's Holy Spirit. For example, we are told in the book of Acts, "it shall come to pass in the last days, saith God, (that) <u>I will pour out my Spirit upon all flesh</u>: and your sons and your daughters shall <u>prophesy</u>, and your young men shall see <u>visions</u>, and your old men shall dream <u>dreams</u>: and on my servants and on my <u>handmaidens I will pour out in those days of my Spirit</u>; and they shall <u>prophesy</u>: and I will shew <u>wonders</u> in heaven above, and <u>signs</u> in the earth beneath; blood, and fire, and vapor of smoke: the sun shall be turned into darkness, and the moon into blood, before the great and notable day of the Lord come: and it shall come to pass, that <u>whosoever shall call on the name of the Lord shall be saved</u>" (Acts 2:17-21). With this outpouring of God's Spirit, it therefore seems that there will be an influx in the occurrence of the supernatural as well – prophesying, visions, dreams, signs and wonders! But as exciting as that may sound, there is probably at the same time an even greater experience that can be expected – WORLDWIDE REVIVAL! That's right, many people coming to know the Lord. And if you think about it, this makes perfect sense. After all, remember that Paul told us that we as Believers are not to be in the dark regarding the Lord's return (1 Thess. 5:4-5). Instead, once the tribulation begins – commencing with the city of Jerusalem being encompassed by Arab armies (see Luke 21:20) – we will therefore KNOW that we have no greater than 3½ years to prepare not only for the Lord's return, but also to get the word out and thereby reach the lost. And the effect of this awareness for Believers can certainly be something that is greatly inspiring. After all, this is just human nature. People generally respond better when they are working with a deadline. And the knowledge that we are in this tribulation period provides this very deadline. Thus, what can the effect of this knowledge be? Essentially two things.

On the one hand, with this increased effort of outreach occurring among the Believers, we can therefore also expect a greater counter-reaction. In other words, we can probably expect from the enemy a rise in Christian persecution. However, although for us individually quite a fearful thing, this as a whole is not necessarily a bad thing. After all, whenever God's people are in the face of trouble and persecution, they tend to more greatly humble themselves. This therefore will result in more of an outpouring of God's grace (see James 4:6). Consequently, God will show up on their behalf in even greater and more mighty ways (Jer. 33:3; 2 Chron. 16:9). This is what happened to the early Church during the 1st Century and the outcome for them was their growing ever stronger as well as their numbers ever increasing (see the book of Acts).

On the other hand, this corresponding increase in numbers is essentially what we call revival, and is therefore what we can also expect to occur during this period! Incidentally, isn't this what we have been continually praying for? God will be providing the very circumstances for this one last great harvest. As a matter of fact, this is deemed in Scripture as the harvest that takes place during the last or "eleventh hour" (see Mt. 20:1-16) – essentially the great harvest that occurs during this last period of time known as the tribulation.

Thus, it seems that this period of time will be quite an interesting scenario for the Christian. However, as opposed to what is popularly believed, it is doubtful that there will be worldwide chaos. Rather, the conflict will be centrally located in the Middle East. With the rise of terrorism however, there definitely could be some backlash that occurs in other places. But nothing on the sort of an all-out world-wide war. Thus, it certainly will be interesting for the rest of the Body of Christ outside of the Middle East. To be able to observe this tribulation conflict between the Jews and Arabs/Moslems, especially live via satellite television, has to be an incredible thought. But will this really be the case? From a Scriptural standpoint, it seems to me that at this particular point, it more than likely is what we can expect. But of course, only time will tell. And for that matter, it may be in very little time that we actually do find this answer out...

"What to Expect for Believers"
Scripturally Explained

To seriously consider the content of this book, one must ultimately entertain the probing question of what this all means for us as Believers, that is, for those of us who are followers of Jesus Christ? In other words, we must ask that all so personal question of "What's in it for me?" This is not to say that we are being self-centered by asking this question because certainly, we all want to know the ramifications thereof of all these end-time prophecies, especially in light of how they might pertain to each one us personally or individually.

Admittedly, the traditional bent of end-time teaching for the tribulation period has included the interpretation that there will be a world-wide government, controlled by an antichrist leader, as well as the sensationalistic idea that there will probably be a nuclear holocaust that will ultimately destroy this world, to include a host of other related details or events associated with these two ideas. At the same time, for many Believers the teaching has also included the belief that the Christians will be removed from this all out chaotic state of affairs, them believing that they instead will be raptured just prior to the start of this tribulation. Of course, the conclusion of this book is that this is hardly the case.

First for the Christian, they will have the opportunity, if you can call it that, to witness this tribulation (or better, to be a witness in this tribulation period!). However instead of it being 7 years long, it will instead be half that length, or 3½ years. But for the Christian, does this then mean that they are to be paralyzed by the fear of those horrific events anticipated? Actually, except for what seems to be a limited number of Believers, practically the opposite is what the Christian should expect. For instance, remember that the end-time events are to be understood primarily in terms of that initial conflict that started way back in the beginning of the Bible, referring to that conflict over the Holy Land that still continues even today between the Jews and Arabs. Essentially then, this very conflict is a significant motivational force behind all the hateful acts that have occurred already as well as those that will continue to take place during this same tribulation period. Again, remember that although the Arabs cannot seem to get along with each other, there is still at least one common factor that they all seem to agree on, and that is their intense hatred for the Jews. Essentially, it helps to try to understand these things from their perspective. In other words, the ramifications in the eyes of the Arabs regarding Jewish religious history, as it is recorded in the Old Testament Scriptures, is that they (the Arabs) have in a sense, been spited by (the Jews') God. Nevertheless the Arabs, with great zeal and determination, continue to pursue the obtaining of this Promised Land. However, from the point of view of these Arabs, it seems that the Jews (though for them it wouldn't be intentional) keep sticking this supposedly "pious" attitude of having God's so-called favor back into their faces. Of course, the Arabs are by no means pushovers and even more so, they have a great deal of dignity and pride. As a result, their efforts to obtain and control this land have been not only historical, but also continue even today. Yet not only that, but they are a greatly religious people too and in fact, their religious ferver is based seemingly upon these same promises – that is, that their "God" has supposedly told them that they really are the "people of God" and that the land rightfully belongs to them. In addition, they are taught that to accordingly deal with the Jew in a justly manner means to retake this land. As a matter of fact, they are even taught that to eliminate the Jew in this process is both a noble feat for them as well as a desirable aim of their god. Ultimately then, the result of this is that there will eventually be a great Middle Eastern showdown between these two peoples during this tribulation period. However, those of us outside of the Middle East will merely witness or observe this jihad, or "holy war," more or less from a distance, which in this case <u>does</u> include Believers (them having not yet been raptured).

In effect, we as Christians will thus be witnesses of this ultimate dealing by God with the Jewish people. Let me for a moment give you a brief Scriptural overview of how this picture has not only developed over time, but also how it has ultimately gotten to this very point. For instance, remember first that in the very heart of God, the Jewish people are considered His beloved. As a matter of fact, God even took them to be His very own wife/bride (Jer. 3:14,20; 31:32; Is. 54:5). Certainly we know that God was truly a faithful husband, however they would ultimately be unfaithful. In fact, they would even betray Him, committing innumerable fornications and spiritual adulteries, such as in their partaking socially with the neighboring heathen peoples (Arabs) as well as in their religiously serving the others' (Arabs') gods. In effect, Israel therefore became a spiritual whore (Ezk. 6:9; Rev. 17:1), but even worse, she would became the spiritual mother of all other spiritual harlots (Hos. 4; Rev. 17:5). The result then spiritually was that, rather than her being a stepping stone for the other "nations" (incidentally, referred to here as Gentiles) through her actions and thereby helping to lead them to her God, Israel instead became a stumbling block for them (Is. 57:14; Ezk. 7:19; 14:3,4,7), even herself consequently falling away from her God. Thus, so grieved in His heart was God that He ultimately ended up divorcing her (Jer. 3:8). However, this was not a typical divorce as we tend to understand them for, as we all already know, God unequivocally hates divorce (Mal. 2:16). However in this case, what the Scriptures actually mean is that what God really hated was being put into the position of <u>having to therefore put away</u> His wife (Mal. 2:14-16). In other words, <u>only because she left Him, and therefore did not want to be with Him</u>, was Israel in turn put away. Of course, God never actually wanted to do this. But because Israel was unbelieving, God in turn let her go her own way (book of Hosea; 1 Cor. 7:10-16). As a matter of fact, His unending desire for her continued, it ultimately being for an eventual reconciliation with her (book of Hosea). Yet this too would not first be without serious and even long-term consequences for her. As a result, Israel would stumble (Is. 8:14; 28:7), even becoming blind (Is. 6:9; Rm. 11:8,25) and yet, although the eventual cost would become very great for her, God (as is His custom) would still cause this overall circumstance to work together for good (Rm. 8:28). In particular, the offer of salvation and the chance to become a part of God's people would now also be extended to the Gentiles (Rm. 11:11-12). This consequence for Israel would therefore be considered a form of God's discipline and chastisement for them (Heb. 12:2-11) — yet even this being a demonstration of His amazing and unceaseless love for His people (Jer. 31:3). This unwavering, unconditional, or "agape" love of God would ultimately and effectively result in an eventual repentance on the part of Israel, as well as a full and complete restoration for her (Joel 2:12-13; 3), thus leading to the amazing reconciliation of her with her Husband and He with His beloved wife (book of Hosea). Thus in contrast, although iniquity would greatly dominate in her life at first (Hos. 4:4), righteousness would still result later and in turn, even ultimately prevail within her (Hos. 2:19-20). Unfortunately, the necessary time period for this outcome to finally find fruition would be that prophetic time period of 70 weeks of years (Dan. 9:24-27) of which would not even be continuous, thereby spanning over a couple of thousand years. On top of that, the last 3½ of these years would in fact be terrible for Israel, described even as "a time of trouble such as never was since" (Dan. 12:1). This is because it will specifically for her be deemed "the time of Jacob's (Israel's) trouble" (Jer. 30:7). Thus we can conclude from this Scriptural picture that for Israel, this tribulation period will be extremely difficult to say the least, especially for everyone who will actually be living in that very land.

At the same time, however, it will be no less difficult for the Arab peoples. Being that it was they of whom historically Israel adulterated with (as in the Babylonians, Philistines, etc.), and since they also harshly treated this beloved wife of God, it has been determined that great punishment for them will likewise be their lot by God. Ultimately, this punishment will climax in what we know to be "the battle of Armageddon" (Rev. 16:16; 19) — for them, a terrible day indeed, even though initially the Arabs will actually seem to prosper, conquer, and even rule during the first part of this tribulation period.

Nevertheless for us as Believers, a key factor to realize is that this end-time scenario is primarily limited to what we know today as the Middle East. As a matter of fact, the Bible actually speaks rather loudly regarding this very factor. As a result, unless as a Christian you find yourself located in the Middle East during this period, it is really unclear as to just what effect on you the tribulation will have. In other words, contrary to what most people believe, what actually could happen for the Christian might not be too out of the ordinary after all. This is because on the one hand, on subjects where the Bible basically seems silent, we therefore really can not know what to expect and, by the way, this pretty much seems to be the case for those of us outside of the Middle East. Thus quite possibly, things may for the most part continue as they already are in areas outside of the Middle East. Yet on the other hand, although it seems that the world at large may (and most likely will) become even more intolerant of the Christian faith, and therefore even more so persecute Believers, nevertheless we can take courage in knowing that when the early Church also had this same experience of being persecuted, it actually led to a host of positive results. In other words, as we know from the book of Acts, it was in the mighty face of persecution that Believers stood tall and got courageous, therefore resulting in extensive and unparalleled growth within the Body of Christ. This, of course, is also a good sign of which, as it seems from Scripture, God has hinted already of a still remaining final great harvest of new Believers. As a matter of fact, the Bible depicts their conversion during this tribulation period as taking place in the very last hour (Mt. 20). Still however, we as Believers cannot be fully sure whether we will therefore "experience" this tribulation first hand — that is, as in the magnitude of how it is recorded in the book of Revelation. This is because for the book of Revelation, it once again speaks of the bulk of these things taking place not throughout the entire world, but rather primarily in just that specific "land" (Greek "ge") as located within the Middle East.

Yet you might ask at this point, "But what about in Revelation where it speaks of the <u>third part</u> of the world being destroyed, as in a <u>third part</u> of the trees, grass, sea, creatures, etc. (Rev. 8:7-12)?" Couldn't this include us and doesn't it obviously extend beyond the Middle East?" Of course as usual, this Biblical reference for the "third part" is not speaking directly about one-third of the entire world or its various elements, but rather is a symbolic reference specifically identifying <u>all of the land of Israel</u>. In other words, this phrase of the "third" or the "third part" is used elsewhere in Scripture to symbolize Israel. Notice the amazing teaching found in this particular verse, "In that day shall Israel be <u>the third</u>..." (Is. 19:24). In addition, speaking of Israel at end of the tribulation, Zechariah 13:9 amazingly says, "And <u>I will bring the third part through the fire</u>, and will refine them as silver is refined, and will try them as gold is tried: they shall call on my name, and I will hear them: I will say, <u>It is my people (Israel)</u>: and they shall say, The Lord is my God." Likewise, some additional references which speak of Israel as being the "third part" are recorded in Ezekiel 5:1-5,12 and Revelation 9:15. Obviously then, the way that we are to understand these events of Revelation 8 about the third part of the creatures, sea, rivers, etc., being destroyed is that this is just giving us a picture of the type of impact on this <u>land of Israel</u>, being now known Scripturally as the "third part," that this tribulation period will have. Once again, when we closely examine the teachings of Scripture, we find that the Bible amazingly and yet clearly speaks not only for itself, but even does its own interpreting for us.

But then you ask, "What about in Revelation 6 where it discusses the <u>fourth part</u> of the world being killed through war, hunger, death, and beasts (Rev. 6:8)? Isn't this a reference that speaks somewhat of worldwide destruction?" Believe it or not but once again, this too is a symbolic reference to Israel. In other words, in addition to being symbolically known as the "third part," the Bible even speaks of Israel as also being the "fourth part" — "Who can count the dust of Jacob, and the number of the <u>fourth part</u> of Israel?" (Num. 23:10). Again, other examples depicting Israel as the "fourth part" can be found in Ezekiel 14:21, Amos 2:6, and Nehemiah 9:3. Thus, we are to understand from this symbol that it is not one-fourth of the world that will experience death, but rather it is actually the people of Israel who will experience a great deal of it. Of course for them, this is very unfortunate. Nevertheless, we once again see that the Bible alone can be used to interpret Revelation for us and in this particular case, we see that it is once again Israel which is to be the primary recipient of these details found in Revelation 6:8. Incidentally, I might add that not only is Israel called both the "third" and the "fourth" in Scripture, but as was earlier pointed out in the chapter on the two witnesses, it is even referred to as the "tenth" (or at least the city of Jerusalem is — see Is. 6:12-13). This was important, if you recall, for interpreting Revelation 11:13, "And the same hour was there a great earthquake, and the <u>tenth part</u> of the city fell." In other words, according to the Scriptures we can interpret this to mean that with the occurrence of this great earthquake, not $1/10^{th}$ of the city will fall, but rather <u>all</u> of the city of Jerusalem will be damaged. Certainly, without having the Bible to inform us that the city as a whole is to be known as the tenth, we would be left to conclude here that merely 1/10th of Jerusalem would fall, which alone would not only be very difficult to measure (I've been to Jerusalem and this would basically be an impossibility, to somehow measure out 1/10th of the city), but would at most, if this were to actually happen as such, result in it being described as something of considerably less magnitude than that of a <u>great</u> earthquake. Again, Jerusalem is not that big of a city. Any <u>great</u> earthquake would by its very nature impact far more than just $1/10^{th}$

of this city. But not only that, realize that unless we are to interpret Revelation as being a compilation of numerous visions or revelations (many of which again are actually different pictures of the same or similar things), as is the case in my approach, we would have to instead conclude that during this tribulation period there is not just one, but in fact three "great earthquakes" which in turn occur – the first being in Revelation 6:12, the second here in Revelation 11:13, and the final one occurring in Revelation 16:18 (of which, by the way, it says that there is none other like it before or since???). And of course, these "great" earthquake references do not even include those of the plain and simple (or minor???) "earthquake(s)," such as in both Revelation 8:5 and 11:19. Likewise, there is a similar problem when it comes to the mention in Revelation of the "great city" falling — that is, how often are we really to interpret that this city is actually going to fall (see Rev. 11:13; 14:8; 16:19; 18:2)? — unless of course we again realize that the book of Revelation is a compilation of many different pictures of the same event taking place. The same can also be said when it comes to the mention of the word "world" in Revelation, wherein many believe that it many times is depicted as incurring worldwide destruction – that is, how many times will it actually experience destruction and in each case, to what extent — unless instead we again realize that we are being given many different perspectives of basically the same event(s) taking place? In other words, the conclusion for us as Believers from all of this is that, unless one is actually living in the Middle East during the tribulation, it is very difficult to assess Scripturally just what we can expect during this same time period. For once again, unless the Bible actually speaks directly regarding an issue, we should be careful not to "add unto" it anything beyond what it already states, especially in these areas in which it chooses to remain silent (Rev. 22:18). And certainly, such seems to be the case for the Christian living outside of the Middle East during this period. Thus, it will definitely be interesting to see how this all unfolds, especially from the perspective of us as Believers. Again, only time will tell...

Chapter 37

"What about the United States?"

Having somewhat established in the last chapter what to expect for the Believers during the 3½ year tribulation period, it now raises the question of what to expect for the United States? Does the Bible specify a role for them? Again, the answer is unfortunately no. That is, the Bible doesn't really identify the United States in any direct manner. Although many Biblical teachers attempt to connect various Scriptures with them, this really is stretching it. Rather at best, all you can do is merely speculate. For that matter, there certainly are enough references in Scripture to do so with. However, there is a risk in so doing in that the possibility always exists that people can be either misled or even erroneously taught. But at the same time, you almost can't help but wonder if God spells out somewhere their role(s). Nevertheless, there are at least a few Scriptures worth considering as food for thought, as well as few from which to truly evaluate them from.

Obviously, since the United States is currently involved in the war against terrorism, they probably already find themselves involved. Although this involvement is not predicted in Scripture, there is a reference to consider as possibly either referring to them, or at least including them. In the book of Daniel, there is a verse which identifies the involvement of forces from some other country (or countries) other than those included as part of the Arab/Moslem empire. As a matter of fact, these forces are actually specified as being ships, "For the <u>ships of Chittim</u> shall come against him (= King of the North - see earlier chapter on "King of the North vs. King of the South")" (Dan. 11:30). This reference to Chittim is depicting the island of Cyprus in the Mediterranean Sea, directly west of the land in the Middle East. Of course at that time (when Daniel wrote this), and actually throughout time, Chittim (Cyprus) has never really been a country with any arsenal of military might, to include having a fleet of ships for their Navy. That is, for them it doesn't exist. However, this reference is given from the point-of-view of Daniel (located in the land), revealing what would take place in the future. Thus, what he sees are ships in the Mediterranean Sea coming against this Arab/Moslem empire. Could they therefore be from the United States' Navy? I think it is very possible. As a matter of fact, the way that the New International Version states it is that the "Ships of the western coastlands will oppose him." Again, this very well could be a description that refers to or even includes the United States, though we won't be able to know in advance. With the current war against terrorism, it seems likely that the United States will probably be involved in some manner. Especially since in the past, the United States has been a strong ally of Israel, though even that could change before too long. For instance, it is difficult to imagine Jerusalem being taken over, and this lasting some 3½ years, without some extent of repercussions from the United States, unless of course the United States for some odd reason were to adjust either its policy towards or its position with Israel. Yet even that, of late, has somewhat already begun to occur at times and in varying degrees.

At any rate, in response to the above thought on Daniel 11:30, I realize that some would be quick to point out that this verse is not even prophetic. That is, they would quickly point out that this verse is not referring to something that is to take place in the future, but rather has already been historically fulfilled, and they are right. Yet, though that may be true, there still remains the possibility that this passage, specifically Daniel 11:21-39, might have a dual fulfillment. This too is not unusual in Scripture though again, only time will ultimately tell for us regarding this particular passage.

Outside of this particular reference, is it possible to imagine the United States involved in this Middle Eastern conflict of 3½ years? Again, although the Scriptures make no other direct or indirect statement regarding them, it still does not mean that they won't be involved. That is, though God's Word might be silent regarding them, it does not mean that they can't be involved. Plus, under the current circumstances, it seems very likely that they will be. But even if so, it would probably be more from a distance, meaning that we probably would find ourselves sending our troops over there. It seems highly unlikely that the Arabs/Moslems would send their personnel over here, at least in a militaristic sense. However, and sadly I might add, we still may have to anticipate here in our lands that which we already have experienced – the fear of additional terroristic acts of violence! This would seem very likely since we have already been told by those such as Osama bin Laden and Saddam Hussein that their two greatest enemies are one and the same – Israel and the United States! As for the recent attack against terrorism in Afghanistan, President George W. Bush has already told us that it is merely the beginning. Currently, a great deal of discussion is taking place regarding who will next be attacked, and the popular thinking is Iraq. Of course, the Iraqis' response has been that this would be a grave mistake on our part, obviously suggesting some form of backlash if this were to occur. And if you use history as a precedent, the Gulf War provides for us an obvious crystal ball from which to predict things. Thus, it would seem that an attack against Iraq would probably mean a counter-attack on their part against not only us, but especially Israel, the same as what occurred back then. This very well could therefore be the catalyst that brings about the fulfillment of Luke 21:20 (Jerusalem being surrounded by Arab armies), accordingly taking us into the tribulation period. But again, only time will really tell for us.

But as far as this war against terrorism goes, some might even wonder what the meaning of a supposed victory against the Taliban and the Al-Qaeda network would be according to Scripture. Interestingly enough, Revelation 13 seems to provide for us such an explanation. John informs us of this possibility in verse 3, "And I saw one of his heads (referring to the beast empire) as it were <u>wounded to death; and his deadly wound was healed</u>: and the world wondered after (or was in great awe of) the beast." John here seems to describe a major setback, or death blow, incurred by the beast empire. However, a miraculous rebound on their part takes place afterwards. This, of course, is NOT to be understood as a person individually dying and then afterwards arising, as has been popularly taught, wherein they often refer to it as their supposed future Antichrist (see again earlier chapter on "Antichrist"), but rather is depicting some type of major defeat on the part of what is a country or alliance that is personified as the beast. Thus, if the United States were to defeat the Taliban, only to have them then rebound, then this could therefore be a possible fulfillment of this very verse. Obviously, this very well might happen, especially if the United States were to defeat them without finding Osama bin Laden. And this possibility is also very likely…

Essentially then, it seems that we should be very alert as a nation during this tense period of time, though not necessarily paralyzed by fear. Actually, what we may in turn witness is a conflict in the Middle East that is not much different from what we already know. Certainly, with an extended role on our part, the expected result could be the loss of even more lives, especially among the forces within our military. In turn, an increase in terrorism within our lands might also result, but at least there would not be this all-out worldwide chaotic state of affairs as has been popularly taught. But again, as far as the United States goes, at best all we can do is speculate, such as in what I just did. As for reality, only time will ultimately tell for us. But we should at least be growing more and more aware of the times that we are in. God has already stated that the Church is not to be in the dark, so it is definitely time for us to wake up, because the end it seems is definitely nigh upon us!

"What about the United States"
Scripturally Explained

Having somewhat addressed the implications of the tribulation period on us as Christians, the same question can be asked regarding its implications on the United States. In other words, will the U.S. play a role in the outcome of these end-time events, especially in terms of what happens in the Middle East? After all, some have attempted to find the United States in Scripture, aiming to determine its end-time role. But again, in all honesty, it seems that the Bible is silent in terms of its speaking about America. But you might say, "What about where the Bible talks of the eagle, for doesn't the book of Revelation even mention that Israel rides on the wings of an eagle? Couldn't this possibly be the United States?" Again, we must seek the Scriptural answer of what an eagle represents to answer this question.

Revelation 12:14 says, "And to the woman were given two wings of a great eagle, that she might fly into the wilderness, into her place, where she is nourished for a time, and times, and half a time, from the face of a serpent." The woman is obviously Israel and we see again that she heads for the wilderness (also mountains as in Mt. 24:16) for 3½ years, or the length of the tribulation period. Of course, the question for us regards this eagle — could it be that the United States is this great eagle? After all, our national symbol is the eagle, so wouldn't that mean that it represents us? Certainly, America is great and yes, her symbol is an eagle. But again, unless the Bible itself states that the United States is an eagle, then for us to interpret it as such would only be speculation, and therefore potentially dangerous. Incidentally, the Bible does NOT, in fact, use an eagle to symbolize America. Nevertheless, the Bible does use an eagle to symbolize more than one thing, of which two of these are worthy of consideration. On the one hand, an eagle is used to depict one of the allies of Israel, being God Himself (in Is. 40:31), in which case it symbolizes the protection that He provides for His people, "Ye have seen...how I bare you on eagles' wings, and brought you unto myself" (Ex. 19:4). On the other hand, the eagle has also been used to depict one of the enemies of Israel — for example, as in the king of Babylon who took Israel captive, "Son of man, put forth a riddle, and speak a parable unto the house of Israel; And say, Thus said the Lord God; A great eagle with great wings...came unto Lebanon, and took the highest branch of the cedar... Say now to the rebellious house, Know ye not what these things mean? tell them, Behold, the king of Babylon is come to Jerusalem, and hath taken the king thereof, and the princes thereof, and led them with him to Babylon" (Ezk. 17:2,3,12). Incidentally in this case, Israel's enemy is referred to as being not just an eagle, but rather as a "great eagle." At the same time, God also informs us in this passage that this great eagle is symbolic, even giving us the meaning of it – Babylon and its king. Thus, when you attempt to interpret Revelation 12:14, although either of these symbolic meanings would potentially seem to fit (that is, that the great eagle is Israel's ally, meaning God, or that it is her enemy, meaning Babylon), it seems that we are more Scripturally consistent if we interpret it to represent her enemy. This, of course, is primarily because the eagle in this verse is actually referred to as the "great eagle," which is also what Babylon was called. Of course, Babylon is representative of the Arab peoples and thus, we can interpret this verse as follows — due to the works of the Arab peoples during this tribulation period, Israel in turn flees to the wilderness. This again is consistent with Scripture (see Lk. 21:20-21). Nevertheless, as far as the United States in concerned, the point here becomes not what the great eagle represents, but rather what it does not represent – the United States, meaning that the U.S. is eliminated from consideration in interpreting this passage.

Incidentally, it seems that additional attempts have been made to assess the role of the United States during the tribulation using other passages as well (in Psalms, Isaiah, etc.). However in each case, all that can really be said from these passages is that the message might relate to, or even apply to, the United States, yet it certainly is not directly about them. In other words, the bottom line here is that the Bible seems to remain silent regarding the role of the United States during this tribulation period.

Nevertheless, probably the best passage to consider in terms of the United States is one that is not about it at all. This passage is in Deuteronomy 28 and, although it is really about Israel, it seems that in an indirect manner it could at least apply to the United States. Without going into great detail verse by verse, it is still worth mentioning a few points here for certainly, as we will see, a great deal can be learned from it with respect to the United States. Specifically, this passage is about the nation of Israel and in it, God lists the various blessings that would result for them if they were to heed His ways (vs. 1-14) as well as the many curses that would result if they were not to (vs. 15-68). Interestingly enough, in the case of the United States historically, what seemed to be true regarding at least its first 150 years (us following God's ways and therefore experiencing His blessings), seems to now be somewhat reversing (us now rejecting God's ways and thus experiencing many of the curses). This is especially true when you evaluate many of the its positions, decisions and actions within just the last century (going deeply into national debt, supporting abortion, removing prayer from school, allowing married couples to easily divorce which indirectly contributes to the break up of many families, the allowance of pornography, etc.). In other words, the warning from this passage is very clear to us if the United States is to continue to exist as a superpower. As a matter of fact, this warning is even more necessary for us if we are to, at the very least, just survive as a nation. For example, observe this warning from Deuteronomy 28, bearing in mind some of these already ungodly positions that the United States has unfortunately embraced:

> vs. 58 - "*If thou wilt not observe to do all the words of this law that are written in this book...*"
> vs. 59 - "*Then the Lord will make thy plagues wonderful, and the plagues of thy seed, even great plagues, and of long continuance...*"
> vs. 62 - "*And ye shall be left few in number...because thou wouldest not obey the voice of the Lord thy God.*"
> vs. 63 - "*And it shall come to pass, that as the Lord rejoiced over you to do you good, and to multiply you; so the Lord will rejoice over you to destroy you, and to bring you to nought...*"

In light of these verses, it seems that the patience of God toward the United States is certainly being tried. Although this passage in Deuteronomy 28 is again a direct warning to the nation of Israel, it nevertheless is worth noting that the deaths of other past nations have at times been traced to their continuous breach of these very same warnings. Hence, we certainly need to acknowledge that it is God who raises up nations. At the same time, we certainly need to also realize that it is God who, because of ungodliness, likewise seals their fate. Thus, in the case of the United States, it is God alone who knows what the future holds for us. Fortunately, we can be thankful to God that He is at least One who is longsuffering, forgiving, and incredibly patient, to say the very least. Thus, we would be wise to bow down to our knees and cry out to Him as the Lord Jesus Christ, the King of all Kings, and the Lord of all Lords:

"Oh Lord, may You bless Your people, and may You bless America, and may you hasten the peace for Jerusalem; even so, come Lord Jesus!"

Appendix

A: A Possibility Worth Considering

"1260, 1290, and 1335 Days"

Many people ask, "Is there anything or are there any events that we can be looking for to be fulfilled in prophecy before the start of the tribulation? Or will the tribulation all of a sudden just begin one day on some future Passover Feast?" I myself have wondered about these same questions and as a result, offer this scenario as a <u>suggested possibility</u>. But I repeat, it is only something to consider!

One night I was studying an idea out in Scripture when I "stumbled" upon what may be the future interpretation for a subject that seemingly may depict an end-time scenario. It involves three periods of time as recorded in the Old Testament book of Daniel, specifically chapter 12. The three periods are as the above title indicates – the 1260 day, the 1290 day, and the 1335 day periods of time. Of course, we know already that the 1260 day period is one that corresponds to the end-times, specifically the 3½ year tribulation. But what about the other two? Are they connected to the end-time picture as well? I believe it is probable, although these are truly difficult to fit together. At the same time, I also believe that they need to be examined. Below is one such possibility.

Essentially, Daniel tells us about these three periods in the following three verses:

> vs. 12:7 – "And I heard the man (the angel Michael) clothed in linen, which was upon the waters of the river, when he held up his right hand and his left hand unto heaven, and sware by him that liveth for ever that it shall be for a <u>time, times, and a half</u>; and when he shall have accomplished to scatter the power of the holy people, all these things shall be finished."
>
> vs. 12:11 – "And from the time that the daily sacrifice shall be taken away, and the abomination that maketh desolate set up, there shall be a <u>thousand two hundred and ninety days</u>."

vs. 12:12 – "*Blessed is he that waiteth, and cometh to the <u>thousand three hundred and five and thirty days</u>.*"

Incidentally, the "time, times, and a half" of verse 7 equates to 3½ years and therefore 1260 days – a "time" corresponds to a year, "times" corresponds to two years, and "a half" equals a half of a year. At any rate, the Scriptural reference that possibly explains these three verses may actually be the previous chapter, or Daniel 11. The following could therefore be the explanation (again, Daniel 11:40-45 is definitely future, verses 36-39 might be future, and verses 21-35 might have a dual fulfillment, being therefore future as well):

A "VILE PERSON"

In Daniel 11:21, we are told that a "vile person" is coming, "*And in his estate shall stand up a vile person, to whom they shall not give the honour of the kingdom: but he shall come in peaceably, and obtain the kingdom by flatteries.*" As was pointed out in the chapter on "The Little Horn (Yasser Arafat?)," based upon all the characteristics listed regarding him in Daniel, Arafat very well could be the "little horn" from Daniel 7:8 and 8:9. Likewise, many of the characteristics of the "little horn" mirror those of this "vile person." Thus, upon the introduction of this "vile person" in Daniel 11:21, you will notice that he (and his people) then come up against or have a conflict with the "king of the south" a certain number of times – THREE:

1. 11:25 – "*And he shall stir up his power and his courage <u>against the king of the south</u> with a great army,*"
2. 11:29 – "*At the time appointed <u>he (this vile person) shall return, and come toward the south</u>,*"
3. 11:40 – "*And at the time of the end shall <u>the king of the south push at him</u>.*"

Amazingly, it seems that Daniel also indicates that there is a DIVINELY APPOINTED time for each conflict.

"1290 DAYS"

The most obvious of these "Divine appointments" is the second conflict of Daniel 11:29. One reason for this is because Daniel, inspired by the Holy Spirit, in fact states that it takes place "at the appointed time." In a study of this word "appointed," it becomes increasingly clear that when God appoints something, He means it. For example, speaking of the very first Passover, Moses wrote, "And the Lord appointed a set time, saying, Tomorrow the Lord shall do this thing in the land" (Ex. 9:5). In fact, so precise and specific was God concerning "appointments" that He established a divine calendar system to validate this, "He appointed the moon for seasons" (Ps. 104:19). Even doing just a casual study of the word "appoint, (ed), (ment)" will reveal the seriousness of God on this matter.

A second reason for the obviousness of this conflict's appointed time is due to a couple of its outcomes, "And arms shall stand on his part, and they shall pollute the sanctuary of strength, and shall take away the daily (sacrifice), and they shall place the abomination that maketh desolate" (Dan. 11:31). Two of the consequences that Daniel reveals here are that the daily sacrifice is taken away and that the abomination of desolation takes place. It is important to note a couple of things at this point. First, the word "sacrifice" is not even listed in the original Hebrew manuscripts, but is rather added by the early translators. Thus, this actually results in the following translation instead, "and (they) shall take away the daily." However in the Hebrew, the word used ("tamiyd") does not necessarily have as its focus a sacrifice. Rather, the emphasis behind this word's usage is the fact that it is to be something done that is on a continual basis. As a result, the best English rendering for this Hebrew word is, in fact, "the continual." Essentially, the "continual" is something that was done every morning and every evening, was at one time an animal sacrifice, but was later fulfilled by the sacrifice of one's prayers. This was revealed to us by David, "Let my prayer be set before You as incense, the lifting up of my hands as the evening sacrifice" (Ps. 141:2). Thus, the future removal of the daily thing (or continual thing) at the hands of this "vile person" can be anticipated to be the denial of prayer for the Jews at their infamous present day holy site known as the "Wailing Wall."

The second consequence listed is the "abomination that maketh desolate." It is unfortunate, but many people do not have a proper Scriptural understanding of this idea. Rather, their understanding is somewhat like what mine used to be. That is, they believe that it is representative of some future antichrist world leader (see chapter on "The Antichrist?"). Rather, it is meant to depict the land of Israel becoming desolate — something that God detests — as a consequence for their persistent hardness of heart (see chapter on "The Tribulation").

Of course, as revealed by Daniel, the fulfillment of both of these consequences is actually according to an appointed time. Amazingly, this is discovered when one looks at what Daniel said in 12:11, "And from the time that the daily sacrifice shall be taken away, and the abomination that maketh desolate set up, there shall be a <u>thousand two hundred and ninety days</u>." Daniel insightfully explains that there is a total of 1290 days from the time that these two consequences occur unto "the time of the end" (12:9) in which "many shall be purified, and made white, and tried" (12:10). Of course, knowing that the tribulation is only 1260 days (Dan. 12:7; Rev. 11:2,3), this gives us an incredible possible revelation, and that is that the second time of conflict between the "little horn" (Arafat and the Palestinians?) and the king of the south (Dan. 11:29) is to take place 30 days prior to the beginning of the tribulation (also, remember that the United States could be considered as being a part of this southern kingdom - see chapter on "The King of the North vs. The King of the South").

"1260 DAYS"

As was just mentioned, we already know that the length of the tribulation is to be 1260 days, or 3½ years, or even 42 months. Amazingly, Daniel instructs us that the third type of conflict that the "little horn" has with the southern kingdom is when the tribulation period actually begins. Notice what he says, "And at the time of the end shall the king of the south push at him" (Dan. 11:40). In fact, it is during this reference to the third conflict that one of the parties of the southern kingdom is actually mentioned (Egypt), "and the land of Egypt shall not escape" (Dan. 11:42). But remember, this is not until it is already that both the "daily is taken away" and "the abomination that maketh desolate is set up," because these occur some thirty days earlier during the previous (or second in this list of three conflicts) little horn/southern kingdom skirmish. Now, what about the first conflict between these two parties, or the one yet to be explained?

"1335 DAYS"

First, remember again that Daniel introduces this first conflict in 11:25, "And he (the vile person/little horn) shall stir up his power and his courage against the king of the south with a great army." Next, remember also that the second battle was mentioned as being divinely appointed in 11:29. Of course, a pattern is given us by God when He validates this second appointment by establishing a certain number of days in conjunction with this event – 1290 (Dan. 12:11). We also see God doing the same with the third conflict of 11:40-43 – 1260 days (Dan. 12:7; Rev. 11:2,3). Thus, this pattern is completed when we see what Daniel instructs us regarding an additional appointment in 12:12, "Blessed is he that waiteth, and cometh to the thousand three hundred and five and thirty days." Amazingly, Daniel lists for us a third already established amount of days that are likewise appointed by God – 1335 days. He also lists some characteristics that will be experienced upon the reaching of these 1335 days. Collectively, these characteristics are God's Divine blessing upon those who by this point have through faith turned to Him and therefore already become a part of His chosen people ("Blessed is he that waiteth, and cometh..."). This is then further established in Daniel 12:13 by the fact that first the end will have been reached by this point ("But go thou way till the end be"), second that God's Sabbath or Millennial rest will have now begun ("for thou shalt rest"), and third that God's people will have finally received their inheritance of the Promised Land ("and stand in thy lot at the end of thy days"). Thus, we see that all three of these established amounts of days (1260, 1290, and 1335) are to be (or at least they might possibly be) consummated jointly at the end of the tribulation period.

Amazingly, this pattern seems to be confirmed by Daniel during the depiction of the second battle when he reveals an amazing characteristic regarding this skirmish. Notice again how Daniel describes this battle, "At the time appointed he shall return, and come toward the south; but it shall not be as the former, or as the latter" (Dan. 11:29). Here, Daniel provides for us a description that gives some further continuity regarding the understanding of these three conflicts along with the three amounts of days.

"WHAT DOES THIS REALLY MEAN?"

If the above possible interpretation is really correct, then the following would be true. Essentially, we know that the 1260 day tribulation is to begin on some future Passover Feast (see chapter on "Holy Days: The Seven Feasts of Israel"). As a result, we would therefore be able to anticipate that 75 days beforehand, there would be some type of conflict between the little horn (and his people) and the southern kingdom. Then, 45 days later (or 30 days prior to the tribulation), a second outbreak or conflict will transpire, also between these same parties. During this conflict, the daily (or continual – prayer at the Wailing Wall?) will be taken away and the Jews will begin to scatter, or flee to the wilderness/mountains. Finally, or 30 days after this second conflict (on Passover), the third outbreak will commence, at which point the tribulation will have begun to occur. The following timeline depicts this scenario:

1260, 1290, & 1335 Days

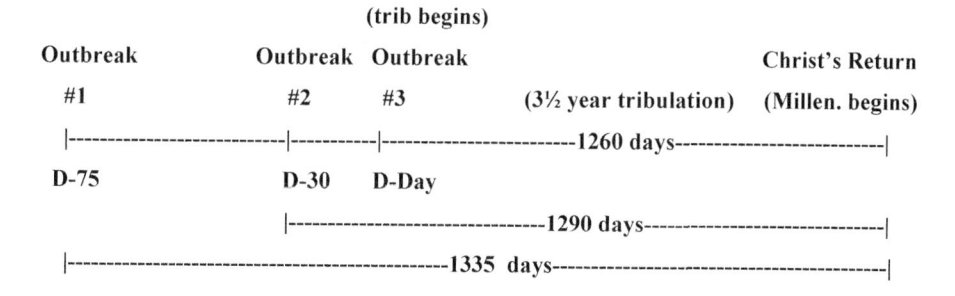

```
                        (trib begins)
 Outbreak          Outbreak  Outbreak                        Christ's Return
    #1                #2        #3     (3½ year tribulation) (Millen. begins)
 |-----------------------|---------|-----------------------1260 days------------------------|
 D-75                   D-30    D-Day
                         |------------------------------1290 days------------------------|
 |---------------------------------------1335 days-------------------------------------|
```

"WHAT DID JESUS "NOT" SAY?"

Does the above interpretation conflict at all with what Jesus said in the Olivet Discourse? He said in Matthew 24:15-16, "When ye therefore shall see the abomination of desolation, spoken of by Daniel the prophet, stand in the holy place, (whoso readeth, let him understand:) Then let them which be in Judaea flee into the mountains." Luke explains this "abomination of desolation" event in a more specific manner, "And when ye shall see Jerusalem compassed with armies, then know that the desolation thereof is nigh. Then let them which are in Judaea flee to the mountains" (Lk. 21:20-21). When Jesus said that "the desolation thereof is nigh," what He was saying was that it was NEAR! He was not necessarily saying that it had begun. In fact, Jesus does not actually state that the tribulation has begun until 6 verses later in Matthew's account when He said, "For then shall be great tribulation" (Mt. 24:21). This would therefore explain or allow for the 30 day gap between the second and third outbreaks of conflict.

"MY SPECULATION..."

In reality, the potential for 3 conflicts to occur in just a 75 day period is really not all that unusual, especially when you think in terms of skirmishes or outbreaks. Sure, most conflicts tend to last far longer than a mere 75 days. However, I would like to parallel for a moment these Scriptures with what already took place during the Gulf War of 1991. If you recall, Iraq invaded Kuwait and then, for no apparent reason, began to launch their Scud missiles at Israel (who was not even involved). Why? It seemed that they were using their obvious conflict with Kuwait to, in turn, provoke Israel into battle. Did this entire ordeal take very long? Not at all. Rather, it all occurred in a matter of just days. Likewise, the same could very well take place with respect to the little horn and southern kingdom.

In other words, consider for example Yasser Arafat representing the little horn. At the same time, consider the southern kingdom as including not only Egypt, but also the United States. Again, as I previously indicated in the chapter entitled "What about the United States?", the U.S., merely by their participation over there in the Middle East, can possibly be considered as also being a part of the southern kingdom. Thus, the following could very well be a possible scenario for fulfilling these three amounts of days. From Daniel 11:25, you could imagine Arafat (or his people) doing something that "stirs up" or even provokes a reaction on the part of the southern kingdom. For example, the suicide bombings, being terrorist activities, might cause the U.S. (and/or any alliance of southern Arab countries) to attack them as part of our war against terrorism. However, it seems that he would then, as a result of this happening, somewhat back down, therefore leaving this as merely an outbreak, if you will. Of course, this "stirring up" only begins to set the tone for the things to come, even establishing an atmosphere of increased tension, prime for the next outbreak. This next outbreak would thus be the one of Daniel 11:29 wherein Arafat could then even further initiate some action, only this time being much more assertive. As a matter of fact, it would be at this point that they would turn on Jerusalem, causing a stoppage of prayer at the Wailing Wall, even causing the Jews to flee. Yet at the same time, we learn from verse 30 that "the ships of Chittim" (possibly being the U.S. military – see chapter on U.S.) accordingly return fire against him. Eventually, Egypt even becomes involved and soon the tribulation has begun (conflict #3 – Dan. 11:40-43). Of course, this would begin on a future Jewish Passover Feast, "And at the time of the end..., and he shall enter into the countries, and shall overflow and pass over (PASSOVER!)" (vs. 40).

"WHICH PASSOVER?"

Of course, if the above is even close to being the case, then the question becomes which Passover for from it, we could then calculate the supposed dates for each of these three conflicts. At the time of my writing this (2001), the next Passover Feast is to begin on March 28th, 2002. Could this be the one? Only time will tell, but to demonstrate this process of calculating, I will use this next Passover for my example:

March 28th – This is the start of the Jewish Passover for 2002. Using this date, you would calculate this as possibly being the beginning of the tribulation. In turn, it would represent the start of the 3rd conflict. From this date to the end of the tribulation would be 1260 days (D-day).

February 26th – This would be the date that is 30 days prior to March 28th, thus representing the start of the 2nd conflict. From this particular date to the end of the tribulation would be 1290 days (D-30).

January 12th – This would be the date that is 75 days prior to March 28th, thus representing the start of the 1st conflict. Of course, from this date to the end of the tribulation would be 1335 days (D-75).

Essentially, you have a Divine appointment represented by each of these dates. Of course, the actual dates would depend upon the actual year of the tribulation, of which I truly don't know (only in hindsight would we really know!). Incidentally, I would like to point out again that at the same time, this entire interpretation for these 1260, 1290, and 1335 day periods is also something of which is just speculation on my part. This I admit. But I do think that it is at least worth considering. Of course, only time will truly tell for us…

[i] - Thomas Kiernan, *Yasir Arafat*, (London: Cox & Wyman, 1976), p. 60
[ii] - Ibid., p. 108.
[iii] - Ibid., p. 138.
[iv] - Ibid., p. 146.
[v] - Ion Mihai Pacepa, *Red Horizons*, (Washington, DC: Regenery-Gateway, 1990), p. 24.
[vi] - "Rabin: Arafat's Call for 'Jihad' Puts Peace Process in Question," *The Jerusalem Post*, May 18, 1994.
[vii] - Danny Rubinstein, *The Mystery of Arafat*, (Vermont: Steerforth Press, 1995), p. 32.
[viii] - "Oh little town of Bethlehem," *Middle East Intelligence Digest*, February 1995, p. 6.
[ix] - "Hussein and Arafat in Conflict," *The Jerusalem Post*, October 28, 1994.
[x] - Ibid.
[xi] - Ibid.
[xii] - "Ramadan Moon Boosts PA'S Mufti," *The Jerusalem Post*, February 3, 1995.
[xiii] - Kiernan, pp. 160-161.
[xiv] - Yasser Arafat, *El Mundo*, Venezuela, February 11, 1980, cited in Bennett, *Philistine*, p. 100.
[xv] - *Logos*, Greek Lexicon, #803.
[xvi] - "A true man of his word," *The Jerusalem Post*, September 13, 1994.
[xvii] - "The earth shakes under our feet," *The Jerusalem Post*, May 5, 1995.
[xviii] - "A curse of death gets the kiss of death," *The Jerusalem Post*, December 8, 1995.
[xix] - Ibid.
[xx] - Ibid.
[xxi] - "Even as they speak peace," *Middle East Intelligence Digest*, November 1994.
[xxii] - "PLO-Hamas connection," *The Jerusalem Post*, January 17, 1993.
[xxiii] - Monitored by BBC Caversham, July 28, 1992, cited in "PLO-Hamas connection," *The Jerusalem Post*, Jan. 17,.1993.
[xxiv] - "Horror show of the absurd," *The Jerusalem Post*, July 7, 1991.
[xxv] - Text of Osama bin Laden's Statement, *USA Today*, October 8, 2001.
[xxvi] - Ibid.

ABOUT THE AUTHOR

Dennis Crump is an ordained Southern Baptist Minister who has been in ministry for over fourteen years since being honorably discharged as an officer from the United States Marine Corps. Having served mostly as a Youth Minister in the past, he currently pastors a new church start, Believers Assembly, in Green Bay, Wisconsin. He has a family of five and currently resides in Green Bay with his wife, Rhonda, of twelve years and his three sons, Cuyler, Callon, and Cana. If you would like to reach him, he can be contacted by email: dennisrcrump@netzero.net.